And Then
Their Hearts Stood Still

He took her again into his arms.
This time she did not resist.

ALSO BY MARY CADOGAN

The Woman Behind William: A Life of Richmal Crompton

Frank Richards: The Chap Behind the Chums

Chin Up, Chest Out, Jemima

The William Companion

Women with Wings: Female Flyers in Fact and Fiction

Just William – Through the Ages

WITH PATRICIA CRAIG

You're a Brick, Angela!

Women and Children First

The Lady Investigates

And Then
Their Hearts Stood Still

An exuberant look at romantic fiction past and present

MARY CADOGAN

M
MACMILLAN
LONDON

First published 1994 by Macmillan London Limited

a division of Pan Macmillan Publishers Limited
Cavaye Place London SW10 9PG
and Basingstoke

Associated companies throughout the world

ISBN 0-333-56486-3

Copyright © 1994 Mary Cadogan

1 3 5 7 9 8 6 4 2

A CIP catalogue record for this book is available from
the British Library

Typeset by CentraCet Limited, Cambridge
Printed and bound in Great Britain by
Mackays of Chatham PLC, Chatham, Kent

For my daughter, Teresa Mary

I should like to thank my Editors at Macmillan, Peta Nightingale and Jane Wood, for their encouragement, suggestions and patience. To Rachel Anderson I owe a special debt because her intriguing book *The Purple Heart Throbs* awakened my interest in romantic fiction when I first read it twenty years ago. Warm thanks are also due to David Pringle, the Editor of *Million* magazine, to Mary Lutyens ('Esther Wyndham') for her most helpful comments, to Margery Hylton, and to my long-suffering husband, Alexander.

Mary Cadogan
Beckenham, Kent, 1994

I have drawn in the main on the first sources referred to in the text of *And Then Their Hearts Stood Still*, but have also consulted Gale's *Twentieth Century Romance and Historical Writers*, *The Purple Heart Throbs* by Rachel Anderson, *Reader, I Married Him* by Patricia Beer, and various articles in *Million* magazine.

Contents

Introduction

♡

And Then Their Hearts Stood Still is an appreciative assessment of twentieth-century romantic fiction from classics to comic-strips; from governess-gothic suspense fantasies to gutsy 'bonking and shopping', bodice-ripping, blood, sweat and semen sagas; from the trademark romances of Mills and Boon, Harlequin and Silhouette to single-sex love-stories; from women's magazine exploits to Ruritanian and Regency romps; from teenage and schoolgirl passions to the second (or third and fourth) time-around affairs of older – though not necessarily wiser – women.

Over 25 million copies of romantic novels are published every year in Britain alone (Mills and Boon sell one every two seconds), while the market in the USA and other countries is enormous. Despite – or possibly because of – the strongly materialistic pressures and shifting patterns of contemporary life, the demand for such stories from women and girls of differing ages and backgrounds continues to grow. During the recession-stricken and acutely realist late 1980s, for example, two of the world's best-selling writers were Janet Dailey, a leading American exponent of contemporaneous love-stories, and Barbara Cartland, the British *grande dame* of Regency-set passionate encounters between strong men and sweet but spirited young women.

Sure signs that the appeal of romantic stories continues on a world-wide basis during the 1990s are the substantial sales in several of the Eastern European countries and the fact that even during the Gulf War ten of Barbara Cartland's titles were bought by Arab publishers. The influence of amatory novels has long been extended by their transmogrification into plays and films and, in recent years, they have reached a new public through adaptations into TV mini-series. However, in spite of their prodigious output and popularity, most writers of love-stories have until very recently worked in comparative obscurity, largely ignored by both literary critics and social commentators. It is often argued that romantic novels are unreviewable because they stick to the same basic plot and because there is no development generally in the genre, but during the last two decades its frontiers have been pushed out to provide intriguing variations on previously accepted formulae. Some stories, of course, still dwell exclusively on the vicissitudes of rather vacuous husband-hunters, but we are now also likely to meet heroines who are concerned with 'finding themselves' and shinning smartly up their career ladders. Feminism – a fairly regular ingredient of romances since the late 1970s – is now often taken seriously and no longer used simply as a device to keep the hero and heroine at arm's length until the traditional clearing-up-of-misunderstandings clinch of the closing paragraphs.

Insights into changing responses to sexual attitudes and identities (both female and masculine) come over clearly when consideration is given to the love-story in all its variations. The religious intensities of the leading ladies of Marie Corelli and Florence Barclay are in sharp contrast with Barbara Cartland's conventionally rapturous heroines. In the magazines, *Woman's Weekly* provides staidly domestic stories while the *Peg's Paper* canon is one of seduction and betrayal. The torrid excitements of E. M. Hull's, Ethel M. Dell's and Elinor Glynn's desert, North-West Frontier and love-on-the-leopard-skin fantasies are of a very different nature from those of Daphne du Maurier's perfect gothic, *Rebecca*, and its successors from Victoria Holt, Mary Stewart, Barbara Michaels, Evelyn Anthony and others. Then there are the earthy but passionate hospital romances and the consciously trendy picture-strip exploits in *Jackie, Valentine, My Guy*, and so on.

The romantic and gothic genres have a long history and are, in fact, rooted in the very origins of the novel. Stories of seduction and tales of terror from the eighteenth century such as Samuel

Richardson's *Clarissa*, Ann Radcliffe's *The Mysteries of Udolpho* and Horace Walpole's *The Castle of Otranto* can be seen as precursors of today's romantic and suspense novels. In particular Jane Austen and the Brontës put their indelible stamp on the love-story: twentieth-century romantic fiction encompasses, extends, sometimes enhances and sometimes debases themes, plots and archetypes which these authors of genius originated. *And Then Their Hearts Stood Still*, therefore, looks back to Austen, the Brontës and some of the luridly intriguing earlier seduction stories in order to trace the development of the genre and the changing status of its heroines. It asks how accurately these mirror the fantasies and aspirations of several generations of women and (perhaps more importantly) reflect the frustrations and fulfilments of their real-life situations.

As well as focusing on the heroines, it looks at the role of the great romantic heroes from those in the classic Lovelace, Darcy, Heathcliff, Rochester and Rhett Butler moulds to the prosaic, living-round-the-corner Mr Rights, for whom less favoured heroines than Elizabeth Bennet, Jane Eyre and Scarlett O'Hara might have to settle.

The genre is often seen as endorsing men's power over women but, ever since Charlotte Brontë maimed and blinded Rochester in *Jane Eyre*, it has frequently reflected female dominance of the male in 'taming-the-beast' tales from writers as distinct in style and approach as D. H. Lawrence, Vera Brittain and Barbara Cartland.

Until fairly recently the love-story genre has been confined within clearly marked boundaries. However, dictionary definitions of romance are so wide-ranging that to cover the field of the romantic story could mean surveying practically the whole of English literature (after all, as we are so often told, it *is* love that makes the world go round or, at any rate, sex that keeps the human race going). From this amatory ubiquitousness it has not been easy to set the parameters of *And Then Their Hearts Stood Still*. Many superb love-stories fall outside the specific romance genre but have profoundly influenced it, so their inclusion in this study seemed essential. It would, for example, be ridiculous to write about romantic suspense stories without mentioning *Rebecca*, although Daphne du Maurier cannot be confined within any category. Similarly, the work of Jilly Cooper, Rosie Thomas, Judith Krantz, Danielle Steel and Barbara Taylor Bradford could not be omitted, because although their stories fit into other genres, are mainstream or stand on their own, there is a natural osmosis between them and romantic fiction.

A difficulty has been the place of the family saga which, popular since the 1930s, has now escalated virtually into a genre of its own. I have dipped into it with relish to pillage some plums for *And Then Their Hearts Stood Still*. However, its comprehensive coverage would require another book. Also, though tempted, I have not even touched upon Catherine Cookson, Lena Kennedy and many other admirable, individualistic writers because there is no space to do them justice. Nor have I taken on board Maeve Binchy whose excellent stories, despite their emotional appeal, seem to me to deal more fully with female friendships and general social issues than with romance. There are also hundreds – or rather thousands – of love-story authors whom I have not mentioned specifically by name. I hope that they will forgive the omission and feel that I have, at least, done justice to their chosen field of creative writing. Lack of space has also precluded a detailed study of the content and style of the wide-ranging, straightforward historical romance: I have discussed only those few novels in this category which are particularly relevant to the development of the love-story – or which have a strong appeal for me. Similarly, I have drawn from one or two serious works which have personally affected me. I should say that I have deliberately not included any sequels by other hands because a full discussion of these would necessitate a book of its own.

The romantic novel has often been condemned for providing fantasy, idealism and adventure which are purely escapist. But just what do we mean by 'escape'? How important a factor is it in all our lives, and does it differ fundamentally from the expansion of our imaginative horizons which occurs in the reading of 'serious' literature? In this context it is possibly significant that many lively-minded girls read Mills and Boon romances because they find a lot of today's 'intelligent' novels formless, unsatisfying and lacking in characters with whom they can identify. At a time when young people are tending to move away from the book to the computer, we should perhaps see what lessons might be learned from branches of popular fiction which still exercise an addictive appeal. The future of the book and its relevance to our lives is under question – but we can be fairly certain that the romantic story at least will continue to roll on resiliently, as it has done for a couple of centuries.

CHAPTER ONE

Governesses and Gothics

THE TWENTIETH-CENTURY love-story has acquired an almost astonishing variety of shape and style, orientation and atmosphere, but despite drastic changes in literary fashions and social attitudes, the 'gothic' romance remains one of the genre's most resilient and satisfying forms. Its roots are in the tales of terror and seduction which were the most popular type of fiction in the eighteenth and early nineteenth centuries; it has, however, largely departed from the authentic gothic mould as the status of the heroine has altered and thus affected her responses to the archetypal male character (the potential rapist villain and the supportive rescuer hero). The more extravagant excesses, both physical and psychological, have been toned down; incarceration in crumbling castles, haunted abbeys, labyrinthine forests or cata-combs has been replaced by sojourns in roomy but not necessarily huge houses, and insane, power-crazed baddies have been replaced by calculating seducers and con-men. However, the central element – woman in jeopardy – has remained comparatively unchanged from the mid-eighteenth-century beginnings of the gothic story to the romantic suspense novels of the 1990s.

Samuel Richardson's *Clarissa, or The History of a Young Lady* set the mood. This seven-volume novel was published over a two-year period, from 1747 to 1749, in the form of a series of letters from over twenty correspondents. Most of these were from the epony-mous heroine to a female friend, and from her unscrupulous admirer, Lovelace, to a male confidant. The letters, which incor-porate conversations, carry this lengthy narrative forward with a sense of drama and immediacy. Clarissa, the archetypal young female innocent, is first locked up and humiliated by her family when she refuses to marry a wealthy suitor whom she hates. Lovelace, who is handsome but rakish, pretends to be her deliverer but, after engineering her escape, establishes her in a London brothel which she has understood to be a respectable lodging-house. They both undergo a whole gamut of confused responses. Clarissa is intrigued by Lovelace's wit and charm but repelled by his obsessiveness. She understandably distrusts his proposals of marriage, and clings to her virginity which becomes symbolic of her sense of independence and identity. His passion and admiration – but also his anger and ruthlessness – increase as she unfalteringly resists his blandishments and advances. His determination to conquer persists until at length, in the fifth volume, he drugs and rapes her, with the horrifically dramatic consequence that, instead of turning to him, as he had predicted, she begins to lose her reason. However, she manages to escape from him and eventually to regain her sanity, although her ultimate release from trauma and terror comes only in a physical decline and death: Lovelace, suitably overtaken by remorse, is then killed by Clarissa's cousin, Colonel Morden, in a duel. Despite the novel's melodramatic nature, the personalities of Lovelace and Clarissa are persuasively developed, and their struggles have, with variations, become formulaic in subsequent tales of seduction.

Other basic ingredients of the gothic romance were provided in Horace Walpole's *The Castle of Otranto*, which was published in 1765. Set in Italy during the thirteenth century, this fairly short novel was to provide the classic pattern of villainous intrigue against a vulnerable heroine who is imprisoned and persecuted in a gloomy pile, and helped to escape by a young man who later becomes her husband. It is plentifully strewn with passion and anguish, as well as with the sinister trappings of ghosts, grisly visions, dank churchyards, vaults, caves, and statues that appear to come to life.

Some three decades later Ann Radcliffe was to become the leading exponent of the gothic novel with *The Romance of the Forest*

(1792), *The Mysteries of Udolpho* (1794) and *The Italian* (1797), all dealing with heroines confined by malevolent male aristocrats in murky, decrepit abbeys and castles. Mrs Radcliffe adroitly prolonged the torments of her heroines – and often those of her heroes – through lengthy three-volume novels, to tease and tantalize her readers. It was the excesses of *Udolpho* in particular that Jane Austen parodied in her *Northanger Abbey* (1817) when gothic romances were very much in vogue. She also referred to M. G. Lewis's *The Monk* (1796) and macabre novels by other writers. Her witty and perceptive indirect critique of the genre helped to redefine and humanize it, and, three decades after the publication of *Northanger Abbey*, Charlotte Brontë so brilliantly balanced imaginative and realistic facets of the 'governess-gothic' that its appeal was to continue until the end of the nineteenth century – and far beyond.

Charlotte and her sisters Emily and Anne all contributed significantly to the development of the romantic suspense story as we know it today, although they wrote from their own direct experiences of a very different society. Each knew instinctively how to harness such individual experiences to create exultantly archetypal romances. Charlotte's *Jane Eyre*, Anne's *Agnes Grey* and Emily's *Wuthering Heights* were all published in 1847. There is nothing governessy about *Wuthering Heights*, of course, but Charlotte and Anne drew on their own teaching experiences for their first published novels. Anne's heroine, Agnes, has her full share of career and social frustration: her tale of governessing and romantic tribulations is shorter and more succinct than Charlotte's, and more open to Christian interpretation than that of fable (or Freud!) which could be applied to the adventures of Charlotte's celebrated protagonist, Jane Eyre. *Agnes Grey* is illuminating about the plight of impoverished, intelligent, single nineteenth-century women who had virtually no other choice of livelihood than teaching, and were often at the mercy of extremely mean-minded employers. Agnes was not merely incarcerated in the houses of people who treated her callously, but was psychologically confined by having to conform to their petty, soul-destroying dictates and regimes.

Tormented by her spoiled young charges and ignored by their parents, she became worn down by drudgery and the desperate loneliness of never making contact with a kindred spirit: 'I seemed to feel my intellect deteriorating, my heart petrifying, my soul contracting; and I trembled lest my very moral perceptions should become deadened ... The gross vapours of earth were gathering around me ...' Happily, however, when Agnes reaches her lowest ebb, consolation is at hand in the sturdy shape of the local curate: 'and thus it was that Mr Weston rose at length upon me, appearing like the morning-star in my horizon, to save me from the fear of utter darkness; and I rejoiced that I had now a subject for contemplation that was above me, not beneath.' There is a lyrical quality about the expression of her love for Mr Weston but also a practical recognition of her vulnerability from which she can be rescued only by someone of the opposite sex who is physically, psychologically and financially stronger than she.

There are gothic strands in the real lives of Anne, Charlotte and Emily. These highly creative sisters were confined, not by seductive villains but by social conventions and family demands, in their father's parsonage which stood apart from the other buildings of the village of Haworth and was, symbolically, next to the graveyard in which so many of their family found premature resting-places. It was also near the edge of the moors which, by turns bleak and brooding, magnificently wild or intricately lovely, seemed to echo and influence the sisters' inner moods, and the secret, dramatic fantasy-worlds that from childhood they created in their imagination to enhance and expand their claustrophobic circumstances. The pressing need to earn a living as well as ambition fired by their extraordinary talent drew them out of the parsonage into governessing. It was hardly fulfilling work for the Brontë girls who, poorly paid, untrained and unrespected, were often very lonely. On top of all this Charlotte suffered the anguish of unrequited passion when she fell in love with a teaching colleague who was married to the principal of the school in Brussels in which she worked. Back in Haworth Parsonage, which offered both the security of the womb and the oppressiveness of being immured (with the latter exacerbated by the drink-and-drug-induced degeneration of their brother Branwell), Charlotte, Emily and Anne used aspects of their lives away from Haworth to give more muscle to their writing.

Charlotte's first published novel, *Jane Eyre*, emerges as the classic formulation of the modern gothic romance, which, unlike the medieval fantasies of Horace Walpole and Ann Radcliffe, puts its main emphasis on love rather than horror elements. Her story has been recycled, refurbished, expanded and sometimes debased by writers of successive generations, from Daphne du Maurier, whose perfect twentieth-century gothic saga, *Rebecca*, echoes *Jane Eyre* not only in plot and structure but in brilliance, to authors who have simply rechauffé the basic Brontë elements into pot-boilers.

The story-line of *Jane Eyre* is well known. Orphaned and at the mercy of an extremely unsympathetic aunt, Jane is sent to Lowood School, a grim and ugly place in which she suffers privations similar to those experienced by Charlotte in real life at Cowan Bridge. It was the hardships of this clergy-daughters' school that she held responsible for the early deaths of her two elder sisters, Maria and Elizabeth. Similarly in the novel, Jane's almost angelic friend, Helen Burns, dies at Lowood. At eighteen Jane is determined to have no further dependence on the aunt who has blighted her childhood, and sets out to earn her own living. She is both frail and indomitable – a perfect fictional example of 'the mouse that roared'. By advertising she secures a position as governess to Adèle Varens, the young Gallic ward of Edward Fairfax Rochester. He is the affluent owner of Thornfield Hall and, when Jane enters his life, he exudes the charismatic aura of a slightly world-weary but highly energized man with a libertine past. It is obvious almost from their first meeting that, although they are apparently opposites in nature and in fortune, there is an intense mental affinity between Rochester and Jane which develops into full-blown love and their determination to marry. This is cruelly thwarted when, at their wedding ceremony, Jane learns, dramatically, that the strange and violent creature who lives in isolation with her nurse in one of Thornfield's upper rooms is, in fact, Rochester's legal – but longstandingly insane – wife. He begs Jane to go away with him to the South of France, but, keeping a hold on the bitter realities of social ostracism (and even perhaps of Rochester tiring of her eventually, just as he has abandoned other loves in the past) she refuses, leaves him and, after a period of desolation and illness, begins to build a new, if drab and joyless, life for herself. At last, however, Jane becomes aware in a psychic vision that Rochester is free to marry her and, even more significantly, that his need for her is now desperate and total. It transpires that his crazed wife has died in the fire she started, which also burnt down Thornfield Hall and permanently maimed Rochester. Jane goes back to him, of course.

Charlotte wrote other novels with governess heroines, and it is interesting to compare *Jane Eyre* with *Villette*, which was published six years later in 1853. There is a flagrant, youthful, imaginative romanticism about the first book which is lacking in *Villette*. Each features an insecure but independently minded, unmarried governess in the leading role and consists of a first-person narrative which starts with the vicissitudes of childhood, probes the problems of women seeking work of dignity and integrity, and ends with actual or promised romantic fulfilment. *Villette* is possibly better crafted than *Jane Eyre* but far lower-key in tone, and it is also less archetypal. It remains a potent study of a young woman who undergoes emotional crises and virtual breakdown, but finds the strength to claw her way back from these and from social humiliations to discover exactly what – and who – she wants from life, and to get both. For Charlotte, there must have been a distinct element of wish-fulfilment in the romance between *Villette*'s heroine, Lucy Snowe, and her fellow-teacher, Paul Emanuel, which was obviously an enhanced fictional representation of her own thwarted love affair. Perhaps honesty dictated that Lucy and Paul's relationship should therefore be less satisfyingly consummated than Rochester and Jane's. Instead of the latter's celebrated and unequivocal declaration of 'Reader, I married him', Lucy has to settle for awaiting the fruition of promises, and asking her readers simply to 'picture union and a happy suceeding life'.

In spite of melodramatic and romantic excesses and some

unsettling, patchy feminism, *Jane Eyre*, as vigorously as ever, seems set to remain the model for the romantic suspense story. Comprising love, betrayal, mysteries of parentage and elements of folk and fairy-tale, it is the stuff from which legends are made. Jane's coming to Mr Rochester's Thornfield Hall can be equated – as the narrative suggests – with the situation of Bluebeard's wife in his castle, or Beauty's at the home of the soon-to-be-mellowed-or-transformed Beast. Like the experiences of these other vulnerable heroines, Jane's story is a compelling amalgam of dream, nightmare and reality that lends itself readily to psychoanalytic as well as fanciful interpretation.

Her special strength lies in the fact that she refuses to allow herself to be trapped by circumstances, however daunting, tantalizing or appealing these might appear to be. She is able physically – if not metaphorically – to shake the dust of Thornfield from her feet and turn her back on the deliciously desirable Rochester as soon as she discovers that he already has a wife, in name if not in actuality. Despite her mouse-like exterior and the streak of submissiveness which Rochester, her 'master' at more than one level, brings out, she retains a measure of independence, even of defiance, so long as she knows that love cannot be utterly reciprocal. In spite of – or possibly because of – her affection-starved childhood, she *demands* the totality of an emotional and status fulfilment that Rochester cannot give while his tragic, raving and revengeful wife retains her mortal form. There are Freudian touches as well as elements of folk-lore in his chastening by fire and consequent crippling and blinding. Jane's return to him when his mad wife and part of his manhood have been consumed by burning is symbolic of her insistence on being loved, needed and absolutely at the centre of his life: for her it is all or nothing. Charlotte certainly started something here. After *Jane Eyre* a succession of apparently fragile but actually very determined heroines were able to accept romantic union only after the heroes had suffered permanent or long-term disability (see Chapter 4).

Emily Brontë's *Wuthering Heights* has also, of course, helped significantly to shape and colour the twentieth-century romantic suspense story. Like *Jane Eyre*, it is a study of archetypal images of inner turbulence and passion which are echoed in Emily's description of the wild, windswept and majestic landscapes of the Yorkshire moors. A celebration of love that is soaring and unfettered, it is also earthed by the physical and psychological violence of the main protagonists, Cathy Earnshaw and Heathcliff, and by death – that ever-present threat of which the Victorians were so acutely aware. It contains many of the trappings of the classic gothic tale: enforced confinement in isolated houses, oppression and exploitation, tortuous family relationships, intrigues over inheritances, desire that is far more violent than tender and amounts to obsession, and so on. At best, Cathy and Heathcliff's mutual passion can be seen as a union of souls: when Cathy almost destroys Heathcliff by agreeing to marry the socially acceptable Edgar Linton, she confides to the family's faithful and much put-upon servant, Nelly Dean, that 'it would degrade me to marry Heathcliff . . . because he's more myself than I am. Whatever our souls are made of, his and mine are the same, and Linton's is as different as a moonbeam from lightning, or frost from fire.' After her death and Heathcliff's anguished 'Be with me always – take any form – drive me mad! Only do not leave me in this abyss, where I cannot find you', she is apparently united with him in ghostly though not fleshly manner. At worst, their arrogantly exclusive passion, and the ruthlessness which it seems to generate in their feelings for everyone else, can be seen as ugly, self-indulgent and destructive in the extreme. *Wuthering Heights*, however, has become emblematic in the genre of the liberating power of love, although Cathy, for all her scorching and swirling intensity, never comes near to achieving the emancipation of Jane Eyre, who could say, with truth, 'I am a free human being with an independent will.'

In fact, modern heroines are far closer to Jane than to Cathy: Emily's permanent legacy to literature and imaginative fantasy was the creation of Heathcliff, whose saturnine appearance and uncontrolled passions have provided the model for innumerable romantic heroes from the middle of the nineteenth century to the present day. Generally speaking, however, these have one quality which

Heathcliff notoriously lacked – the ability to soften brutishness in response to love or compassion. Most heroes, however tough and unfeeling they may appear on the surface, have hidden areas of vulnerability and tenderness, but, as Charlotte was to comment in a preface to an edition of *Wuthering Heights* which appeared after Emily's death, 'Heathcliff, indeed, stands unredeemed; never once swerving in his arrow-straight course to perdition.' She sees him as a 'demon' or 'ghoul' animating 'a man's shape'. A strange masculine role-model for future generations – but there it is. Possibly it is Heathcliff's entry into the saga as an abandoned waif – 'a little, black-haired swarthy thing' – which has appealed to the protectiveness of women readers, but it is difficult to sustain pity for him when one contemplates the horrors of his callous treatment of Linton's sister, Isabella, whom he marries as an act of spiteful revenge; of his bullying of the male Earnshaws, whom he dispossesses and reduces to servitude, and even of his own son.

Romantic fiction is often inaccurately assessed as being restricted to just one or two basic plots. It can more truly be said that there are only one or two real heroes, and that in essence these have changed and metamorphosed over the decades less strikingly than the extremely varied heroines who have featured in amatory tales from the time of Samuel Richardson's *Clarissa* to the present day. Lovelace was a fusion of romantic hero and rapist villain, a handsome, persuasive, dashing but dominating and obsessive rake, who could charm and chill his female victims in equal measure.

There are elements of him in both Jane Austen's Darcy and Charlotte Brontë's Rochester, who were certainly to become archetypal heroes of the love-story. For all his good manners and high breeding, Jane Austen conveys a sense of Darcy's having a contained libido which could at any time erupt into overpowering sexual demand. The fact that his magnetism is masked by hauteur and arrogance often enhances his appeal for the reader who, like *Pride and Prejudice*'s heroine Elizabeth Bennet, is challenged to strip these away and reveal the raw passion beneath the impeccably polished exterior. It is significant that although we have an indelible mental picture of a tall, wonderfully handsome and magnificently rich young man, we are not given much detail about his appearance – we are not even told if he is dark or fair, brown- or blue-eyed – but we respond to his challenging perceptiveness, his intelligence and inability to take fools gladly. Interestingly, although Darcy has become established as a romantic archetype, and his love affair with Elizabeth as one of the most celebrated and sparkling in fiction, Jane Austen consistently eschewed the sentimental. When asked to write a historical romance about the House of Saxe-Coburg, she protested: 'I could not . . . write a serious romance under any other motive than to save my life; and if it were indispensable for me to keep it up and never relax into laughing at myself or at other people, I am sure I would be hung before I had finished the first chapter.'

We *are* provided with a clear physical picture of Rochester. Jane Eyre tells us that he is 'of middle-height and considerable breadth of chest', 'clean-flanked', with 'a dark face . . . stern features and a heavy brow'. Like Darcy, he has a decisive, occasionally sardonic manner; he is an experienced sensualist who constantly, and sometimes sadistically, tries to tease Jane out of independence and dignity and to arouse her passions. Time and again their duels are refought and their qualities reflected by different heroes and heroines in much later love-stories.

The last, ever-resilient male role-model in the genre was created in 1936, although, as for Lovelace, Darcy and Rochester, his setting is many decades earlier. Margaret Mitchell's *Gone with the Wind* covers the period of the American Civil War and its aftermath (the 1860s), but its undisputed hero, the dark, truly dashing, high-powered, keen-witted and caustically perceptive Rhett Butler, is both of his time and timeless. Sensuality glints in his eyes, energy emanates from his athletic frame, and charisma from his pores. He is, however, in full command of his convictions, appetites and desires, unswayed by either the vagaries of public opinion or Scarlett O'Hara's whims and waywardness. Although his creator suggested that aspects of Rhett were inspired by Charlotte Brontë's Rochester and Augusta Jane Evans Wilson's St Elmo (see Chapter 10), Rhett is in fact an original from whom many imitations have since been spawned. (The hero of Daphne du Maurier's *Rebecca*, Maxim de Winter, appeared on the scene two years after Rhett Butler. It is tempting to add his name to this quintet of role-models but, despite his undeniably heart-stabbing appeal and magnetism, he seems in essence derivative of both Darcy and Rochester.)

After the input of the Brontës, the main developments in the romantic suspense story came in the 1860s with Wilkie Collins's *The Woman in White* and Mary Elizabeth Braddon's *Lady Audley's Secret* in England, and Louisa May Alcott's thrillers of thwarted love and vengeance in America.

In *The Woman in White* (1860), Sir Percival Glyde has mysterious connections with Italian secret societies and is involved in several extremely shady business affairs. He tries to persuade his wife, Laura, to make her fortune over to him and is amazed when she questions the contents of the document which he askes her to sign: '"I have not time to explain," he answered ... "Besides, if I had time you wouldn't understand ... What have women to do with business?"' She continues to demur, but pays a heavy price for her independence. Her repulsive husband contrives to have her incarcerated in a mental asylum. Then Anne Catherick, a woman whom he has previously wronged, dies, and he arranges for her to be buried under Laura's identity, a neat but nasty way of prematurely inheriting a wife's property. In the end it is Laura's half-sister, Marian, who intrepidly uncovers the truth and effects a rescue as well as the downfall of Sir Percival who, felicitously, burns to death while trying to tamper with a parish register.

The Woman in White has one foot in the romance genre, and the other in the fiction of mystery and detection, which was, of course, to become immensely popular in the late Victorian and Edwardian periods. Collins's novel was followed two years later by another melodrama of defrauding, extortion and mental asylums – with murder and bigamy thrown in. *Lady Audley's Secret* was unusual in having a beautiful woman, and one-time governess, at the centre of events, not, as in the Brontë books, in the role of heroine but as the villain of the piece. The novel is strong stuff, full of lurid events and social challenges, which are possibly to an extent reflections of the real-life experiences of the author. Mary Braddon started off as an actress, fell in love with an already married publisher, James Maxwell, went to live with him and bore him six children. She also managed to write some sixty novels. Possibly the paciness of these owes something to the energy which she must have had to find to get them written.

The plot is complex and involves the anti-heroine in having several different identities and five different names. Its apex – or nadir – occurs when, now bigamously married and known as Lady Audley, she murders (or, rather, thinks that she has murdered) her first and still legal spouse. She also ingeniously contrives to burn to death a man who, claiming to have witnessed her dire and dirty deed, is blackmailing her. There are many more layers of deception and intrigue, all of which are eventually unravelled by her nephew by marriage, Robert Audley. Her husband decides not to bring disgrace on the family name by handing Lady Audley over to justice but, instead, to have her confined under a false name in a lunatic asylum in a particularly remote area of Belgium. He – like Robert who conducts her there – feels quite sanguine about this because she has, in expiation of her gruesome actions, revealed to them her secret: she is mad, and has known this nearly all her life. With this strange farrago, Mary Braddon neatly turned the governess-gothic romance on its head.

So too did Louisa M. Alcott in a series of novellas and short stories which were published anonymously or pseudonymously during the 1860s, and only attributed to her as recently as the 1940s, after diligent research by her biographer, Madeleine Stern, and her colleague, Leona Rostenberg. Louisa wrote and published several of these 'shockers' before she produced *Little Women* and its sequels and became known as 'The Children's Friend'. The many thousands of women and girls who vicariously participated in the changing fortunes of the March sisters, weeping over Jo cutting and selling the long chestnut hair which was her 'one beauty' or angushing over poor Beth's uncomplaining illness and early death, might well have been astounded to know of their author's addiction to 'blood-and-thunder' and romances of 'the lurid style'. In fact Louisa Alcott continued to write these tales from her 'witch's cauldron' in parallel with her domestic sagas for some time, recording tersely in her journal in 1877 that she 'enjoyed doing it, being tired of providing moral pap for the young'.

The gothic style suited Louisa's flair for the dramatic, which had found respectable expression in her juveniles' stories with the characters dressing up, writing flamboyant plays and participating in amateur theatricals. Her inventiveness and, one suspects, her frustration at being trapped in the restrictive social conventions of her time, poured out in sensational, ghostly, violent and gruesome tales whose obliquely feminist heroines, often prompted by vengeance against some perfidious male, were far removed from the rather passive female victims of early gothic romances. In common with Charlotte Brontë's leading ladies, they were characters to be reckoned with, like the *femme fatale* who is at the centre of 'Pauline's Passion and Punishment', or Jean Muir, the governess with a past in 'Behind a Mask, or A Woman's Power'. In the manner of the 'heroine' of *Lady Audley's Secret*, Jean enters an aristocratic household as a humble governess and schemes with success to take it over and defraud various members of the family of their rightful financial expectations by marrying its elderly head. She sets about becoming Lady Coventry in a business-like way: an important tool of her deceptive trade is of course her ability to enhance her physical attractions. In a startling description at the beginning of the story we see how the governess achieves this – and are also given disturbing insights into the speed at which girls in Alcott's time began to age and lose their sexual appeal:

> she unbound and removed the long abundant braids from her head, wiped the pink from her face, took out several pearly teeth, and slipping off her dress, appeared herself indeed, a haggard, worn and moody woman of thirty at least. The metamorphosis was wonderful . . .

No wonder the wronged and vengeful Jean felt that she had to make up for lost time in her power-gaining schemes and stratagems.

From the 1880s it seemed as if the romantic suspense novel had begun to side-step its gothic mood and settings. The public's appetite for mystery and intrigue was finding satisfaction in the detective story genre which had begun in 1841 with Edgar Allan Poe's 'The Murders in the Rue Morgue' and had been given enormous impetus in the 1880s by the exploits of its most enduring hero, Arthur Conan Doyle's Sherlock Holmes. Late-Victorian and Edwardian writers began to cast their heroines in sleuthing roles: they were usually unpaid, rather unprofessional, and attracted to detection for romantic reasons, such as proving the innocence of a husband or lover. Baroness Orczy, for example, whose main contribution to the romance genre was her novels in the *Scarlet Pimpernel* series (see Chapter 8), created *Lady Molly of Scotland Yard* (1910) in which the eponymous heroine has become an unraveller of crime mysteries in order to vindicate her husband, who is unjustly serving a life sentence for murder. In 1909 the penny weekly *Forget-Me-Not* ran a series featuring 'Janet Darling, the Love Detective'. Janet was described as 'the Girl Detective who will only help lovers', and, if the process of smoothing the path to nuptial bliss for various couples limited her scope as a sleuth, it kept her within the field of romantic suspense which continued to exert wide appeal.

It is intriguing that Daphne du Maurier's *Rebecca*, published in 1938, which injected new vitality into the gothic novel and became a prototype for modern versions of it, should hark back unashamedly to the early-Victorian *Jane Eyre*. As mentioned previously, there are vivid parallels between the two novels' first-person narratives, their penniless, orphaned, unassuming, Cinderella-like heroines, their rich, experienced, self-assured heroes and the shadows cast on the second marriages by ghostly, vengeful first wives. Just as Jane's marital happiness with Rochester is at first denied because of the existence of his insane, discarded spouse, so *Rebecca*'s unnamed heroine finds that her dream of achieving romantic fulfilment in her seemingly ideal marriage to the widowed Maxim de Winter is shattered by the tenaciously haunting influences of his first wife, the beautiful, confident and glamorous

Rebecca. Both books followed the formula, established by Mrs Radcliffe in *The Mysteries of Udolpho*, of the heroine being dangerously enclosed in 'the master's house' which did the double duty of fictional setting and dominant symbol. In each case the solid, dignified, sheltering but challenging house is surrounded by potentially wild and threatening natural elements: Thornfield Hall stands on the Yorkshire moors, and the grounds of Manderley in Cornwall run down to the sea.

At twenty-one, the second Mrs de Winter is only half Maxim's age. She constantly bows to his superior knowledge and experience; everything – even at the most mundane level – is on his terms:

> We watched the car disappear round the sweep of the drive, and then Maxim took my arm and said, 'Thank God that's that. Get a coat quickly, and come out. Damn the rain, I want a walk. I can't stand this sitting about.'

There is no discussion. He is the indisputable controller and he talks to her in the same peremptory tones that he uses for Jasper, their dog. Even his proposal of marriage has been brusque to the point of rudeness:

> '... I repeat to you, the choice is open to you. Either you go to America with Mrs Van Hopper or you come home to Manderley with me.'
>
> 'Do you mean you want a secretary or something?'
>
> 'No, I'm asking you to marry me, you little fool.'

It is no wonder that after a few weeks at Manderley she is sick of Maxim treating her like a child – 'someone to be petted from time to time when the mood came upon him but more often forgotten ... and told to run away and play'. She despairs of ever being a real partner to him: 'I did not want to be a child. I wanted to be his wife, his mother. I wanted to be old.' Ironically, of course, after she learns the grim secret of his murder of the mocking and faithless Rebecca, he does begin to treat her as a responsible adult, and to depend on her psychologically. And after the hateful, brooding housekeeper, Mrs Danvers, who remains obsessively loyal to her gilded memories of Rebecca, burns Manderley down and in consequence disables Maxim, his mousy but determined second wife begins to roar a little, coming into her own and establishing at last a vital relationship with her husband (see Chapter 4).

Daphne du Maurier combines the elements of mystery, murder, suspense, irony and romance so skilfully that no word or nuance of *Rebecca* seems out of place. The specific 'Cornish-gothic' atmosphere that she was possibly the first author to establish proved so indelible that, although the backcloths of the 1940 Hollywood version of the story seemed to be made of painted cardboard, the authentic mood and scene somehow prevailed. (It should, of course, be said that Joan Fontaine and Laurence Olivier were perfectly cast and wonderfully convincing in the leading roles.) The overall romantic tone of *Rebecca* finds echoes in two other du Maurier gothic novels, *Jamaica Inn* (1936) and *Frenchman's Creek* (1942), whose respective heroines Mary Yellan and Dona St Columb tangle with ruthless men and follow their passionate loves at high cost. In the more tormented *My Cousin Rachel*, which appeared some time after the other suspense novels in 1952, the main protagonist is a young man, rather than a girl, whose interests are centred more on family and heritage than on sweeping desire.

Rebecca quickly became a cult novel which fascinated not only enthusiasts of romantic stories but men and women from extremely diverse cultural and national backgrounds who had no special interest in the genre. Du Maurier, of course, achieved tremendous success with several different strands of fiction; despite looking back over her shoulder to the Brontës, she was an innovator of power and zest. Authors who produced emotional adventures from the 1940s onwards tended to regard not only *Jane Eyre* as a model but also *Rebecca*, which had firmly transplanted the gothic suspense story into the modern world.

In 1961 Eleanor Burford Hibbert, as 'Victoria Holt', gave a new thrust to the governess tale with *Mistress of Mellyn*. (From the 1940s this truly prolific author, as Jean Plaidy, had been producing very popular historical novels, and, as Eleanor Burford, main-stream romances. From the 1950s she was also writing as Elbur Ford,

Ellalice Tate and Kathleen Kellow, and, from the early 1970s, as Philippa Carr.)

Mistress of Mellyn, which has a Victorian Cornish setting and a persuasively direct first-person narrative, resounds with echoes of *Jane Eyre* and *Rebecca*. Martha Leigh, the orphaned daughter of a country vicar, finds herself, at twenty-four, penniless, and with no prospect of matrimony. Her only resource is 'to find a post in keeping with her gentility', which, of course, means governessing. She is soon installed in Mount Mellyn. Being a castle, this offers even greater splendours than Thornfield or Manderley, but it is also more forbidding. Perched high on a misty cliff-top, with the sea constantly pounding the shore below, it seems 'a tomb' or prison of a place rather than a haven. Martha is employed to look after Alvean, the small daughter of Connan TreMellyn who, in the tradition of masculine employers of Victorian governesses, on their first meeting emanates challenge rather than chumminess:

> His voice was strong – arrogant . . . I was immediately conscious of his great height . . . His hair was black but his eyes were light. His hands were thrust into the pockets of his riding breeches and he wore a dark blue coat and a white cravat. There was an air of careless elegance about him, as though he cared nothing for his clothes but could not help looking well in them.
>
> He gave an impression of strength and cruelty. There was sensuality in that face . . . but there was much else that was hidden . . . his manner seemed insolent as though he were reminding me that I was only a governess . . .

Naturally Martha gradually uncovers the warm sensitive being beneath the chilly exterior – but it is a long time before she becomes mistress of the situation, let alone of Mellyn. Connan's wife, Alice, who disappeared and died in mysterious circumstances, appears to linger in ghostly form around the castle; servants and visitors to Mellyn drop hints to Martha that suggest she was the victim of murky violence, and even the waves crashing against the cliffs seem to whisper, whine or shriek her name.

Martha shows great spirit and enterprise. She tames her wild and spoilt young charge and inspires at first respect then passion in Connan who, in the manner of Rochester verbally duelling with Jane, initially responds to her mind and then to her physical charms which, in keeping with her governess role, she keeps somewhat subdued. He eventually proposes: she rapturously accepts but is then brutally brought down to earth by an ever-strengthening belief that he has murdered his first wife. She has to call on all her courage and intelligence to unravel strange secrets, and in the process is nearly murdered by a rival contender for Connan's heart and stately home, before she can eventually be sure of his innocence and true devotion to herself.

Martha then joyously becomes the Mistress of Mellyn, and in a postscriptorial note to the main saga proudly and engagingly informs us that during her long, 'stormy' but blissful life with her 'self-willed' hero she has produced five sons and five daughters who have 'in their turn' also been 'fruitful'. (Thus fictional passion goes the real-life way of all flesh – into domesticity.)

Throughout the 1960s, in the wake of the enormous success of *Mistress of Mellyn* and Victoria Holt's similarly atmospheric *Bride of Pendorric* (1963), there was a greater demand for 'modern gothics' than for any other type of romantic story. Among its outstanding exponents were Catherine Gaskin, Dorothy Eden, Phyllis Witney and the pre-eminent crime writer who was equally at home with the mystery emotional adventure, Mignon C. Eberhart.

Mary Stewart, whose first novel, *Madam, Will You Talk?*, was published in 1955, is in a class of her own. Her books can be seen as extremely satisfying contributions to the suspenseful love-story but, in fact, she transcends restrictions of genre and formula. Her fourteen romances have an almost forty-year span, the most recent being *Stormy Petrel* which was published in 1992. (During the 1980s she turned away for a period from contemporary suspense novels to produce four devastatingly effective sagas of Merlin, Arthur and Dark Age Britain which are indeed chronicles of 'power and terror and bright vision'.)

More than the works of any other author in the field, Mary Stewart's illustrate how the quality of the gothic adventure has altered as its heroines have become (at serious as well as superficial levels), intelligent, assured and responsible. Active in their own interests with a force and dynamic denied to most pre-1950s heroines, they have commitments to careers and society, as well as to the unravelling of the particular mystery and complex love affair in which they have become entangled.

Even when a Stewart leading lady succumbs most ardently to the attractions of the hero, she is capable of sacrificing a romantic relationship if the demands of justice, compassion or intelligence so dictate. She grows in psychological stature during the course of overcoming the hazards which surround her, and emotional fulfilment is the outcome of self-understanding and maturity rather than an end in itself. Nevertheless Mary Stewart manages to sweep her characters – and readers – along on a surging tide of truly gripping tension and flaring romance, with wryly humoured awareness thrown in for good measure. Vivid locational atmosphere from the Scottish islands to the South of France, from Cumbria to Corfu, and satisfying links with history, literature and legend, are not just mood-setting trappings but integral elements in the unfolding of the dramas.

Nine Coaches Waiting (1959) is Stewart's only true governess-gothic. Linda Martin is twenty-three and, at the beginning of the story, leaves London for the remote Savoyard valley where she is to become nursery-governess to nine-year-old Philippe, Comte de Valmy. He, like herself, is an orphan; he lives in the Château Valmy in the care of his uncle, Léon de Valmy, whom he seems to fear. Léon manages Philippe's vast estates with energy and fierce dedication despite being severely disabled after a motor accident and confined to a wheelchair: he projects an aura of enormous power and is 'the handsomest man' Linda has ever seen, although his slightly haggard intensity and sharp, almost psychic comments cause her mentally to dub him 'the Demon King'. Before she recovers from the shock of his impact she meets his son, Raoul, who strongly resembles Léon in looks but not in personality. While the 'fallen-angel ... kept himself banked down, so to speak, and burning secretly, Raoul was at full blaze'.

Half-French and half-English, Linda is delighted to be back in France after an absence of nine years spent in the kindly but unimaginative atmosphere of the Constance Butcher Home for Orphans in London. As soon as she arrives at Valmy she responds to its rivers, gorges, winding roads and forests:

> What met me with the rush almost of a wind was the sunlight and space and the music of the trees. Everywhere was the golden light of late afternoon. The air was cool and sweet and very pure, heady with the smell of pines and with the faint tang of the snows.
>
> A far cry, certainly from Camden Town.

Soon, however, she discovers that there is menace as well as beauty at Château Valmy. Someone is trying to kill Philippe, and, because it is to them that the inheritance would come should he be murdered, Linda's suspicions fall on Léon and Raoul.

It is particularly bitter gall for her to feel that Raoul might be implicated because, from the first moments of their meeting, when she almost crashes into his Cadillac (rather as Jane Eyre collides with Rochester's horse), there is a rapport between them. After an evening out together, which is hastily arranged to help Linda get over the shock of having been fired at by an unknown assailant, it is obvious that the attraction between them is physical as well as mental:

> It wasn't the brandy . . . It was a much more deadly draught. There was one thing that stood like stone among the music and moonfroth of the evening's gaities. It was stupid, it was terrifying, it was wonderful . . .
>
> For better or worse, I was head over ears in love with Raoul de Valmy.

Linda realizes that she must escape from the château with Philippe in order to save him, and knows that this puts paid to any chance of romance developing between herself and Raoul. If, as she fervently hopes, he *is* innocent, how could he ever forgive her for suspecting him? However, 'there it was. For Philippe's sake I had to assume Raoul's guilt . . . The child had only one life to lose, and I couldn't stake it.'

Mary Stewart harnesses all the elements of fear and flight and Philippe's extreme vulnerability to build up a climax of suspense. Almost to the end Linda does not know whether or not the dishy Raoul de Valmy is a villain or a hero – but, of course, there is eventually a splendidly romantic resolution to the story. Although strictly speaking this is the author's only gothic exploit, she has used the ingredients of menace, deception, murderous intrigue and intense sexual response in most of her non-Arthurian novels, notably *Wildfire at Midnight* (1956), *Thunder on the Right* (1958) and arguably the most compelling of her suspense stories, *The Ivy Tree* (1962). A measure of the richness of these is that even when they have been read several times, and provide no further surprises or revelations, the frisson and the romance remain.

M. M. Kaye is best known for her novels which are set in the India that she and several generations of her family knew so well. However, over twenty years before she wrote *The Far Pavilions* she produced half a dozen mystery romance stories, each of which was set in a different country. Lush emotional dramas in exotic locations, these were often also infused with gothic elements, with the heroine imprisoned on a boat or in some seedy hotel room, for instance. Like Mary Stewart's feminine leads, M. M. Kaye's heroines are lively, intelligent and slow to be put down by arrogant or scheming males. The titles generally indicate the setting – *Death Walked in Kashmir* (1953), *Death Walked in Berlin* (1955), and so on. Two of the most atmospheric are *Death in Zanzibar* (originally published as *The House of Shade* in 1959) and *Death Walks in Cyprus* (1956). *Zanzibar* is particularly pacey: not long out of school, Dany Ashton has to rely on guts rather than experience when she is entrusted with conveying a mysterious package to her family in Zanzibar. Her way is cluttered with corpses and colourful but dubious characters of various nationalities. International intrigue, a popular fictional subject in the 1950s, rears its weary head, and she gamely sets about sorting the baddies (communist agitators) from the goodies (supporters of the Western democracies). Fortunately she is eventually able to obtain assistance from a handsome and enigmatic male stranger although at first she cannot make up her mind whether he is the suspected murderer or her perfect potential lover.

In *Cyprus* the heroine, Amanda Deringham, also starts off as an innocent, but like all Kaye's leading lights, she becomes a fast learner in order to survive. She leaves her guardian in Egypt and sets out to visit Cyprus. Even before her ship docks, a female travelling companion drops dead in Amanda's cabin – and this is only the beginning. She is plunged into a vortex of fear as several of her acquaintances meet violent, inexplicable deaths and she realizes that she is at the top of the hit-list. In sharp contrast to all this murky menace, there are the compensations of olive groves, sun-baked slopes, cobalt seas and – most comforting of all – the attractive hero's supportive shoulder.

'Barbara Michaels' and 'Elizabeth Peters' are pseudonyms of the American Egyptologist Barbara G. Mertz, who helped significantly to update the tone of romantic suspense novels during the 1970s and 1980s. Like Mary Stewart, she writes beyond the strict confines of any genre; she has commented that she abhors 'the word gothic as applied to anything except the novels of Mrs Radcliffe and "Monk" Lewis', and that her own books are 'mysteries . . . written from the point of view of a female protagonist' and incorporating 'romantic plot elements' (*Twentieth Century Romance and Historical Writers*). Her engaging heroines are intelligent enough to take feminism for granted, and to be more concerned with their scholarly researches and demanding careers than, initially at least, with responding to the hunky heroes, or solving the mystery puzzles which confront them. Plots are tautly structured and lucidly presented but, despite their general air of erudition, never over-earnest or pretentious. Historical, mythic and supernatural elements are often slotted persuasively into the action.

New slants are given to vignettes of old houses with ghostly denizens and dark, ancient, apparently unfathomable secrets. *Greygallows* (1972), *Someone in the House* (1981) and *There I Stay* (1983) are, in spite of the author's resistance to their being classified as such, among the most arresting gothic adventures of the last quarter-century. Whether they are set in Cornwall or Pennsylvania, these mysteries continue to compel the imagination after the book has been read and put down. *Black Rainbow* (1982), for example, has an ingenuity of plot resolution that brings intriguing new dimensions to the Victorian governess fantasy. It harks back to upper-crust rural society during the 1850s. Megan O'Neill displays more than the customary measure of governessy determination in ensnaring the affections of her employer, Edmund Mandeville, who is the master of Greyhaven Manor and its spreading acres in deepest Warwickshire. With a refreshing disregard for the English story-book heroine's traditional sense of decorum, Megan unashamedly eavesdrops, schemes and outwits an affluent rival, thus triumphantly achieving her emotional and social ambitions. But she gets more – far more – than she bargains for.

The appearance of an eerie black rainbow presages disaster. Clever, calculating Megan finds herself increasingly menaced by the uncontrollable forces of primitive fear and superstition, violent social disruption and – most pernicious of all – by the horrifying irrationality of her husband's behaviour. It is no wonder that by the end of the book Megan and her sister-in-law Jane have to take the law uncompromisingly into their own hands, and Megan finds herself reflecting that 'perhaps marriage is not always the best for everyone'.

Another author with a gutsy approach to the mystery romance is 'Hilary Ford' (real name Samuel Youd, but probably best known under another of his pseudonyms, John Christopher). As Hilary Ford he wrote three romantic suspense stories – *Sarnia* (1974), *Castle Malindine* (1975) and *A Bride for Bedivere* (1976) – in response to his agent's suggestion of his 'having a go at the gothic'. Inquiring cautiously just what *was* a gothic, the author received the reply, 'really I suppose it's about a girl in danger, and a smell of money'. There is no doubt that by the 1970s the boundaries of the genre were loosening. Samuel Youd makes the point in an article in *Million* magazine of May/June 1991 that what his agent should have suggested was humiliating the girl at the centre of the action rather than putting her in danger. He reaches this conclusion because he had toughened up his heroines in the course of his three gothics but, apparently, the more robust they became the more readers turned away. It seems to him that 'there is a suppressed masochism in women readers to which the gothic novel, in particular, ministers'.

The darker faces of romance were recognized in 'Nightshades', Fontana's stylish early-1980s series designed to give a 'modern slant to the age-old pattern of courtship and love'. These uprooted the gothic formula of romance titillated by outrage, intrigue and seduction, and transplanted it into modern settings. The heroines are competent, jet-setting career girls who manage to cope with a bizarre range of hazards from psychic manipulation to gangland warfare. They are, of course, no longer confined in crumbling old houses where something horrid clumps threateningly around the corridors, nor are they passive victims of masculine lust. The mood is consciously glossy, with the leading characters cutting a dash in Porsches and Ferraris, while dazzling real-life celebrities sometimes pop in to adorn the plots: 'Guy told her that Anthony Burgess and Bjorn Borg bought their croissants there.'

Sticking closer to tradition and heralded in a *Daily Mirror* review as 'a marvellous blend of *Gone with the Wind* and *The Thorn Birds*', Reay Tannahill's *A Dark and Distant Shore* (1983) can hardly live up to this hype, but it is full-blooded, fiery and atmospheric. Its heroine, Vilia Cameron, is one of those born-before-their-time ladies whose ambitions know few limits. The story sweeps (and there is no other word to describe its momentum) through the lives of three generations of a divided and tempestuous family. At the centre of events stands the castle of Kinveil, wind-raked, mist-swirled, set in the wild Scottish Highlands and overlooking the sea towards Skye. Vilia, deprived of Kinveil, is determined to recover her heritage by whatever means are necessary. *A Dark and Distant Shore* not only deals with the relentless pursuit of her individual dream but covers highpoints in Victorian history and Empire-building.

Reay Tannahill faithfully reiterates the intensities of the nineteenth-century romance, but in *A Bloodsmoor Romance* by Joyce Carol Oates, which also appeared in 1983, these are raised to the level of flamboyantly imaginative black comedy. The circumlocutory, euphemistic narrative style is exactly appropriate, and much of this pastiche's effectiveness lies in the contrast between its admonitory tone and the outré events that it has to convey. The physical setting is vast (Pennsylvania, New York City, the Wild West) and so too is the range of characters, from social and spiritual revolutionaries like the mountainous Madame Blavatsky at one extreme to young virgin innocents at the other. The story starts with the five daughters of a genius inventor doing their fancy sewing and discussing how they can genteelly capture the right kind of husband. The youngest girl, Deirdre, running away from her sisters after a squabble, becomes the prey of an aerial balloonist abductor. An adopted child whose ingratitude and deviousness have sometimes shocked her family, she is hurtled after her kidnap into the occult manoeuvres of the early Theosophists, becomes a skilled and celebrated medium, and chooses to remain completely cut off from her parents.

She is not the only daughter to be lost to them. Malvinia succumbs to the degradations of a theatrical career, while Constance adroitly escapes her husband's over-athletic sexual attentions on her wedding night by slipping a dressmaker's dummy beneath the sheets – which he mounts before even noticing the substitution! She disappears, finding the courage to follow her real inclinations and assume a male identity. Samantha elopes with an admirer who is unacceptable to her family. Only Octavia settles for 'respectable' Christian marriage, and she certainly gets the worst bargain of all the sisters through enforced participation in the bewildering sexual rituals demanded by her apparently conventional but actually convoluted spouse. Joyce Carol Oates provides gothic accoutrements in abundance, although, despite the book's title, romance of the genuine rather than the send-up variety is intentionally sparse.

Mary Higgins Clark has pushed the emotional macabre tale into greater realism and sharper-edged horror than many of her predecessors. Her 1975 *Where Are the Children?*, for example, has the grimly compelling theme of a child-molester murdering his own children, while the girl who answers a personal ad in *Loves Music*,

Loves to Dance (1991) meets a serial killer. However, like Mary Stewart and Barbara Michaels, she is adept at introducing romantic elements into her suspense stories as well as focusing on heroines who are intelligent and likeable. They clearly illustrate how the role of the young woman in a gothic story has changed from the beginning of the genre when she was far less active in her own interests. The author has commented that in all her books 'the woman is strong. She's *vulnerable* often; she is being drawn into a net she doesn't understand, but she always helps in her own salvation.' She also braves extremely hazardous situations in order to protect those who are dear to her, as in *Where Are the Children?* when she goes alone to a house to save her offspring although she knows she will have to confront a man who is mentally deranged, and in *While My Pretty One Sleeps* (1989) when she expects to be killed but tries to warn her father to keep away.

She considers that the appeal of her stories 'lies in the fact that they are about ordinary people whose lives have been invaded by malign forces' – which, of course, might happen to almost anyone in today's unsettled society. She also tries to present the victims of crime more cogently and hauntingly than as just 'chalk marks on the floor . . . It's somebody's mother, somebody's wife, somebody's sister' – and eschews gratuitous sex or violence partly because she knows she is read by twelve-year-olds as well as adults, and partly because she believes that better results are achieved when quite a lot is merely suggested and then left to the reader's imagination.

She has given the gothic arena wider boundaries by introducing moral and political issues. For example, in *The Cradle Will Fall* (1980) the leading lady, Kate DeMaio, is a lawyer who, confined briefly in hospital after a minor accident, discovers and has to unravel a grisly project that violates medical principles and decent human feelings. In *Stillwatch* (1984) we are in the world of television and top-of-the-heap American politics. The story is spiced with stimulating or bizarre trappings, with old, unsolved mysteries, resurrected love-affairs, designer clothes, death, disablement, houses of menace and secrets, the wheeling and dealing of high-powered TV executives and statesmen, the Oval Office – and even touches of the Kennedys in their 'pre-Camelot' period.

At twenty-seven, Pat Traymore, a successful TV presenter and interviewer, has made the decision to move back into the family house in Georgetown, a Washington suburb. She wants to be in political circles because she is planning to make a documentary about Abigail Jennings, a woman Senator who is in the running for the Vice-Presidency, but her decision to return to the house signals something far more important in Pat's personal life. She has decided to confront the gruesome mystery of her childhood. She last lived there when she was only three years old, and her memories of the event that traumatically changed her life are only half-conscious. She knows, however, that her Congressman father is supposed to have killed her mother and himself in the Georgetown house and left Pat so badly injured with a fractured skull and a shattered leg that she was in a coma for a year. To protect her from scandal and gossip, her grandparents gave her a new identity and for years Pat has been under the misapprehension that she had been adopted.

Yet another reason for her wanting to return to Washington is to pick up, if possible, the threads of an affair with Congressman Samuel Kingsley; their romance had ended some time ago because he could not leave his badly disabled wife, but since the latter's death Pat has cherished hopes of being with Sam again. His reluctance to revivify the relationship springs from their age difference – he is twenty years older than she – and his fear that he is now too jaded to begin to match up to her vitality, competence and 'smouldering sexuality'. But he does, of course, eventually – Pat is not the sort of girl to take no for an answer, and anyway Sam cannot help succumbing to her proximity and the admiration he feels for her bravery in uncovering the truth about her horrific family tragedy.

Pat seems to be surrounded by mysteries and intrigue; as soon as she has moved back into her old home she begins to receive threatening telephone calls from someone who quotes from retributive scriptural texts, is determined to kybosh her proposed feature on Abigail Jennings and to punish her (Pat) in revenge for her father's supposed crimes (even though she was of course the innocent victim of these). The caller is obviously mentally disturbed, but knowing this doesn't by any means lessen the sense of fear and threat that hangs over the house; in fact it probably sharpens it.

The tensions and triumphs of Pat's TV work are conveyed with colourful immediacy: she rubs shoulders with the rich and famous from showbiz to the seat of government, she looks fetching and can afford arresting clothes which women envy and men admire: to a White House dinner she wears an Oscar de la Renta green satin gown with her grandmother's emeralds and, for daytime business functions, a 'burgundy-and-grey tweed suit, obviously a designer original ... burgundy leather boots with the small gold Gucci trademark [American authors always seem to use Gucci as a symbol of life in the fast and affluent lane, see Chapter 13]; the matching shoulder bag; the Burberry over her arm'.

However, in spite of the glamorous aura which she projects, Pat is still, like so many other heroines before and after her, trapped in the terrors of being shut up in a house in which lurks a hostile and probably a homicidal presence:

> Pat stood with her hand resting on the telephone as though by touching it, she could hear again every single word Sam had uttered. Finally, still smiling softly, she started up the stairs. A sudden creaking sound overhead started her. She knew what it was. That one board on the upstairs landing which always moved when she stepped on it ...

Worse is to follow; before she manages to clear up the secret which broods over her own past – and an intrigue which surrounds Senator Jennings – she is not only immured in the house against her will but tied hand and foot, with her mouth taped, and flames licking all around her. Nevertheless Mary Higgins Clark manages to extract her intact from these 'Perils of Pauline' situations, *and* to reward her with romantic fulfilment.

During the 1990s there seems to be no slowing down in the production of variations on the gothic amatory tale. Some of these, like the novels of Mary Higgins Clark, have settings of today, but most look back to earlier, and particularly to the late-Victorian or Edwardian, periods. One of the most evocative and appealing is *Malina* (1993) by Penny Perrick, which has as its backcloth the west of Ireland from the 1880s to 1917. The appropriate mood of mists and murkiness (both physical and psychological) is established in the opening sentence: 'My husband's first wife threw herself off the dunes at Horam's Cove and died.' (Arresting first sentences have of course become statutory ever since Daphne du Maurier's now classic start for *Rebecca*, 'Last night I dreamt I went to Manderley again.')

Celtic backgrounds and cultures, however vaguely defined, seem especially appropriate for sagas of great houses which are solidly built but surrounded by disturbing human or natural elements. Cornwall, Wales and areas of Scotland have been well used for this purpose, and now Connemara comes into its own as the site for Malina, a residence on the edge of a lake, with wooded slopes behind it, which was designed and built for the English Charles Trewin. Like its owner, Malina suffers many mood-changes: To the robust, twelve-year-old Rose Erris McCalla, who is brought there by Charles ostensibly to help with the horses because of her 'way with animals', it seems 'grand', 'a fairy palace growing out of the glittering water', but bleakly unlived-in, a kind of empty mirage which reflects the failure of Charles's wife Harriet to put her mark upon it, or indeed on their married life. She is pale, thin, childless and frightened: the energetic, over-confident and, at this point, insensitive Rose is irked to the edge of hatred by her lack of spirit: 'Harriet wore wanness like a badge of suffering. That's what I couldn't abide.' Her resentment goes almost beyond reason: 'I could not acknowledge or explain what was almost a lust in me to make Harriet unhappy, or why, where she was concerned, I was as taunting and unscrupulous as any playground bully.' Although Rose responds to Charles's wit and exuberance, she does not realize how strongly he is attracted to her or that he has already marked her out as a future mistress of Malina. With the thoughtless arrogance of youth she becomes his unwitting abettor in the tormenting of Harriet which ultimately drives her to suicide.

So far, so gutsy. Our sympathies tend to be with the beleaguered wife rather than the brash young thing, but the author then cleverly effects changes in Rose's attitude and circumstances that enlist our emotions on her behalf. Charles remains the villain of the piece; having destroyed one wife he now proceeds to do a psychological demolition job on her successor, but, happily, Rose is made of sturdy enough stuff to cope with his miseries and machinations. More and more she finds consolation in Malina which in her care seems to develop a lambent personality of its own. Even its many enchantments, however, begin to fade when she meets Irish-American Peadar Griffin and discovers that

> Everything is moonshine compared to the education of the heart. I, a horse-trader's daughter, who had viewed life as a transaction, giving nothing unless sure of a return on my investment, had learnt how to squander myself, to give and give and ask for nothing in return.

Peadar is not obviously the material of which heroes are made. 'Blinking and stringy and prone to stomach disorders', he nevertheless has fiery visions of freeing Ireland from its English oppressors, and in the 1916 Easter Rising he dies – ingloriously – accidentally shot by another of the Volunteers. Rose is left, a year after his death, with the knowledge that at last the English are beginning to think of going home, that she now has a child (surprisingly, as it turns out, not Peadar's but Charles's), that her husband has been mellowed by events into an almost tolerable companion – and that she still has Malina.

Malina stands apart from other contemporary big-house romantic mysteries because of its vivid, allusive language, which, though both lyrical and dramatic, is perfectly attuned to the unfolding of the story's relationships and events. Atmospherically it is highly charged, but never over the top even though wild or lugubrious Irishness can so easily become over-lush. The author remains satisfyingly aware of this; despite the fact that everything Irish tends to be untrammelled and free while Englishness is represented as heavy, restrictive and unimaginative, Harriet, the sadly persecuted bride from across the water, is allowed just one spirited and perceptive comment: 'my ears are dinged with the Irish howl'. It is part of the same howl that began in Otranto, reached its crescendo at Thornfield Hall and Manderley and seems set to continue into the twenty-first century.

CHAPTER TWO

Piety and Passion

W**HEN STRIPPED** of their gothic elements, Victorian
novels which targeted female audiences often became little
more than watered-down expressions of religiosity. Heroines had
to prove their worth as potential wives by ministering earnestly to
the poor, practising self-denial and domestic economies and dem-
onstrating their amiable submissiveness to the all-providing male
in general and to their fathers, fiancés and husbands in particular.
The moulding of spirited young leading ladies into subordinate
characters hardly produced stimulating or entertaining reading,
and many so-called romances of the mid-nineteenth century were
in fact little more than religious tracts.

Charlotte M. Yonge's *The Heir of Redclyffe*, published in 1853,
was primarily concerned with moral uplift but also provided a
dramatic story-line and plenty of powerful emotion. It was to
delight a wide variety of readers with its concepts of chivalry,
honour and romance – although the latter was firmly of the non-
sexual variety. Charlotte's constant desire to point a moral had
inspired her to become a Sunday School teacher and, in her teens,
to write religious features for *Magazine for the Young*. In 1843,
when she was just twenty, her first novel was published. As its title,
Abbey Church, or Self-Control And Self-Conceit suggests, it was not of
a frivolous nature. Her preoccupation with sin and self-sacrifice,
springing from her extremely religious upbringing, was to provide
the theme for *The Heir of Redclyffe*, which graphically illustrated
how the sins of one generation could poison the lives of its

descendants, and how redemption might come about by religious humility and selfless love.

Sir Guy, the eponymous heir to a great estate, also (quite injustifiably) inherits the dire reputation of his 'fiery violent' and murderous forebears. He loses his parents in infancy and, later on, goes to live with his uncle, whose daughter Amabel ('Amy') Edmonstone is particularly pretty and sweet-natured. She and Guy fall in love, but he is deeply aware that because of his supposed bad blood he has little to offer her. Nevertheless, it is made clear to the reader from the beginning that he is every inch the hero, with a wonderfully handsome, open face, incredibly lustrous eyes, an utterly truthful nature and an unquenchable nobility of soul. His love for Amy, 'beyond all power of telling', is courtly and reverential rather than physical or passionate. Even before he finds the courage to declare it, however, she feels so attracted to him that 'her shrinking modesty and maidenly feeling' drive her to pray about her apparently over-warm and even possibly impure responses. (Charlotte was always very keen on young girls searching their hearts and souls for evidence of unwholesome feeling and behaviour. In her own life, prompted by 'high-minded admonitions' from her parents, she rooted out any 'temptation to personal vanity' or passion that she could find.)

It is a long time before the lovers can be united in matrimony. The villain of the piece, a cousin of Guy's called Philip, further vilifies the heir of Redclyffe's reputation by falsely telling Amy's father that Guy has gambled away much of his fortune. It is only after his being barred from the Edmonstone home, suffering hardships and performing a gallant rescue at sea, that Guy's real worth is recognized by Amy's family.

Amy and Guy marry, and he further demonstrates his dedication to religion and virtue by suggesting that they spend their honeymoon visiting 'all the cathedral towns of England'. In the end, Switzerland is settled upon as a more suitable location. For the first part of the honeymoon they are idyllically happy, although readers are given no evidence of physical consummation – throughout the long saga Guy and Amy do not even exchange kisses. But bliss is rudely interrupted when Philip crops up once again. He is also on the Continent, and the lovers learn that he is suffering from malaria and is close to death. They hurry off to nurse him, apparently bearing no malice for his earlier attempts to wreck their romance, but although Philip recovers, Guy succumbs to the fever and, after a long and uplifting death-bed scene, leaves Amy and the world of the living for ever.

Of course, the ignoble Philip is so moved by Guy's self-sacrificial devotion to himself that he becomes a reformed character. Despite the fact that the text has steered Guy and Amy well clear of sex, she gives birth to his daughter, who cannot inherit Redclyffe because it has to go to the male who stands first in the line of succession. Ironically, this is Philip. However, Charlotte sugars the pill of his taking over the home and estates of the man whom he had wronged: she provides several chapters about the desirability of reconciliation and forgiveness – and Philip marries Amy's sister, Laura, thus tenuously keeping Redclyffe in the family.

The Heir of Redclyffe was widely read and appreciated in its time. It started a vogue for high-flown and religiously inspired romantic novels which was to continue for almost seventy years. With Guy and Amy putting their moral principles above everything else, and with death so abruptly curtailing their marital happiness, Charlotte's book was seen as representing the triumph of idealized or spiritual love over temporal satisfaction.

Two notable and still-remembered novels dealing with the conflicting pulls of religion and physical fulfilment were published in 1867, fourteen years after *The Heir of Redclyffe*. These were Augusta Jane Evans Wilson's *St Elmo* (in America) and Rhoda Broughton's *Not Wisely But Too Well* (in England).

St Elmo appeared only a year or two after the ending of the Civil War whose upheavals might indirectly have helped to bring about the book's occasionally innovative tone. By today's standards, however, it is not exactly revolutionary, and there is a curate's egg approach in its progressiveness. Its heroine, Edna Earl, achieves literary success after some tough struggles against prejudice, but abandons all career aspirations when she has – after even tougher struggles – converted the eponymous hero from thoughtless and sometimes sadistic hedonism to caring Christianity, and consented to marry him. However, with the character of St Elmo the author created a cult figure which several decades later was to inspire Margaret Mitchell, who, of course, with *Gone with the Wind*, wrote the most addictive story ever about the American Civil War and its immediate aftermath.

It is difficult at times to realize that aspects of St Elmo helped to stimulate the creation of Rhett Butler because Augusta Wilson's hero lacks the sustained, virile and fully-fleshed appeal of the man who was to woo, win and eventually walk out on the wayward Scarlett O'Hara. A great deal of Butler's appeal lies in the fact that he always remained true to his own lights and his own instincts, undeflected by passion or circumstances. St Elmo, who starts out promisingly enough with loads of colour and charisma, is eventually flawed by his conversion. Somewhere along the rocky road to salvation he is transformed from macho-lord-of-creation to meek-and-long-suffering lover.

Augusta Wilson was born in 1835 at Columbus, Georgia, on the Alabama border. Rather like Ouida (see Chapter 3), in all her novels she gave her heroines interesting and unusual roles and insisted that every woman should make the most of her talents and capacities. However, also like Ouida, she did not support women's suffrage and, somewhat dauntingly, prefaced *St Elmo* with an anti-feminist quotation from Ruskin: 'Ah, the true rule is – a true wife in her husband's house is his servant; it is in his heart that she is queen.' Ruskin, of course, could allow women to rule his heart but not other important organs: it is possible that Augusta did not realize this at the time but, even so, the quotation seems a cold douche to the flames of romance.

St Elmo was Augusta Wilson's fourth novel and, like all her books, is studded with gems from other writers, including Keats, Dante, John Stuart Mill, Goethe, Scott, Tennyson, Schiller, Byron, Pope, the classics, scriptures and popular hymns of her day. The action is also enhanced – and/or held up – by lengthy pages of argument about marriage, love, Darwinism, women's duties and rights. From this background of earnest verbiage, St Elmo stands out like a streak of lightning against the night sky. His character unfolds through the eyes of Edna Earl who, at the beginning of the story, is 'that pure-hearted Tennessee child' with black eyes, shining hair and an 'unusually transparent complexion which is rouged by early exercise and mountain air'. She is, we are told, completely free from the corrupting influences of society, and without ambition or greed. Orphaned as a baby, she has been brought up by her blacksmith grandfather who, though keeping her free from the conditioning of society, has exposed her to massive indoctrination from the Bible, *The Pilgrim's Progress*, *Irving's Sermons and Parables* and other religious tracts, as well as *Guy Mannering* and 'the Greek Sages and Hebrew prophets'.

With her parents having died long ago, she suddenly loses both her grandfather and step-grandmother. Leaving the old rustic home to work in a factory in Columbus, she travels by train, accompanied only by her grandfather's dog, to whom she is devoted. The train crashes and many passengers, including the dog, are killed. Edna suffers a dislocated shoulder and broken bones in her feet which for a time make walking impossible. Small wonder that, for her, 'the chilling belief was fast gaining ground that God had cursed and forsaken her . . .'

Happily, Mrs Murray, a gracious and affluent lady, befriends and adopts Edna. In the warmth of her kindness, Edna's religious convictions are quickly restored, although she is sad to find that she cannot respond positively to Mrs Murray's son, St Elmo. He is twenty years older than Edna, and chivalry is not one of his strong points. He jeers at his mother for taking Edna in and suggests with blood-chilling offensiveness that her protégée will make off with the family's 'silver forks, diamonds, and gold spoons' and that even his watch will not be safe in his pocket.

St Elmo is tall, athletic and physically impressive, even though his looks have been flawed by 'the ungovernable flames of [undefined] sin'. He has thick, waving brown hair . . . his features were bold but very regular: the piercing steel-grey eyes were unusually large, and beautifully shaded with long, heavy, black lashes, but repelled by their cynical glare: and the finely formed mouth, which might have imparted a wonderful charm to the countenance, wore a chronic savage sneer . . .

Although Edna can hardly bear to look at this renegade, he gets under her skin. She regards him as a Satanic incarnation and, almost as soon as she is well enough to walk again, gamely defies him in the name of God when he is savagely beating one of his dogs which has got out of control.

During Edna's progression from early to late teens, every encounter between St Elmo and herself increases their mutual antipathy. This is, of course, a sure signal to the reader that they will eventually fall into each other's arms – but the author makes everyone wait a very long time for this.

St Elmo continues in his questionable ways, frequently travelling abroad and, when he is at home, smoking cigars by the hour in his own part of the Murray home which is furnished with distinctly un-Christian trappings intended to underline his depravity. However, even while Edna's spirituality expands by leaps and bounds, she finds herself becoming attracted to this 'tempting demon'.

We are given frequent glimpses of Edna and St Elmo casting secret, yearning looks at each other, and when Edna has made up her mind to leave the protection of Mrs Murray's home and go to New York as a governess St Elmo brings matters to a head. He declares his love in extravagant terms – 'my pearl, my sole hope, my only love, my own pure Edna' – but she rejects him because he is still an unrepentant, atheistic sinner. Much as she loves St Elmo, and wishes to redeem him for Christ, Edna does not weaken. Giving him as a consolation a copy of a very earmarked and annotated Bible, she sternly spells out her situation: 'Mr Murray – I cannot lift up your darkened soul: you would only drag mine down.'

He, of course, cannot pretend to religious feelings which are not sincere. With characteristic arrogance, he is convinced that Edna will be unable to forget him, claims that he is her 'conqueror' and, forcing her to kiss him, swears to wear this kiss 'on his lips till death stiffens them'.

It comes as no surprise to the reader that, from the moment of her rejection of St Elmo, Edna begins to receive frequent proof of the virtues which underlie his irreligious exterior. (What moves her most of all is his erection of an obelisk for her dead grandfather's hitherto humble grave.)

She goes to New York and not only pursues a governessing career but becomes a successful writer.

She is horribly insulted and browbeaten by several male editors (as well as St Elmo and an elderly minister of religion who befriends her) for thinking that, as a mere woman, she has something important to write about. There is also plenty of condemnative narrative comment about women writers (surely an irony, considering the author's own gender) in whom, apparently, the creative spark is likely to become 'a flame which generally consumes the female in whose heart it burns ... She may write well but she would be better and her life would be sweeter if she earned her living at the wash-tub, or in the dairy or by the needle.' The subjects of Edna's writings, by the way, were unsensational to the point of innocuousness: they included aspects of fifth-century Athenian life and 'a glowing tribute to the liberators of Helvetia' entitled *Keeping the Vigil of St Martin under the Pines of Grütli*.

Undeterred by criticism, Edna continues to struggle with governessing and writing until she collapses into 'hypertrophy of the heart'. Her doctor prescribes complete rest but she drives herself on. She is, however, by now anxious to reveal to her readers that the only worthwhile career for a woman is that of homemaker. The flagrant anti-feminism of Edna's new – and last – novel, *Shining Thrones of the Hearth*, is made clear by Augusta Wilson in several thousand words of text which applaud it but do not explain her heroine's change of view.

While in this mood of womanly surrender, Edna again encounters St Elmo who has by now been redeemed by her noble influence (and, presumably, that annotated Bible). He has been ordained into the Christian ministry, and his new-found humility seems quite awful to the reader (though not to Edna who agrees to marry him): 'the dare-man, dare-brute, dare-devil expression had given place to a stern mournfulness and the softening shadow of deep contrition . . .' The subdued St Elmo prepares to lead his shattered-by-over-work bride to the altar. She lapses into unconsciousness for two hours before he can get her into the church, during which time he experiences the delectation of kissing her lips repeatedly until 'the blood shows itself again' in them.

Just before the marriage ceremony, in which 'they earnestly consecrate their lives to the service of Jesus Christ', St Elmo has a flash of his old manly and masterful spirit, although the expression of this is hardly flattering to Edna:

'Today I snap the fetters of your literary bondage. There shall be no more books written! . . . And the dear public you love so well must whistle for a new pet. You belong solely to me now and I shall take care of the life you have nearly destroyed in your inordinate ambition . . .'

After all this, one might well wonder if *St Elmo* was to be Augusta Wilson's literary swan-song, but, in fact she went on to produce several more novels although she never achieved another hero who caught the public imagination as St Elmo had done.

Rhoda Broughton's first novel, *Not Wisely But Too Well*, as mentioned earlier, was published in the same year as *St Elmo* – 1867. Rhoda littered her narrative with telling quotations as liberally as Augusta Evans Wilson and also shared that author's determination to stress how easily a young woman might be deflected from godliness to ruin. However, she wrote more zest-fully, was not afraid to describe physical passion, and carried the fictional kiss to hitherto unrecorded heights and depths.

Kate Chester, the seventeen-year-old heroine, starts out with an appealing natural vivacity and a robust attitude towards social niceties and relationships generally. She seems, despite her youth, to be very contained and in control of her life, but Colonel Dare

Stamer, the son of family friends, manages to put her at a disadvantage whenever they meet. He oozes not only charm but power: six foot two against Kate's five foot three, he is 'deep-chested, clean-limbed, thin-flanked . . . with long sinewy arms and a great columnar throat'. His face is described as extremely intelligent, and 'ugly' but 'magnificent'. His hair is dark and thick and his moustache of the 'great, soft, black-brown . . . and drooping silky' variety that was so much admired by the Victorians. To set off his arresting looks he sports an eyeglass.

At social gatherings he flirts with Kate, stirs her to a 'new-born, uncalculating passion' and then simply ignores her. Just when it seems, however, that Kate is 'casting her soul's costly pearls before swine', Dare turns the full force of his virile power upon her 'soft luxuriance' by inviting her to take unchaperoned walks with him without the knowledge of her family. Fate, thus tempted, soon gets out of hand and Kate finds herself every morning and evening fantasizing about the dashing Colonel Dare when she should have been starting and ending her days with prayer. Dare lives up to his reputation as a cad and a roué. He is already married – although Kate does not then know this – but deliberately sets out to seduce her. He exploits to the full his wide experience with women which is contrasted with Kate's innocence, and looking up into his 'rapt green eyes' that have become 'wells of liquid fire', she succumbs to his kiss:

> off went the last rags of restraint, and he wrapped his arms around her as she stood before him, tighter, tighter, and bent down his head from its stately height to her small uplifted face, nearer, nearer, till their lips met, and were joined in a wedlock so fast, so long enduring, so firm, that it seemed as if they could never be divorced again.

Rhoda Broughton cannot resist a quotation from Fatima here: 'Once he drew/In one long kiss my whole soul through/My lips, as sunlight drinketh dew.'

Dare then shows the full force of his ruthlessness (and the Victorian double standard, because we know only too well that he has no intention of remaining entirely faithful to Kate). He swears,

'I'd cut your dear little soft throat here, this very minute, if I thought any other man would ever kiss you as I have done today.'

It should be remembered that in 1867 a fairly full-blooded description of a kiss was just about as shocking as one of explicit sex might have been. Indeed, having brought her plot – and her two main characters – almost to a climax, Rhoda Broughton seems not quite to have known how to proceed. She falls back on her sometimes engaging and sometimes irritating habit of throwing asides into her narratives:

> 'I've done. I'm tired of writing about love-making. When two people have climbed up to the extremest pinnacle of insane bliss, it is best to leave them alone there. They come tumbling down quick enough, without any one's help: and so there I leave Dare and Kate.'

Of course she doesn't leave them long. The first of Kate's battles between good (chasteness) and evil (passion) takes place on page 101, and these continue for another 250 pages. Dare persuades her to elope, but at the eleventh hour she realizes her folly and draws back from the brink of ruin. She has, nevertheless, become the classic woman-as-victim – initially because of Dare's exploitativeness and then because of her own over-developed conscience and sense of sin. Her young and vital life seems besmirched for ever: there are many references, although she is still only in her teens, to the imminence of death, with Kate having visions of herself expiring, loudly panting and gasping for breath (and 'who would care to kiss her then?'). However, 'she has been given yet a little space – a little space to do evil or to do good in'. Kate chooses the latter and throws her abundant youthful energy into a dreary round of do-gooding and spiritual studies under the guidance and encouragement of a thin, hungry and absolutely uncharismatic curate called James. He falls in love with her but dies of malaria before he can do much about this, knowing that Kate, in spite of all her noble works, still hankers for the deep but destructive passion that only Dare could bring into her life.

She suffers a bout of brain-fever, but *does* meet him again, when she goes with friends to an exhibition at the Crystal Palace. Even then he is dallying with another woman of the obviously 'fast' type whom he quickly casts aside on seeing Kate. Once again he woos her with wild and loving words and more of his scorching kisses. There is also recrimination and self-pity. Flagrantly distorting the facts, he blames her for his own vices and for having sent him 'galloping along the road to hell ... You saved your own soul, I daresay, very comfortably and properly, but you ruined mine.'

Poor Kate is torn apart. She feels that his kisses 'would make up for anything ... would compensate ... and far more than compensate' for the loss of 'virtue and respectability, and duty, and plenty of friendly relations', but knows that going off with the already married Dare would literally sentence both the lovers to the eventual fires of hell. She can, if they agree to part, offer one profound consolation: 'Just think what a short wretched span life is ... Dare, Dare, I know – I feel certain – that Heaven will be pitiful to us; and not let either you or me drag our weary years to anywhere near three score-and-ten.'

Despite kisses and cajoling, meaningful moustache-stroking and blood throbbing vigorously through his veins (a sure signal of Dare's sexual arousal), he fails to persuade Kate to live 'in sin' with him. Having escaped ruin by a hair's-breadth for a second time, Kate (after another spell of brain-fever) devotes herself entirely to charitable works 'among the smoky reeking alleys and courts of filthy, heart-rending London'. She decides at last to become a Sister of Mercy, having already, so as 'not to be taken unconsciously by the Great Reaper', put aside 'all decoration and gaiety'.

However, before finally renouncing the world, she attends a ball with her family. Dare rushes there to make yet another desperate bid for her affections. His carriage is overturned just as it reaches the ballroom: he is mortally injured and, despite several pages of Kate's pleading for him to throw himself on God's forgiveness, or at least to let her 'say one little prayer for him', he refuses to repent.

Kate has only two solaces. The first is that on Dare's deathbed he asks for the 'withered poppy' which she had given him long ago 'when their love was young' to be buried with him. For the second she has to wait until 'many days had come and gone, when youth was just beginning to merge into grey beautyless middle age' and – worn out with good works – she follows Dare into a fairly early grave.

Although at its worst *Not Wisely But Too Well* seems yet another dispiriting saga of woman destroyed for ever by man, in its more positive moments it broke new ground through Rhoda Broughton's uncompromising focus on physical fulfilment. She was only twenty-two when she wrote the novel: a parson's daughter, she obeyed the moral edicts of her time by never competely allowing the passions of her leading characters to find resolution outside matrimony. Despite this restraint, her early books were considered so scandalous that for some time they were taboo in polite society. Later in her career she produced witty novels which were as much concerned with sharp observations of the social scene as with romance (*Mrs Bligh* (1892), *A Waif's Progress* (1905), among others).

She published her first few books anonymously. In the 1860s, of course, there was still a sense of the risqué about women writers, so several were tempted to follow the example of the Brontës and use pseudonyms which could be masculine, neutral, or flamboyantly unreal in order to hide their true identity. This subterfuge was employed to placate authors' parents or husbands as well as to protect themselves.

Marie Corelli had no such inhibitions. She was not only an immensely popular romance writer but, for about fifteen years around the turn of the nineteenth century, almost certainly the most successful of all living English authors. Her books were bizarre mixtures of quasi-mystical morality and pseudo-science which, although practically unreadable today, obviously struck the right note with late-Victorian and Edwardian audiences. With hindsight it is difficult to understand exactly why they were so appealing. Even in their time they found scant favour with critics who were so mocking and derisive that after the mid-1890s Marie refused to send out review copies. (She dismissed her critics' antipathy as jealousy of her 'genius'.) Her style is fuzzy and inflated; her narrative view is self-indulgent; her plots are rambling and unconvincing, and none of her characters lifts off the printed page. Yet her fans, who included Queen Victoria, Mr Gladstone, the then Prince of Wales, the Dean of Westminster and Ella Wheeler Wilcox, remained tremendously loyal. What she *did* offer was enormous dollops of passion, sentimentality, proseletyzing zeal and a belief in herself that was assured to the point of arrogance; of course, many people, then as now, were attracted to certainty and positivism.

For Marie, whose real name was Minnie, fact and fantasy were always blurred. Claiming aristocratic Venetian parentage, she was apparently born in 1855 in modest circumstances in London, the illegitimate daughter of Charles Mackay, a song-writer whom she was to call her 'stepfather'. Possibly the insecurity of her early background prompted some of her later excesses, when her life became as extravagant and overblown as her novels. She became the self-appointed guardian not only of the interests of the Almighty but of Shakespeare when in 1899, at the height of her literary success, she took up residence in Stratford-upon-Avon where she lived until her death in 1924. (During this time she imported a gondola from Venice, plus a gondolier in full regalia, to shuttle her up and down the Avon.)

With an extraordinary capacity to distort the truth of any situation for her own ends, Marie made enemies wholesale. She had no sense of humour (as indicated by her books) and was an inveterate name-dropper and lionizer. Mark Twain, who suffered her attentions, described her as 'the most offensive sham'.

Minnie Mackay took the name of Marie Corelli in 1884 when she began to write. Her first novel, *A Romance of Two Worlds*, published in 1886, is a narcissistic fancy which sets the tone of her whole canon. It describes a love affair of larger-than-human proportions: in fact a celebration of the 'divine' two-way love with which the author is constantly preoccupied. Its unnamed heroine is an 'improvisatrice' pianist – surely based on Marie who had described herself in these terms when, before becoming a writer, she had embarked on a brief career as a professional pianist. The fictional music-maker in *A Romance of Two Worlds* is suffering fromn acute nervous debility, but this is quickly put right by Heliobas, an occultist from an ancient Chaldean culture, who not only gives her an elixir which renews her soul-substance but transports her – in the flesh, one gathers, as well as in dreams and visions – throughout the universe to learn its uttermost secrets. It is a difficult book to get to grips with because the heroine spends so much time floating through the ether 'in a sea of translucent light' and, in an extremely meandering, amorphous manner, discussing the sweet mysteries of life with Heliobas, the angels, Jesus Christ and God himself.

What makes us tick is at last revealed to the reader. It is, quite simply, 'human electricity'. Electrical impulses are the essence of everything in the universe – charging, sustaining, transforming, renewing. It is all extremely vague and unsatisfying. However, Corelli provides some specific and helpful details about Heaven, which is not only, of course, sizzling with electricity but quintessentially circular. It is, overall, a 'Fiery Ring' which is made up of smaller circles and spheres, illuminated by 'rainbows' and 'opal tinted lights'. The whole place is 'scintillating' and 'jewel-like', with God and 'all pure souls dwelling' at its centre.

Marie saw nothing pretentious or absurd about all this and went on to produce further books of mystical revelation. *Ardath* (1889) features a male in the leading role, who not only hobnobs with angels but becomes one of them and marries another. *Barabbas* (1893), as its title suggests, is a biblical saga which gives a graphic, emotional account of the Crucifixion, explains exactly why Judas betrayed Jesus (it was all to do with his sneaky sister Judith Escariot!) and stresses Christianity, rather than the occultism of her earlier books, as the means of human redemption. *The Sorrows of Satan* (1895) shows Marie Corelli on intimate terms with the Devil, who has repented of his rebellion against God and is fervently yearning to get back on to the side of the good and conformist angels. Satan is encouraged in this aspiration by the saintly Mavis Clare (who not only shares Marie's novel-writing profession but her initials) with whom he falls in love. The insinuation, of course, is that Marie is so charged with grace and goodness that she can redeem even the Devil.

More straightforward love between men and women does crop up from time to time in the books, but the earthbound activities of Eros are a poor second to the doings of the high-flying, semi-celestial beings who can say, with absolute conviction, that 'In Life's great choral symphony, the keynote of the dominant melody is Love!', and that this Love is 'the Breath of God', and so on, and so on.

In 1897, when Marie Corelli's novels were in their heyday, the *Publisher's Circular* declared that 'of all forms of fiction the semi-religious is the most popular!' A lot, of course, depends on the definition of 'semi-' and 'religious' here. Late-Victorian authors of romances must have been extremely aware of the need to perform constant balancing acts between temporal and spiritual needs and passions; to know just when the religious motif could enhance or dramatize a plot, and when it might simply submerge the story. It worked efficaciously for Florence Barclay, who used it in many of her novels as a catalyst to the flowering – or recognition – of earthly desires. As befitted a minister's wife, she stuck strictly to the symbols and tenets of Christianity. For her the heady and hazardous occult trappings employed so frequently by Corelli seemed strictly taboo. Probably because she was helpmate to a busy parson husband as well as being the mother of two sons and six daughters, her output is low in comparison with that of Marie Corelli, Elinor Glyn and Ethel M. Dell who were writing at approximately the same time. She produced only thirteen novels over a thirty-year period compared with Corelli's twenty-seven, Dell's thirty-eight and Glyn's twenty-five.

Florence Barclay was born in 1862 and her first novel, *Guy Mervyn*, which she wrote under the pseudonym of Brandon Roy, was published in 1891. In this she tackled the theme of love between a young man and a much older woman which was to recur in several of her novels in parallel with the predominant motif of the effects of religious conversion on her leading characters.

Time and again, for her heroes and heroines, divine and mortal love became intricately intertwined. In the author's eyes, love between man and woman, however deep and passionate, was a fraught, inadequate and tacky business unless both partners had opened themselves up to Christianity, in other words, 'come home to the Father's house'. Barclay's books are still readable and persuasive because, in spite of their heavy sentimentality, she wrote with fervour and sincerity, was a good story-spinner and – unlike Corelli – did not completely drown her characters' humanity beneath highly wrought, pseudo-spiritual attitudes.

Her declared aim was 'never to write a line which could introduce the taint of sin or the shadow of shame into any home', and she firmly adhered to the idea that 'The only excuse for fiction is that it should be more beautiful than fact.' These precepts could, of course, make for fictional blandness, but she managed to introduce dramatic light and shade into her narratives, even though she avoided creating those 'mean' and 'morbid' characters who she felt were far too evident in real life.

Her most triumphant fusion of sacred and spiritual love, and her most intense story, was *The Rosary*, which was published in 1909. Florence sets her scene at a typically Edwardian aristocratic house-party where the guests of the elderly Duchess of Meldrum include her niece, the Honourable Jane Champion, and the artist, Garth Dalmain (often known as 'Dal'). The contrasts between these two are incisively drawn. Jane, at thirty, is pretty well 'on the shelf': Garth, at twenty-seven, is in the full flood of his vitality, achievement and sexual magnetism. Jane at five foot eleven and twelve stone is distinctly hefty (though full of feminine fragility under the skin). Her 'massiveness' and plainness of features are constantly referred to, but it is made clear that she is 'a perfectly beautiful woman in a plain shell ... no man had as yet looked beneath the shell and seen the woman in her perfection'. 'The absolute perfections' of Garth's fine-featured, dark-haired good looks are, however, obvious to all. As his upper-crust hostess comments:

'Really, Dal, it is positively wicked for any man, off the stage, to look as you do, in that pale violet shirt, and dark violet tie and those white flannels . . .'

At one level Jane is a representation of the Edwardian 'new [liberated] woman'; the educated girl; the sport or tomboy who would prefer to play a vigorous round of golf with a man than to go to bed with him. Garth and other young men of her acquaintance tend to call her 'old chap' and see her as a great chum but not as a romantic partner. Nevertheless her athletic wholesomeness makes them respect her enormously:

> Old Jane was superb! Fancy! . . . She drives like a rifle shot, and when she lofts you'd think the ball was a swallow; and she beat me three holes up and never mentioned it. By Jove, a fellow wants to have a clean bill when he shakes hands with her!'

Like most of the young women at the Duchess's house-party, Jane cannot fail to respond to Garth. She is even more aware of his inner beauty than his outward charms: 'She knew the beautiful story of Garth's boyhood with his widowed mother. She knew his passionate adoration of her sainted memory.' Jane realizes that Garth often hides his sensitivity beneath an exuberant extroversion, and she too keeps her deepest feelings under wraps: for her it is music that 'is a sort of holy of holies in the tabernacle of one's inner being. And it is not easy to lift the veil.' It is typical of the self-effacing Jane that this profound passion for music is normally only expressed in public when she accompanies others on the piano, although she has a magnificent singing voice. However, she stands in at short notice for a visiting singer who is indisposed, and overwhelms everyone with her rendition of *The Rosary*. 'The deep, perfect voice thrilled through the room. A sudden breathless hush fell upon the audience.' Garth in particular is transfixed and transformed. With his eyes shining 'like burning stars', he commands her to sing it again – which she does, several times in the course of the narrative. Her wonderful voice has 'lifted the veil' of her inner being and Garth 'has passed within'.

Once again, as it so often does in popular fiction, music has acted as the catalyst to love: 'I have found her,' he said, in low terms of rapture, 'the ideal woman, the crown of womanhood, the perfect mate for the spirit, soul and body of the man who can win her ...' There is a great deal more in this vein but sadly the confident, charismatic Garth is unable to persuade Jane to become his wife. She loves him, of course, but is so conscious of her own plainness compared with his magnificence that she fears his sudden, wildly romantic passion for her will as quickly evaporate. She rushes away out of his life, and it is only when fate cuts Garth's glories down to size by blinding him (see Chapter 4) that Jane feels she can become his (almost) equal partner. Even so, she has first to be with him in his hour of need, disguised and incognito. As 'Nurse Rosemary' she cares for him, and helps him to come to terms with his terrible disability. (She manages adroitly to protect her anonymity by nursing him without ever touching him – surely a remarkable feat.) Astoundingly he does not recognize his nurse's speaking voice as Jane's. He confides deeply, desperately and frequently to 'Nurse Rosemary' how much he loves and longs for Jane; she eventually puts him out of his misery by – guess what? – singing *The Rosary* to him so that he will know her true identity, and understand that she is now prepared to marry him. She realizes that he has now also learnt, as demanded in the climax of the song, not only to respond to romantic love but 'to kiss the cross' of suffering or renunciation. In other words, his conversion to Christianity is complete. He can accept everything, even his blindness, as the will of God, so there is no further barrier to the fulfilment of Jane and Garth's mortal passion. There follow scenes of intense but fairly unphysical lovemaking, with Jane's womanliness at last finally unleashed. Readers are given the additional satisfaction of learning that Garth's creativity flowers again in the light of their happiness; no longer able to paint, he discovers and develops a flair for musical composition.

One of the first skills that an Edwardian romantic author had to master was, of course, to manipulate her plots and her characters' desires so that the hero and heroine do not fall too fixedly into each other's arms until the closing paragraphs. Florence Barclay was particularly adept at finding ways to postpone or prevent altogether the final physical consummation – which in her canon took second place anyway to religious fulfilment.

In *The Following of the Star* (1911) it is the hero's missionary work and subsequent life-threatening illness which separate the lovers. The marriage of Diana, a wealthy heiress, and Rivers, an impoverished missionary, is supposedly one of convenience which will make it possible for her to share and donate lavishly for his noble work in a typhoid-infested area of Africa. After the wedding ceremony he takes off to his sad and swampy mission-field while Diana languishes for a while in her comfortable, gracious home in England. The author provides plentiful clues about the Rivers' true emotional state: it becomes evident to the reader – though not to them – that they are terribly in love with each other. A curiously convoluted and long-drawn-out courtship by correspondence takes place which seems dogged by misunderstandings and crossed or delayed letters. When at last they are reunited, Rivers is apparently on his death-bed and Diana's first moments of physical intercourse with him are uncomfortable rather than ecstatic. She has to kneel at his bedside, cradle his head on her breast and clasp her arms around him. His doctor encouragingly suggests that if she can maintain this awkward position 'all night', her husband might be saved: 'your vital force is vitalizing him. It is like pouring blood into empty veins; only a more subtle and mysterious process, and more wonderful in results.' Diana is nothing if not game, and, as well as following the doctor's urgings, she also throws in for good measure, as it is Christmas Eve, a few verses of 'Hark the Herald Angels Sing'. Needless to say, this combination of physical and spiritual intensity does the trick.

For the lovers in *The Broken Halo* (1913) things are less simplistic. Dick is a young doctor with little interest in the spiritual life but a dedication to helping his patients through their physical difficulties. Somewhat tainted by ambition (he hopes to buy an affluent city practice), he marries a wealthy woman who will help financially to forward his career. She is older than he – a lot older, in fact, somewhere in her seventies – *and* suffering from a weak heart.

From the beginning of their marriage they have separate rooms (nominally because of her delicacy) and at first it seems that Dick will simply hang on to the shell of this strange marriage until he can collect the expected rich pickings. However, it is not long before he begins to be deeply influenced by the faith of his 'Little White Lady' wife, which lifts him out of the doldrums of his materialistic attitudes into a strong spiritual and emotive bonding with her. Touchingly, he discovers that he is profoundly in love with his undemanding spouse: 'Earthly and heavenly love, in the fullness of their perfection, had been revealed to him together: and his heart stood still on the threshold of these holy sanctuaries . . .' Alas, he never gets beyond the threshold and into the Little White Lady's bedroom. Before their wonderful mutual love can be consummated she has a heart attack and expires, obligingly leaving him all her worldly goods so that he can carry on his medical work and find himself a younger – and, one has to surmise, a more suitable – romantic partner.

Florence Barclay made no extravagant claims about her own work although *The Rosary* and several of her other novels were to provide inspiration for several generations of readers. As noted in *The Life of Florence Barclay* (attributed simply to 'one of her daughters'), she recognized that those who read her books did not demand 'art for art's sake' or some 'literary *tour de force*' but asked 'merely to be pleased, rested, interested, amused, inspired to a more living faith in the beauty of human affection and the goodness of God'. She successfully harnessed the tricky theme of love between a young man and a considerably older woman (often frowned upon by society: see Chapter 12) to stress the importance of divine love and human self-sacrifice – particularly in the case of the female partner.

Annie S. Swan, who was to become one of the most prolific writers in the genre with some 250 novels to her credit, gave kissing and close physical contact a fairly wide berth in her early 1880s novels. She used religious themes in several of her books but less intensely than Florence Barclay. Her career spanned almost half a century which, of course, allowed her fictional love-making eventually to hot up considerably. She saw herself not so much as a reformer or revolutionary but as a kind of agony aunt: from the beginning of her literary career, advice on emotional and social problems flowed from her pen almost as readily as novels and short stories. The protectiveness she felt for her readers was potently conveyed in books such as *Courtship and Marriage, and the Gentle Art of Home-Making* (1893) and *Letters to a War Bride* (1915) as well as in her many articles on etiquette and romantic problems written for the monthly magazine *The Woman at Home* which she edited from 1893 to 1917. (She was also to edit *The Annie S. Swan Penny Stories* from 1898 to 1899 and the *Annie S. Swan Annual* from 1924 until the 1930s.) Her advice to the lovelorn was frank and down to earth:

> Do not marry the man ... Better a little heartache now than a lifetime of unavailing regret ... What if you have to earn your own living? Anything is preferable to the desolate wifehood which, in the circumstances would certainly be yours.

Frustratingly, we do not know the vices of the man in question which have prompted so uncompromising a reply, but one imagines that Annie is dealing here with the demon drink. The last words of her reply to this particular correspondent illustrate her care and conscientiousness: 'Let me know your decision, which, I trust, will be a refusal.' Much of her advice ends on a religious note – 'Bear ye one another's burdens, and so fulfil the law of Christ' – and similar gems of spirituality also punctuate her novels and factitious works such as *Elizabeth Glen, M.D.: The Experiences of a Lady Doctor* and *Memories of Margaret Grainger, Schoolmistress*.

Her novels are often concerned with missing or defrauded heirs, secret marriages and young people driven from home to seek pastures new by unimaginative or ruthless elders. Many of her heroines have a tough time: they endure their suffering with a patience that harks back to early Victorian tales.

Downtrodden skivvies and shop-girls receive a lot of attention, possibly because many of Annie's readers came from this section of society, but there is also romance in high places where fierce pride and false hopes lead affluent young ladies into melodramatic situations. Everything is seen from the woman's point of view, which is the general rule of the genre, but has the effect in many of her novels of emasculating the hero by making him a cypher. It is hard to find a Swan male with charisma. Despite her popularity she was not an innovator: the most interesting of her novels are those that provide insights into contemporary issues, for example the suffragette campaign in *Margaret Holroyd* (1910). There is also a specially intense atmosphere to be found in the books which she located in her native Scotland, where her heroines seem even more oppressed than their English counterparts, although her use of local dialect makes the reading of certain passages a daunting task.

In her agony-aunt role Annie frequently encouraged girl readers to take up paid work, but her novels stress that women should be protected by men and are not fitted to play an active part in public or business life. When, for example, in *The Curse of Cowden* (1897) the father of Janet and Lizzie Leslie dies, they realize with something akin to horror that in order to survive they will have to open a small private school. Even though 'Janet is by nature brave and self-reliant ... her five and twenty years' experience of life, and her own powers of observation, had taught her that it is a pitiful thing when a woman, gently nurtured, has to take her place in the fighting ranks of life.'

Incidentally Janet is eventually on the receiving end of one of the least rapturous proposals ever offered to the heroine of a romantic story: the Laird's long-estranged son, Ludovic Bonthron, who had once shown distinct partiality for Janet, returns after an absence of several years, during which he has never even sent a letter. He visits Janet and, after commenting bleakly that 'the years have told' on her and he hopes she hasn't forgotten him, Ludovic adds: 'And you'll let me begin where I left off – only with some new privileges. You'll be my wife, Janet?' Her response to having inspired a proposal is, like that of most Swan heroines, 'trembling', 'blushing' and 'wavering' – but positive. When she indicates her acceptance she is 'gathered close to his heart' in what appears to be a kiss-less embrace.

In spite of their staid and homely tone, Annie's romances appealed so much to different generations of readers that with only minimal updating many were relaunched decades after their original publication. Her 1898 *Shadowed Lives* was reissued and well received over half a century later (its subject was the dire social repercussions of alcoholism, a theme which has remained sadly and perpetually relevant).

Annie's long-suffering female characters were permitted little or no lip-contact with their lovers but, as long as descriptions of the sexual act or even heavy petting remained beyond the literary pale, other authors emulated Rhoda Broughton's emphasis on kissing as the ultimate expression of passion. Berta Ruck was born in 1878 and lived for exactly a hundred years. She was to become another prolific romance writer whose stories were published from 1914 until the end of the 1960s. Kisses and kissing cropped up in several of her titles, from *Khaki and Kisses* (1915) and *The Bridge of Kisses* (1917) to *Half-Past Kissing Time* (1936) and *Quarrel and Kiss* (1942).

Joey Dale, the heroine of *The Bridge of Kisses*, which has a Great War Home Front setting, is positively preoccupied with kisses, although at the beginning of the story no man's lips have ever touched hers, not even those of Hilary Sykes, the affluent but dull architect to whom she has just become engaged. This relationship has been foisted on her by circumstances: she is marrying to provide financial security not so much for herself as for her mother and sister, and her two little cousins, Cecil and Harry, who live with them. Her father is abroad on active service and, apparently, money is terribly tight. After Hilary has invited her to become 'the fairy of his hearth and the angel in the home', he begins to realize that he has taken on more than he bargained for because although Joey has all the 'womanly, old-fashioned virtues' she is also spirited and independent, used to running her family, and wants a say in how her future will be managed. Hilary tries to seal their engagement with a kiss, but is interrupted by a minor but literally bloody fracas brought about by the small but 'wicked' cousins. Days afterwards, when her fiancé has been whisked off to Scotland, Joey is still rejoicing that he has done so before she 'had to put up with so much as a first kiss'. It is obvious that Hilary is on a losing wicket. Joey says, in her chatty, first-person narrative:

> The first kiss! Of course, one reads about the wonderfulness of it, and the throbs and thrills and the feeling that life will never seem dull or ordinary again. All those girls in books like it so awfully . . .

but goes on to comment that with Hilary she is sure she would 'simply loathe it'.

Because of her young cousins' illicit activities, Joey has a series of skirmishes with Dick Rowlands, a good-looking army officer who is in charge of building an important bridge near her home. To her amazement she finds herself speculating about how she would respond to *his* kisses, and then she actually takes the initiative. By this time, he has become a friend of the family and is present when she receives a letter confirming that her father has been wounded in action. When she breaks into fearful sobs he hugs her comfortingly and Joey reacts by kissing him – though only in a sisterly way: 'The kiss was just a very little one, under the bridge-builder's ear.'

She still cannot bring herself to allow Hilary to kiss her. His petty and patronizing ways compare unsympathetically with Dick's imaginative flights of fancy. Joey is particularly impressed when he gives his version of how the gap between the sexes can be spanned:

> 'There's a bridge there already,' said Dick Rowlands in that soft voice of his. 'The only one that could ever be put across such a gap.'
> 'What is that?'
> 'Love,' replied the bridge-builder, simply. 'The Bridge of Kisses'.

It is, of course, only a question of time before he is 'showering down' on Joey's eyes and lips and throat kisses which more than live up to her image of what these should be.

Throughout the 1920s and 1930s fictional passion continued to peak in the kiss. However, with the wartime lifting of many social restraints during the 1940s and the increasingly liberal mores of the 1960s and afterwards, romantic authors were soon able to write without restriction about every aspect of physical relationships between men and women – and between members of the same sex. The kiss as a symbol of release or rapture or union then became far less prominent in the general run of love-stories, although naturally it continued to be a keystone of plots which were set in pre-war and pre-contraceptive pill eras.

In the 1990s, Barbara Cartland must be the greatest exponent of the kiss, because so many of her amatory fantasies are set in Regency or Victorian times, and because she never allows her leading men and women, of whatever period, to get into the bedroom together unless they have first been respectably wed (see Chapter 7).

There are countless examples of kissing in the Cartland canon: their essence is summed up in the closing lines of *Dollars for the Duke* (1981) when Magnolia, a nineteenth-century heiress, has at last resolved all her misunderstandings with the dishy, Byronic Duke of Otterburn:

'I love you! I adore you! I worship you!' the Duke cried.

Then their hearts were beating against each other's and his kiss was that of a fighter, a conqueror who had fought against tremendous odds and was the victor.

Yet he was very gentle as she surrendered herself to the insistence of his mouth . . .

Then love carried them on the waves of ecstasy into the starlit sky, and they knew that nothing mattered now except that as a man and woman they were one now and through all eternity.

Dame Barbara provides us with many slight variations on the theme, but waves of physical rapture opening out into the eternal and the infinite and the divine are constant ingredients of her kisses.

Judith McNaught, who like Cartland also draws on the Regency period for many of her settings, is another contemporary writer who lingers long and lovingly on the kiss. She gives rather more anatomical information, however. In *Whitney, My Love* (1987) the different stages in the lengthy process of sexual sparring between the hero and heroine are summed up in the changing quality of their kisses. When she is angrily resistant, for instance, his mouth throttles her screams 'to an hysterical whisper' as his lips move on hers 'with fierce tenderness, shaping their soft curves to his own'. By the time she has come to want his kisses, 'dazed with passion and longing', he crushes her to him with his mouth opening over hers, 'slanting fiercely back and forth', and while she 'glories in the wild excitement', his hands shift 'possessively across her back and down her spine, then lower to cup her buttocks, moulding her closer against his hard legs and thighs, forging their two bodies into one'. And, as if this isn't enough, 'an eternity later' he deepens his kisses until flames are 'shooting through her veins' (see Chapter 7).

There are, of course, many more kisses in romantic extravaganzas which are described with matching relish. One of the most touching of all, however, is conveyed in simple, direct and low-key terms at the end of Mary Webb's *Precious Bane*, which was first published in 1924. Prue Sarn, the rustic heroine who is cursed with a hare-lip and by the primitive superstitions of the people living in her village, has become the repository of blame for every tragedy that affects the community. She is set upon by an angry mob, accused of murder and witchcraft and tied to a ducking-stool. Only the sudden appearance of Kester Woodseaves the weaver, whom Prue has for some time loved in secret, saves her from drowning. He restores the violent crowd to sense and order, takes Prue up on to his horse and, like a knight of old, rides off with her:

> all faded in the quiet air. There was only the evening wind lifting the boughs, like a lover lifting his maid's long hair . . . and we were going at a canter towards the blue and purple mountains.
>
> 'But no!' I said . . . 'You mun marry a girl like a lily. See, I be hare-shotten!'
>
> But he wouldna listen. He wouldna argufy. Only after I'd pleaded agen myself a long while, he pulled up sharp, and looking down into my eyes, he said –
>
> 'No more sad talk! I've chosen my bit of Paradise. 'Tis on your breast, my dear acquaintance!'
>
> And when he'd said those words, he bent his comely head and kissed me full upon the mouth.

CHAPTER THREE

Stronger-Minded Heroines

OUIDA (Marie Louise Ramé) whose books began to be published in the 1860s, quickly established a reputation for flamboyant and daring fiction which found echoes in her own bizarre and extravagant life-style. With a deadly earnest belief in her own literary greatness she claimed, after George Eliot died in 1880, to be her natural – indeed her only – successor, declaring with absolute confidence, 'There is no one else who can write English.'

Her pen-name derived from her childish mispronunciation of her middle name, Louise. She lived from 1839 to 1908, was half-English and half-French, and played up her Gallic glamour for all she was worth. What she lacked in good looks and figure, she made up for in vanity, ostentation and self-aggrandisement, casting herself in the role of cultural *grande-dame*, adorning herself in designer gowns and blatantly embellishing the facts of her life with fanciful illusions and anecdotes. She saw herself as a campaigning, reforming writer who seriously challenged the currently accepted morality, but the ultra-fashionable, showily upper-crust settings of her novels removed them, and her social indictments, far from reality to what some contemporary critics dismissed as 'romantic absurdity'. However, she had her champions too – reviewers' assessments ranged from ridicule to near-reverence: her narrative force, graphic vocabulary and truly sweeping imagination compensated for the social and political inaccuracies which punctuated her outpourings. She was, despite her voluptuous fantasizing, eminently readable. Many critics played safe by barbing their compliments; the *Spectator*, for example, commenting in 1875 that Ouida's *Pascarel* was 'preposterous' but 'wild, luscious and beautiful'.

What she offered was certainly a welcome change from those staid stories of hearth and home that were becoming staple fare in 'women's' novels. Her heroes, whose over-the-top strength and courage sometimes seemed laughable rather than impressive even in their own time, can with hindsight be seen as distinct improvements on the worthy but wooden Sir Guy of *The Heir of Redclyffe*, just as her colourfully depicted and generally robust heroines were several steps up from Charlotte M. Yonge's rather insipid Amy. Cigarette, the girl soldier in Ouida's *Under Two Flags*, who dances 'with the wild grace of an Almeh, of a Bayadêre, or a Nautch girl' for the Algerian soldiers and then goes into battle with them, is certainly more arresting than Amy, constantly praying about her own imperfections.

Ouida saw herself not as a romance *raconteur* but as a serious, innovative writer whose realism would give new form, impetus and style to the novel. And of course she never regarded herself as catering for the female-escapist market. Encouraged by its distinguished editor, Harrison Ainsworth, she started her career by producing stories for *Bentley's Miscellany*, while *Under Two Flags* was first published in a military periodical. In fact when this, her best-known novel, appeared in 1867 it *was* influential though possibly not in the way which Ouida had predicted. Called by the critics everything from 'naughty', 'immoral' and 'outrageous' to 'sincere' and 'splendid', its heroine, Cigarette, was the archetypal fictional tomboy, the girl whose tough exterior hides a heart of gold; who claims equality of opportunity – and risk – with men, but also offers them her love and loyalty, and would have been the type to settle down in the story's final paragraphs as a conventional wife and fecund mother. There had been tomboys of a kind in novels written before *Under Two Flags* but compared with Cigarette these had been fairly bland.

Ouida's fantasies did enliven the romantic novels which flowed from many late-Victorian pens, and they also had a strong influence on the development of another genre: stories for girls in their early teens. There seems little doubt that the heroines of Bessie Marchant's thrilling 1890s' tales, who intrepidly tackled fearful hazards in the outposts of Empire and other far-flung regions, owed something to the soldiering-adventuress Cigarette. It is, of course, always difficult to know the extent to which an author is in the vanguard of accepted attitudes and how much he or she is simply quick to reflect these. It is interesting that in the same year that *Under Two Flags* was published in England, on the other side of the Atlantic Louisa M. Alcott launched her own break-through tomboy character, Jo March, in *Little Women*. More perceptively than preceding writers, Ouida and Alcott seem simultaneously to have recognized in their fiction the early stirrings of the contemporary girl's struggles for education, career opportunities and fuller participation in the social set-up.

Ouida was almost certainly the first woman to create a block-busting adventure-romance; she was also in advance of her time in exploiting (long before Robert Hichens, P. C. Wren and E. M. Hull, see Chapter 5) the alternately rhapsodic and ruthless fictional potential of the Arabian desert as a background for eroticism and/or derring-do. *Under Two Flags* was a best-seller from the 1860s at least until the 1920s. It was made into a play, and then filmed three times, in 1916, 1922 and 1936, with Cigarette played respectively by Theda Bara, Priscilla Dean and Claudette Colbert. Its rather complex plot begins to unfold in comfortable, upper-class England, with Bertie Cecil feeling forced to assume the identity of a brother whose name has been dishonoured. His determination to redeem his sibling's reputation takes him away from England, Home and Beauty (in the shape of the well-born woman whom he appears to love nearly as much as he does his magnificent horse, Forest King) to French Algeria where he joins the army. At times it is easy to lose the thread of how his subsequent exploits have any connection with achieving his avowed purpose, but all that really matters is the gusto with which Ouida hurls Bertie into different roles (from society swell to fugitive to soldier-hero) and into one adventure after another. During the course of these he meets and captivates the affections of Cigarette and overcomes not only the enemies of France but the savage challenges of the desert, taking in his manly stride many hair's-breadth escapes from death – for example, surviving gunshot wounds and having two horses killed beneath him.

Despite – or possibly because of – the vast differences in their backgrounds, the gritty Gallic girl fighter continues to fancy Bertie heavily. However, given little encouragement by him, she learns to play her romantic cards close to her chest. In recounting their bizarre relationship, Ouida turns several social and fictional traditions on their heads. Time and again Cigarette (though rather patronizingly referred to as 'the Little One') seems to be the tougher of the two: she adroitly extracts Bertie from frightful situations, hauling him out, when he is buried just-about-alive, from under a pile-up of dead and wounded men, and in the end sacrificing her own life for his. Bertie finds himself – terribly unjustly – facing a firing squad and, at the moment when the order to shoot is given, the doggedly devoted Cigarette staggers on to the scene and flings her own body between Bertie and the murderous bullets. (This interruption, rather surprisingly, brings about Bertie's reprieve.) She is allowed the supreme satisfaction of being clasped in his arms as she expires, with 'the unconscious tenderness of his kisses that had the anguish of farewell in them', and – at last – the opportunity to come clean about her ill-fated but undying passion. Her sacrifice has awakened Bertie into loving her although, of course, 'it came too late, this warmth of love' and in a matter of seconds, 'with the dauntless heroism of her smile upon her face like light . . . and in the midst of her Army of Africa the Little One lay dead.'

If Cigarette had survived and become Bertie's wife or long-term companion, there seems little likelihood that their relationship would have run smooth: one suspects that it would have proved even more disastrous than if the innocent and idealistic Juliet had lived to become bound for ever in matrimony to Romeo. It appears that Bertie quickly became aware of this too, because in spite of his affirmation of love for the Little One he soon returned to England where, with the family honour restored, and without any doubts or qualms, he married his former lady-love.

The progressiveness which Ouida demonstrated in allowing her heroines to break new ground was not always echoed in her own actions and responses. For example, she opposed female suffrage, preferring not to be 'a New Woman' but to influence events through her friendships with powerful men. It was in keeping with her self-appointed role of campaigning literary queen that she could support women as long as they were the under-dogs of society but felt it would not do for there to be too many queens in the hive. However, she was sufficiently liberal-minded to oppose the imprisonment of Oscar Wilde, and the fervour with which she embraced the causes of animal welfare and 'green' issues was wholehearted. One suspects that she was really more at home writing about dogs and horses than human beings, and indeed her most charismatic heroes were often described in terms of animal imagery (Bertie Cecil's eyes being, apparently, like those of a spaniel, and thus a touch more droopy than one might have imagined in such a vigorous and fanciable man of action). When Ouida abandoned England and Bury St Edmunds for Italy and Florence, she became known as La Signora De Cani (The Dog Lady). She gave sanctuary to every stray canine who came her way (being lady bountiful to the under-dog again) and it was said that she once had thirty strays in her home. Several of her novels feature dogs: a poodle answering to the name of Flick-Flack improbably trots along by Bertie's side during his time in the Algerian army, and in addition to writing *A Dog of Flanders* and *Bimbi* (animal stories for children), Ouida ambitiously produced *Puck*, a novel which has a first-person narrative from one dog and is dedicated to another.

Her feelings for nature were often sentimentally expressed by positive presentation of the peasantry in contrast with denigration of fashionable men and women. This is a recurring motif in much Victorian and Edwardian fiction but, as Ouida really relished writing about over-dressed and over-indulged trend-setters and sophisticates, her drooling over rustic roots did not always convince, despite the fact that, in real life, she campaigned sturdily to improve the lot of the Italian peasants.

According to contemporary accounts, Ouida was extremely plain, so she has to be admired for creating her own myth of beauty, elegance and genius and living this to the full. She never married but fell in love with an Italian marquis, and then with an operatic tenor named Mario, who was the inspiration for de Corrèze, the hero of her 1880 novel, *Moths*. In this, as well as playing out conflicts between real and false glamour (good symbolized as rustic simplicity and evil as sophistication), Ouida sybaritically indulges her love of music, and explores another theme which was to recur frequently in romantic fiction – the older woman's fear of losing her looks and appeal, and her hatred of the young.

Music of the sentimental variety was to become a key and catalytic element in the genre from *The Heir of Redclyffe* onwards (it is while his cousin Amy is playing the piano that Guy falls for her). On numerous occasions heroines captivate heroes by their warbling, piano-thumping and even whistling (the *siffleuse* achieved surprising popularity in late-Victorian novels). Many an erring man was abruptly pulled up in his wayward track by a musical reminder of the innocence of his childhood home, the brain-numbing nobility of his mother or the honeyed recollection of his first love.

In *Moths* it is music which brings and binds together the hero, de Corrèze, and the sixteen-year-old heroine, Vere. Ouida injects even more passion and intensity into *Moths* than *Under Two Flags*. Love is lushly idealistic but also at times unashamedly physical. Reflecting the author's unusual (for the period) tolerance of extramarital relationships, Vere eventually achieves romantic fulfilment by leaving her absolutely horrible husband and living illicitly with de Corrèze. Liberalism of this nature, plus passages which satirize not only social but literary and cultural pretentiousness – with which Ouida herself was, of course, generously endowed! – intrigued her fans but affronted many readers, to say nothing of alienating certain reviewers.

Vere's mother, Lady Dolly, a fluffily pretty but slightly fading matron, is addicted to city lights and plush pursuits. At the beginning of the book she is living it up at Trouville in France:

> She had floated and bobbed and swum and splashed semi-nude, with all the other mermaids *à la mode*, and had shown that she must still be a pretty woman, pretty even in daylight, or the men would not have looked at her so . . .

Her superficiality is further established by listings of her empty activities and bitchy 'friendships' with other women who also have more leisure and lucre than they can creatively cope with. She is one of the frequently mentioned 'moths' who give the novel its title: these are desirable but decadent ladies who nibble away at 'the ermine of life' feeding on the decency of others and giving nothing back.

Lady Dolly's seaside capers are drastically curtailed when Vere comes from England to join her. The mother resents the daughter on two counts: Vere is so obviously trembling on the threshold of young and vital womanhood that her presence suggests Lady Dolly's age to be higher than her publicly declared one, and the girl, whose soul is obviously sated with noble precepts and who looks 'like Burne-Jones's things' might well draw to herself and away from Lady D the fires of admiration that burn in many an ardent masculine breast. Like the wicked Queen in *Snow White*, the older woman is desperate in her desire to remain 'the fairest in the land' and will stop at nothing to counter the challenge of the young pretender. The struggle between Evil and Good is played out in constant personality clashes between the super-sophisticated Lady Dolly and Vere, who is not only an unspoilt child of nature but an athletic and somewhat androgynous one who can ride and shoot like a man whilst looking – without making any effort – fearfully fetching.

Lady D adroitly and autocratically removes Vere from Trouville's competitive social arena by marrying her off to one of her own former flames, Prince Zouroff, an immensely rich but depraved Russian. It is difficult to understand why Vere placates her mean-minded mama by agreeing to the match, especially as she has recently come under the spell of de Corrèze, whom, on one of her walks along the shore, she hears belting out chunks of Mozart's *Requiem* in a voice which is, appropriately, 'rich as an organ's swell, tender as love's first embrace'.

Vere's response is ecstatic and physical. Her heart leaps around in her breast like 'a throb of new warm life', and the burgeoning of passion between her and de Corrèze, intertwined always with music, is rapturously described. Despite his attraction to Vere, the tenor stands on the sidelines while she marries the beastly Zouroff (although he moralizes heavily about those 'ermine-eating moths' that then surround her). As de Corrèze fears, far from flowering in the Prince's gorgeous and glittering St Petersburg palace, Vere simply wilts; Ouida determinedly maintains this 'mothy' image of her heroine's finer feelings being devoured by Zouroff's worldliness and cynicism. Vere dutifully tries to please him but her evident physical unresponsiveness goads him into fury and further depravities.

Flowery images then begin to replace those of the ever-hungry moths: 'Beautiful but scentless' – and expensive – camellias and azaleas emphasize the barren-at-root splendours of the palace and the life of its court. Increasingly frustrated by Vere's coldness ('purity'), Zouroff spends a lot of time crushing roses and tearing off their petals; after giving birth to a sickly and sadly short-lived baby, Vere also starts shredding roses, and the 'despair that numbed her' is equated with frost killing a flower.

Vere finds consolation in occasional meetings with de Corrèze whose singing never fails to thrill and uplift her. They admit that they are in love but, as Vere is too noble to break her marriage vows, their passion is at first denied physical expression. Nevertheless, Ouida describes their responses to each other in strongly sensual terms, with hearts and other parts of their bodies aching in 'trances of ecstasy and pain' and with the lovers nearly 'drawn downward to their doom as a boat into a whirlpool'.

Zouroff (not unnaturally) gives up on Vere, and insults her by going off all over Europe on gambling, drinking and womanizing sprees. Eventually he fights a duel with de Corrèze. Astoundingly, although the singer is only too well aware of the Prince's ruthless, stop-at-nothing nature, he does not aim at his opponent but into the air. Zouroff basely shoots at the tenor's throat so that, although he survives, his wonderful voice is stilled, 'as a flower broken off in full blossom'. All is not lost, however. This barbarous act finally severs the thread of Vere's wifely allegiance to Zouroff. She rushes off to join the mute but still musical Corrèze, who manages to transfer his creative talents from singing to composing. Unmarried but undivided, and living quietly in a remote mountain village, they achieve a true partnership of mind and body, and Vere's ultimate fulfilment is sharply contrasted with the frustrations which beset the dismal and now undeniably middle-aged Lady Dolly who, despite her comfortable, cosmopolitan life, finds that flirtations, fashions and fripperies have lost their savour.

By the standards of today, sex in Ouida's novels was hardly explicit, but she packed her prose with a punch which left only the details of romantic close encounters to her readers' imagination. Her books are memorable for an overall atmosphere of intensity and outspokenness, although, with the exception of Cigarette, her characters have neither stimulated lasting affection nor become role-models.

The novels of Mrs Eliza Margaret Humphreys came to prominence in the 1880s and were supposedly written by 'Rita', an exotic-sounding name that seems more appropriate to a music-hall performer or a bare-back rider than a middle-class married lady. Like those of Ouida and Broughton, her romances were streaked with defiance of social conventions, as their titles suggest, from *Peg, the Rake* (1894) to *Betty Brent, Typist* (1908). The last-named book adroitly bridged the gap between Victorian romantic melodrama and career stories highlighting the struggles of the 'New Woman' which were to become extremely popular in Edwardian England. Rita was unable to create characters of conviction such as Ouida's Cigarette, or stereotypes like Broughton's self-centred, unchivalrous male, Dale Stamer, but her stories had rather more pace and action than many contemporary love-stories. Her *Two*

Bad Blue Eyes (1884) strikes echoes of *Moths* with its theme of a young woman whose betrayal by an older one might debar her forever from romantic fulfilment. But love *is* allowed, eventually, to rule over everything. Lovely Lauraine is virtually sold off by her mother to Sir Francis, an old and unappetizing roué. Just before her wedding day, Keith, her real love (and the eponymous 'two bad blue eyes' of the book's title), turns up, too late to snatch her from the ugly clutches of Sir Francis at the altar but in time to become a constant challenge to the marriage. Lauraine and her husband, of course, become part of high society which, we are told in strait-laced Victorian tones, is shot through and through with men – and women – who are as depraved as Sir Francis. There is, apparently, lots of money but little happiness in life at the top.

For several years Lauraine is pretty well trapped, although the still amorous Keith provides occasional outlets for her dreams and desires. Their paths cross only rarely and their sufferings remain intense, coming to a climax when Keith is brought to his deathbed in France after a duel, at the same time as Sir Francis who, in Italy, has succumbed to the less romantic afflictions of typhoid fever. Torn between duty to her husband and longing for her lover, Lauraine plumps – surprisingly, perhaps – for Sir Francis's bedside. Her loyalty to her almost enforced and distant marriage vows pays off: under her noble influence, her husband repents of his wicked ways in time to reap eternal salvation.

She is unable to wallow for long in this solacing situation, as she has to scuttle off to Paris to share what she expects to be the last moments of her 'two Bad Blue Eyes'. Happily, however, her arrival injects sufficient strength into Keith to enable him to recover, so that Lauraine, with the satisfaction of duty well done, can now look forward at last to the total flowering of true love.

'Rita' was better at conveying the untangling of complicated relationships and intrigues than describing romantic clinches. Kisses came far less frequently in her novels than, for example, in Rhoda Broughton's (see Chapter 2).

Elinor Glyn in her notorious *Three Weeks* (1907) exploited similar circumstances to celebrate blazing passion and sensuality.

The five novels which preceded her major opus were pert and basically unmemorable comedies of manners, morals, marriages and mismatches set in the worlds of high rank and fashion. *Three Weeks* also provides plenty of snobbish social comment but it is in a class of its own amongst Glyn's novels and a pioneering pace-setter in the romance genre generally.

Its fantasy-fulfilling plot is well known. 'Young and fresh and foolish' Paul Verdayne, a 'beautiful Englishman', ex-Eton and Oxford, is sent by his parents on a European tour to sort out his feelings for Isabella Waring, the local parson's daughter with whom he thinks he is in love. Amiable, but hardly the most seductive of young females, Isabella is six foot tall and 'broad in proportion': she plays golf and hockey, 'has a good run ... with the hounds' and sportily calls Paul 'old chap'.

Paul takes off to Paris, finds Versailles and Fontainebleau boring ('beastly rot') and flees to Switzerland where he meets an older, darkly handsome Slavic woman who, travelling alone and incognito, seems to him to be the quintessence of glamour, mystery and sexual allure. She soon erases Isabella from his consciousness. He does not learn her real name (though he eventually realizes that she is married to the ruler of a Balkan state) but simply thinks of her as 'the Lady'. During their three weeks together, she initiates him into the rituals and raptures of sex, enacted against voluptuous backgrounds with sybaritic props (tiger-skins, purple velvet pillows, couches covered with red roses, fountains of the Lady's favourite perfume, and music from apparently invisible violins). At the end of these nights of instructive passion, she has to return to her Baltic kingdom, taking with her not only the satisfaction of a job well done and a sense of ecstatic fulfilment, but also Paul's embryonic child (who will, it seems, be accepted without question as heir apparent to her husband's throne).

Such extravagantly celebrated adulterous love was, of course, heady stuff for readers in 1907, and when *Three Weeks* first appeared, in spite of its general popularity, strong objections were raised by many bishops, teachers and critics, to the amazement of its author who felt that she had written a highly moral tale which had been grossly misrepresented. In her view, love triggered off in Paul and the Lady an inspirational, soul-awakening nobility that more than justified the illicit nature of their mutual passion. There was also a kind of moral retribution in the book's ending. Soon after the Lady has been safely delivered of her and Paul's offspring – 'a fair rosy-cheeked ... golden haired' boy – she is stabbed to death by her 'evil-living', drunken husband. Paul suffers a desperate sense of loss (which eventually affects even his hunting prowess!) for death has snatched his peerless inamorata from him, and left him without interest in putting to the test with other women the sexual mysteries and techniques she has passed on to him. Also, of course, he can never claim his king-in-waiting son.

With hindsight it can be argued that *Three Weeks* broke down a great deal of Edwardian sexual prejudice and hypocrisy: it can, however, also be seen as a wildly titillating fantasy and a foray into voyeurism. In her 1937 autobiography Elinor wrote: 'It seems incredible now that it should have been thought so highly improper.' By 1990s' standards its detail is innocently inexplicit and its eroticism miasmic. It has assumed the nature of high camp, but remains far more readable than many early-twentieth-century romances.

Elinor lived from 1864 to 1943. With red hair, emerald eyes and an astoundingly white skin, she appears to have been the physical prototype for many of her own heroines. Her stories explored greater heights – or depths – of escapist fantasy after her marriage to Henry Clayton Glyn had turned out to be disappointing. His romantic interest in her rapidly evaporated: apparently he found the attractions of sport, gambling and good food more appealing and longer-lasting than those his wife could offer.

The escapism of *Three Weeks* is social as well as passionate: good character, physical beauty and spirituality are narratively equated with aristocratic lineage. All this, of course, gave the author opportunities to dwell on the sumptuous splendours of dress and décor which so delighted her. One of the most classic and colourful descriptions occurs after Paul has given the Lady a tiger-skin which he sees as symbolizing her untamable nature:

in front of the fire, stretched at full length, was his tiger – and on him – also at full length – reclined the Lady, garbed in some strange clinging garment of heavy purple crepe, its hem embroidered with gold, one white arm resting on the beast's head, her back supported by a pile of velvet cushions, and a heap of rarely bound books at her side, while between her red lips was a rose not redder than they – an almost scarlet rose . . .

Paul's lover is nothing if not animalistic:

She purred as a tiger might have done, while she undulated like a snake. She touched him with her finger-tips, she kissed his throat, his wrists, the palm of his hands, his eyelids, his hair. Strange subtle kisses, unlike the kisses of women . . .

(By the way, she manages all this while Paul remains fast asleep, because 'the Eastern perfume' which makes the air around the Lady so alluring 'drugs his senses'.)

One has to say that despite the Lady's sexual expertise and vast experience of men, she gives Paul some questionable advice which might well have backfired if he'd later applied it to relationships with other and reasonably intelligent women:

'You see, Paul, a man can always keep a woman loving him if he kiss her enough, and make her feel that there is no use struggling because he is too strong to resist. A woman will stand almost anything from a passionate lover. He may beat her and pain her soft flesh; he may shut her up and deprive her of all other friends – while the motive is raging love and interest in herself on his part, it only makes her love him the more . . .'

and

'Do you know . . . when a woman's love for a man rises to the highest point . . . however wayward and tigerish and undomestic she may be, she then desires to be the acknowledged possession and belonging of the man, even to her own dishonour.'

Although she constantly flatters Paul and suggests that he is the natural lord and master of herself and everything he surveys, she also – without apparently realizing that she is demeaning him –

strips him of his dignity by, for example, refusing to let him even share the expenses of their travels and entertainments and, when she is at her most complimentary, describing him in terms that seem to equate him with the sentimental *Bubbles* picture by Millais: 'You are beautiful, you know, Paul . . . So tall and straight . . . with curly hair of gold. Your mother must have loved you as a baby.'

All this, perhaps, is carping: the overriding image of *Three Weeks* is of love flaring between a man and a woman despite the difference in their backgrounds and ages: 'But what was age or youth? And what was beauty itself, when a woman whose face was neither young nor beautiful could make him feel he was looking at a divine goddess?' The book offered escape and consolation to millions of readers over several decades and heralded a new sensuality in the romantic novel, as well as affirming that women as well as men could really enjoy the act which Elinor Glyn did not literally describe but suggested by use of dotted lines, or exclamations which celebrated the aftermath of passionate fulfilment: 'Who can tell the joy of their awakening?', and so on.

After the phenomenal success of *Three Weeks* she wrote several more romances, although none captured the public imagination on a mass scale. She worked as a film producer in the USA during the 1920s, when she popularized the word 'It' to describe sex appeal and taught Rudolph Valentino the romantic trick of kissing the heroine's palm rather than the back of her hand.

Ethel M. Dell's first novel, *The Way of an Eagle*, was published in 1912 after being rejected over a period of two years by eight publishers. It became an immediate as well as a long-lasting bestseller. This author brought a breath of fresh air into the rather foetid atmosphere that had characterized many earlier romance stories and, as the century advanced and her heroines abandoned high-necked blouses and smothering, bulky skirts for the less restrictive fashions of the 1920s and 1930s, they also freed themselves increasingly from socially claustrophobic conventions. In a *Dad's Army* episode fairly recently repeated on BBC TV, a character remarked that he had just visited the local library to pick up 'the latest Ethel M. Dell' for his sister. The choice of writer was appropriate: in 1933 Ray Smith's Twopenny Library put her at the top of their list of popular women authors, with Elinor Glyn and Marie Corelli as runners-up. Although Ethel died in 1939, her novels remained attractive fare for wartime readers who sought fictional escape from blackouts, bomb-threats, Home Front rationing and austerities, through her sagas of scorching sexual intensity.

Of course, by today's standards, her leading ladies were neither liberated nor even on the fringes of feminism. Generally speaking, they were a leisured lot who did precious little reading, writing or studying, and for whom careers were rarely a serious consideration. Their main activity of socializing was counterbalanced by a great deal of introspection about their individual relationships with God, nature, their peers and – most important of all – men. Ethel's dramas were set essentially in 'a man's world', although events were seen through firmly feminine eyes. Shy and unassuming, Ethel was for many years dominated by her stronger sister, Ella. Possibly because of this, she was always sympathetic with the under-dog and contemptuous of social climbers (though she was fired with admiration for the upper crust and its activities). The stories which she began to contribute to magazines in 1899 when she was only eighteen featured 'ordinary' heroines with whom readers such as domestic servants, shop assistants, ladies' companions and housewives could easily identify. (Ethel's own background was middle-class.) She transported her readers into satisfyingly unfamiliar settings, thrilling situations and, of course, lushly romantic encounters. She was rather more realistic with her heroes than her heroines: male leads in the stories were quirkily appealing but often physically unprepossessing (the baddies, on the whole, were more handsome). It seemed that Ethel's heroines generally only responded to men who were to some extent handicapped, either physically or psychologically. For example, *The Way of an Eagle* introduces Captain Nick Ratcliffe who has only one arm and pinched, wrinkled and 'monkey-like' features. In *The Knave of Diamonds* (1913) we find a male character with a 'swarthy' and 'unmistakable foreign touch to his appearance', with a tread as 'light and wary as a cat's': in *Greatheart* (1918) the hero, ungallantly called 'Stumpy' by his sister, limps about unimpressively with one leg shorter than the other, while in another story the hero is handicapped by being thirty years older than the heroine. Generally her female characters are spared the sufferings of physical disability but have to undergo a great deal of mental torment. Amongst romantic novelists Ethel was one of the most adept exponents of the popular theatrical adage, 'Let them laugh, let them cry, let them *wait!*' She teased her readers with fictional stop–go love affairs in which attraction between man and woman flames, surges rapturously and rapidly forward but is checked again and again not only by social misunderstandings but by the heroine's having to wrestle with fearful doubts about the rightness and respectability of her responses to the hero, about his baffling, alternately tender and violent moods and her own virginal-but-longing-to-be-awakened state. Usually the final flowering of romance and sexuality comes only in parallel with the heroine's 'finding herself' by going through a quasi-spiritual revelation. This is likely to be triggered off by some potent symbol or other which is suggested by the title of the relevant book: *The Keeper of the Door* (1915): *The Rose of Dawn* (1917): *The Altar of Honour* (1929): *The Serpent in the Garden* (1938), and so on. In *The Way of an Eagle* (1912) the eponymous bird's swooping, diving, thrusting and soaring are used as metaphors of masculine strength and dominance, and feminine surrender not only to the sexual urge but to God, religion or simply some vague, primeval power.

This first book introduced many of the motifs which were to recur in Ethel's subsequent thirty-seven novels and eight volumes of short stories. As well as romance it provides mystical revelations and bloody, thunderous struggles between sturdy white officers and the savage native tribesmen who attack and outnumber them. Some natural disasters are thrown in for good measure while lower-key but equally effective drama is conveyed in the heroine's grappling with rigid social restraints and taboos. Like several other of Ethel's novels, *The Way of an Eagle* is set in India. Captain Nick Ratcliffe saves Muriel Roscoe, a brigadier's daughter, from death and/or dishonour when the British fort is surrounded by hordes of hostile natives. He smuggles her out of their backs-to-the-wall predicament and escorts her across wild, mountainous and ever-threatened terrain to eventual safety. During the course of their wanderings her antipathy towards his 'clever, whimsical' cocksure-ness changes into attraction, but she is not able to yield to him completely until she is absolutely assured that he needs her. Only then can her ugly, one-armed hero assume his true eagle-lover role. (This disabled-hero theme is recurrent and significant in the genre: see Chapter 4.)

Chivalry comes across compellingly, if somewhat bizarrely (with Nick 'whistling a music-hall ballad' in the midst of their dangers while he is determined to defend Muriel to the death), and, as the E. M. Dell canon developed, it was to be liberally strewn with upright young Englishmen of the same calibre. In contrast, other recurring motifs, such as wife-beating and strong men going suddenly and brutishly beserk, are melodramatically sadistic.

The sheer gusto of Ethel M. Dell's sweeping romances ensured their early success. Refinements came later. Although many of her books had Indian backgrounds she had never been there. In fact, apart from a rather unhappy visit to France she never went abroad; however, limitation of travel possibly provides a romance writer with the best opportunities for creating exotic, foreign settings, because imagination can be allowed full play. As a girl, Ethel devoured Kipling's and Flora Annie Steele's Indian novels, and in 1922, when she was forty-one years old, she married Gerald Tahourdin Savage, a lieutenant-colonel in the Royal Army Service Corps who was able to help her to round out her descriptions of the minuntiae of the military, social and sexual actualities of the Raj.

After her marriage, her stories remained essentially colourful and her vocabulary still depended on the untoned-down short-hand symbols of sexual excitement. Kisses and breath still scorched, flamed or were fiery: arms gripped with 'unshackled savagery' and blood throbbed 'tumultuously' through heroines and heroes alike. After the mid-1920s, however, passion (and beatings and kickings) became somewhat muted. The security of her relationship with Gerald was mellowing the excesses of her earlier writing. Until her marriage she had written largely to escape from unpleasant family pressures: her father was a heavy drinker with a violent temper; her sister Ella, who was big, gawky and unattractive, expressed her devotion to Ethel in an oppressive way, and their only brother, Reggie, seems like his father to have had a penchant for liquor and achieved little success in his career or marriage. Until the advent of Gerald, there had never been a satisfactory male figure or role-model on Ethel's domestic scene. Not surprisingly, her later heroes were less Quixotic and more dependable than her early ones.

For much of her writing life Ethel was able to earn the then near-fortune of £30,000 a year, but although publishers tried to promote her personality, she preferred obscurity. At a time when she could well have afforded designer clothes she preferred to knit her own; although a handsome woman, she rarely allowed herself to be photographed. She knew what her readers wanted and she provided this without any fuss, frills or self-aggrandisement. Her romantic novels remained popular for well over half a century, many of these first appearing as short stories or serials in magazines. From the 1890s, when she contributed to the *Royal Magazine*, until the 1930s when she was writing for *Woman and Home*, many readers knew her work mainly through the ephemeral press. In particular, *Sunday Stories*, which started in 1896, was to prove a kind of practice-ground for Ethel in the early years of the twentieth century. Recognizing that her stories then reached an audience of women and girls in tiring, dreary, badly paid jobs, she wrote without patronage and was sincere in her wish to inject glamour and touches of excitement into her readers' lives.

There was often, of course, a considerable gulf between the types of popular fiction published in books and in magazines. With the expansion of state education and literacy, late-Victorian and Edwardian England saw the creation of many cheap pulp paper weeklies for women as well as the better-produced journals such as the *Girl's Own Paper* and *Girl's Realm*. Alfred Harmsworth, who founded the *Daily Mail* in 1896 and the *Daily Mirror* in 1903, becoming Lord Northcliffe in 1905, built his publishing empire on his ability to provide lively reading for 'the commom man', woman and child. His penny weekly, the *Girls' Friend* (1899–31) and its companion papers, the *Girls' Reader* (1908–1915) and the *Girls' Home* (1910–1915), catered largely for working-girl readers in their late teens and early twenties. Their employment conditions were often appalling: in spite of the increasing influence of the Trades Union movement, which doubled its membership between 1901 and 1913, the unions had done little to improve the position of girl employees in shops and factories, fearing that women's work would undercut and reduce men's wages. Marriage gave such working girls their only escape from mills, sweat-shops or domestic service, but in fact it generally offered nothing more than a change from one kind of unremitting drudgery to another, in which they had to produce and bring up many children, with the whole family living in one room, and several houses sharing a single water tap.

In 1906 girls carded hooks and eyes at home and earned only five shillings weekly for an eighteen-hour day. In London the wage for a female factory worker was between seven and sixteen shillings a week. Almost two million girls were in service as hard-pressed, poorly paid maids of all work. The mill-girls and below-stairs household skivvies formed the sub-stratum of Edwardian society, which of course became celebrated for its elegance. In factories and sewing rooms, for only a subsistence wage, they produced the elaborate corsets, extravagant hats and gracious dresses which were the quintessential adornments of upper-class women.

Alfred Harmsworth's 'mill-girl papers' were more concerned with romance and entertainment than serious social issues. However, in an engagingly iconoclastic manner, their stories conveyed a responsiveness to new ideas and a challenge of accepted authority, which was often personified in beastly bosses or autocratic lovers and husbands. Non-servile working-class heroines were beginning to emerge in a wide range of popular fiction, and the pulp weeklies were to provide interesting insights into Edwardian society from the viewpoint of the skivvies, shop-girls and factory-hands who were not always as loyal and loving to the 'toffs' who employed them as the 'better-class' fiction of the period often suggests. Titles taken at random from the *Girls' Friend* in its 1908 heyday confirm the type of readership as well as the themes of the short stories and serials: 'Only a Barmaid', *Slave of the Shop*, 'Madge O'The Mill', 'Only a Laundry Girl', *Bride's Veil or Nun's*, and so on. (It is interesting that there were many tales of convent life. These were probably included to attract readers among the Roman Catholic Irish girl immigrants who worked in English factories: nunnish labours and leisure activities, considerably glamorized, might occasionally have been seen as an alternative to the sweat-shop, or to marriage.)

Most *Girls' Friend* readers knew that their only escape from hard-working routines lay in romantic fantasies and fiction. Love-stories which improved the heroine's social status were particularly popular, although the rigidity of Edwardian class structures meant that few girls married outside their accepted place in the community. Harmsworth's enterprising authors were able to break down such barriers convincingly: the generally accepted way for a working girl to embark upon a romantic but respectable relationship with a man from the more favoured classes was to get herself run over by his bicycle, carriage or motor-car. He would then lug her insensible but lovely form to the nearest house and, in relief at her revival from the point of death, fall head-over-heels in love with her. There remained the daunting business of demolishing the prejudices of the hero's upper-crust family, but love could usually be relied upon to find the way.

Two of the *Girls' Friend*'s most popular and prolific writers were Mrs de Winter Baker and Mabel St John. Little is known about the former, who may have been a man, and specialized in convent stories, many of which featured Glory O'Shea, a stereotyped story-book Irish girl who spread warmth, cheer and her very broad brogue all around her. She started off as the darling of her school-mates and most of her holy-sister teachers; managing to achieve a great deal of freedom during her convent school-days, she took off occasionally to Paris and other exotic places, and was abducted by gipsies as well as by frustrated, unrequited lovers. Her exploits were triumphantly closed and crowned by marriage to a suitably handsome and well-off admirer. Mrs de Winter then immediately demonstrated her versatility by producing a melodramatic serial called *Convict Chains*. Not surprisingly, however, this lacked the appeal of her convent-bells themes, so she quickly switched to a long-running saga about Glory O'Shea's daughter, who was cast in the same mould as her irrepressible mother, and seemed to grow up into romantic maturity with astounding speed.

'Mabel' was in fact Henry St John Cooper, a writer of women's romances and boys' school and adventure stories who bred bulldogs in his spare time and was the half-brother of the celebrated stage star, Gladys Cooper. (It was Alfred Harmsworth's belief that male authors were better than female ones at producing robust stories and role-models for teenage girl readers. His later 'schoolgirl' papers, for nine- to twelve-year-olds, published from 1919 to 1941, were written, illustrated and edited almost entirely by men who used a variety of colourful feminine pseudonyms. Certainly Henry St John Cooper as Mabel St John gave credence to Harmsworth's beliefs. His spirited and inquiring heroines were generally in advance of their time.)

Mabel St John was always firmly on the side of the under-dog. Her 1909 serial, *Plain Jane*, features a young, orphaned 'slavey' in the dingy home of a brutal employer who kicks, beats and generally humiliates her: she is eventually released from drudgery by a rather improbable romance. Like many writers for this group of papers, Mabel St John, despite frequent moments of melodrama, had little difficulty in creating believable heroines. Their male admirers were often mere cyphers, however, the 'goodies' being bland to the point of boredom while less-favoured wooers appeared to be derived from Victorian moustache-waggling villains.

The most popular and longest-running leading lady of the *Girls' Friend, Girls' Reader* and *Girls' Home* (and also of *Forget-me-Not*) was St John's Pollie Green, who was launched in 1908, and whose saga began with teenage schooldays, progressed through college life, flirtations and love affairs and, of course, ended in marriage. In chronological order the serials are *Pollie Green, Pollie Green and*

Coosha, Pollie Green at Cambridge, Pollie Green in Society, Pollie Green Engaged and *Pollie Green at Twenty-one.*

Pollie managed to live up to the euphoric banner headlines which blazed her attractions ('She's as fair as the heather is Pollie Green': 'The queen of our heart is Pollie Green': 'The pride of the country is Pollie Green', and so on). Her appeal resulted in the widespread issue of paper patterns for the blouses which she was supposed to wear and, as well as starting new fashions, she must have influenced the thinking of the *Girls' Friend* readers on various social issues. One of the paper's many madcap heroines, she also had sufficient intelligence to approach new situations without prejudice. Her contempt for convention is expressed in the informal garb which she favours in the first story, when she is seventeen. She wears a rough fisherman's jersey, a faded old shirt and boys' hobnailed boots, making the point of course, that the freedom of comfortable clothes is more important than the so-called elegance of fashionable but restrictive styles (high collars, wasp-waists, long tight skirts and spindly-heeled shoes were then in vogue). Sartorial simplicity in no way detracts from Pollie's prettiness: to use only a few of Mabel St John's plentiful epiphets, she is 'tall and slender' with 'a dainty, impudent and entirely charming face' which is 'crowned by a tumbled mane of hair ... neither golden nor brown nor red, but which was either – or all three – just as the sun and the shadows ordained'.

There was a touch of the Edwardian New Woman about Pollie. Her desire for education takes her beyond school to a rather quirky college at Cambridge: when, after that, she has London society at her feet, and has accepted a proposal of marriage from a duke, she realizes that money and prestige are not enough. Her aristocratic fiancé begins to reveal his inherent condescension and ruthlessness, and she has the good sense to throw him over immediately. He then not only shoots himself but obligingly leaves Pollie his fortune, thus smoothing her way to a happy marriage with the besotted but hard-up Bruce Hardaker, who has always loved her. The emphasis is on character rather than social class, with Mabel St John championing the under-dog again.

Pollie's various romances make light-hearted but satisfying reading. She never exploits the male college students or even the cads and bounders in whom she inspires adulation. She insists, with the exception of Bruce and, briefly, with her affianced Duke, on putting each relationship on a platonic footing. Marriage of minds – as well as eventually of bodies – is important to her. She is in advance of her time by several decades in her robust friendship with Coosha, the vivacious daughter of a Zulu chieftain, who is being educated in England. This must be one of the first relationships in fiction between black and white conducted on absolutely equal terms. (Its only known precedent was the friendship in a Northcliffe boys' paper, *The Marvel*, between Jack, Sam and Pete, a strangely assorted trio of Oxford undergraduate, American trapper and Zanzibar native. This was created in 1901 by S. Clarke Hook and continued until the stories ended in the early 1920s.) At first St John overdraws Coosha, foisting on to her a wild-eyed and woolly-haired appearance, and idiomatic English of a very bizarre nature: '"You de ugliest ole woman I neber did see ... you old monkey-face ... I get a big knife and cut off yo' head!"' Soon, however, she settles down and becomes convincing, although she remains irreverent and completely unpatronizable. Abetted by Pollie, Coosha is quick to inflict drastic retribution on anyone who tries to treat her as an inferior. There is a marvellous moment when, at Cambridge, Coosha avenges herself on a tutor who has victimized her. Miss Trumpinshaw is a grim-faced lady whose astringency is emphasized by pince-nez and a mannish trilby. At a college charity fête the African girl neatly appends to the tutor's stalwart rear a notice advertising 'One Kiss – 3 Pens [pence]'. Predictably, trade is not brisk, although Miss Trumpinshaw has to ward off one unappetizing but over-enthusiastic military man. Coosha mellowed as she reached maturity, and became involved in several colourful love affairs. Both she and Pollie were potent symbols of tolerance and liberality to the working girls who followed their fortunes.

Of course it was not only in the Harmsworth pulp papers that authors focused on heroines' attitudes towards work as well as marriage. As mentioned on page 72, 'Rita' had her book *Betty Brent, Typist* published in 1908, the year when Pollie's adventures began in the *Girls' Friend*. This was primarily a romance but it made token recognition of the heroine's interest in a career. The Religious Tract Society's *Girl's Own Paper* (*GOP*) featured somewhat low-key romances with the emphasis on domesticity rather than passion. It recognized with reluctance that young women, though still wanting marriage and motherhood, were also beginning to demand better education and career opportunities. However, it resolutely turned its back on the campaign for the vote which was being waged in earnest by the suffragettes and others in the decade and a half before the beginning of the First World War. The paper had a male editor, Charles Peters, from its beginning in 1880 until he died in 1907. He achieved an even greater circulation than the earlier-established *Boy's Own Paper*, but determinedly steered the *GOP* through safe waters, so that its romantic fiction would remain acceptable to the conservative mothers of its younger readers and to the husbands of older ones. Apparently men as well as women read this paper. John Ruskin was amongst those who expressed appreciation of it, and his ideas of a woman's place were notoriously unprogressive (see page 41).

Conflict between love and feminine self-fulfilment or self-expression became a popular theme in Edwardian light fiction. A nauseating example of this is provided in the September 1914 issue of Cassell's quality monthly, the *Girl's Realm*. Eva Bretherton's story, 'A Serious Woman', describes a young married couple, very much in love. The husband is tolerant, wise and forebearing: the wife is 'a little woman, plump and round and delightfully, comfortably soft, with tiny dimpled hands and feet like a baby's'. Everything else about her, especially her intellect, seems correspondingly infantile. She is meant to be the pseudo-serious but actually stupid kind of woman who, in the author's estimation, typified those who had embraced the cause of female suffrage. The 'little woman' joins the militants and, hurling a hammer through a shop window, injures her husband who happens to be there at that precise moment to buy her a generous birthday present. She is not even adept at window-breaking: 'hands like a baby's are not the very best kind for effectually wielding a hammer'. All this banality gives her husband opportunities to show manly strength and understanding; his love weans 'the serious woman' off intelligent causes and persuades her to whisper repentantly that 'the only things that matter to a woman are close at hand and have nothing to do with votes'.

Mrs George de Horne Vaizey was another early-nineteenth-century writer who explored the apparent conflict for girls between romance and careers or education. She frequently championed the cause of the working girl, and sent a string of lively heroines to school or college in search of independence. Her stories injected new vigour into the *Girl's Own Paper* when Flora Klickmann took over its editorship after Charles Peters's death. She wrote intelligent romances, but disapproved of women's suffrage and considered that men should manage the world of politics and business. Her 1914 *GOP* serial, *The Independence of Claire*, is a fascinating and factually reflective study of a nineteen-year-old high-school teacher's struggles against prejudice and poverty, and of her satisfying eventual romance. Like so many of this author's characters, Claire almost eagerly abandons ideas of independence and self-expression as 'from the shelter of her lover's arms her heart went out in a wave of tenderness towards ... the countless hordes of women workers for whom life was a monotonous round of grey hued days shadowed by the prospect of age and want'. Claire's experiences highlighted the fact that she lived in 'a man's world', and in a society ridden with class distinction and mistrust of the intelligent girl who (even unwillingly) pursues a career.

The eponymous heroine of H. G. Wells's *Ann Veronica* (1909) did rather better, and, like Claire, was fortunate enough to get a good man. After leaving school, Ann, who is both athletic and questioning, soon exhausts the activities that society then offered to its middle-class girls. The 'valiant fight for Newnham or Somerville' is lost because her father thinks 'that sort of thing unsexed a girl'. Prevalent attitudes are summed up in her brother's comment that 'Babies and females have got to keep hold of somebody or go under ...' However, Ann Veronica does manage to leave home and achieve some measure of economic and psychological freedom. Her search for a reasonable means of self-assertion leads her into romance, but not respectability: she ends up living with a man to whom she is not married, which was so shocking to the conventions of 1909 that Wells's plea through this novel for more liberal attitudes almost certainly achieved the reverse effect.

Romantic fiction is not, of course, expected to reflect or comment on public or historical events, and it generally ignored the shake-up of values in the early years of the twentieth-century, which had been brought about by competition in world markets, demands for better wages and working conditions at home, the growth of socialism and the demand for female suffrage. It is often left to authors working several decades later to recapitulate with the benefit of hindsight a period's atmosphere, events and mores. For example, Howard Spring's *Fame is the Spur*, which was published in 1940, chronicled the lives and loves of John Hamer Shawcross, an ambitious Edwardian Labour politician, and Ann Artinstall, whom he woos and weds but who proves to be an uneasy partner because she passionately espouses the suffragette cause, to the possible detriment of his career. Their intense feeling for each other somehow survives their bitter personal and political conflicts: Hamer's gradual departure from idealistic socialism to sleek opportunistic success, and Ann's near-breakdown after her angry years of frustration and spells of imprisonment, force-feeding and other humiliations are vividly described. In the end, Hamer loses his parliamentary seat and Ann's health is totally destroyed: they are both well into middle age and have apparently been relegated to the sidelines of the society they have both tried to serve. Nothing remains but their relationship. A new, more tender love has arisen from the ashes of former passions. Facing the prospect of death, Ann comments: 'The world is dying of causes and committees. Why can't we just love one another and leave one another alone?' Hamer more poetically reflects that 'a little light is enough to love by'.

Just over a century later, Barbara Cartland in *A Virgin in Paris*

(1966) also focuses on how an Edwardian heroine's commitment to the suffragette cause could seem sufficiently unladylike to undermine her love life. Gardenia is disturbed when Bertie, her admirer, rants about the women who 'are making a blasted nuisance of themselves' by tying themselves to railings and 'screaming' for the vote. She reassures him that she is not identified with the campaign but, in a flash of spirit, reminds him that 'women have a very raw deal all round. Look how they are ordered about, first by their parents, and then by their husbands . . .' Bertie obligingly takes his romantic cue, and mutters, 'I will let you do anything you want to do' – so, for Gardenia at least, self-assertion as well as romance is achieved.

CHAPTER FOUR

Taming the Beast

A LTHOUGH MANY fictional heroines switched with relief from pursuing careers to becoming housewives, they – or their creators – still had reservations about living intimately with full-blooded men. This was hardly surprising in mid-nineteenth-century England where wives had virtually no protection against husbandly abuse of power. Men not only owned their wives physically and legally but their property as well. The British Empire had officially freed its slaves in 1833 but liberation for home-grown women was not to come for many decades. We are reminded of women's direly dependent state by a chilling passage in *Wuthering Heights* when, after Heathcliff has forced Catherine (Cathy and Edgar Linton's daughter) to marry his peevish and ailing son, the latter remarks:

'. . . uncle is dying truly, at last – I'm glad, for I shall be master of the Grange after him – and Catherine always spoke of it as *her* house. It isn't hers! It's mine – papa says everything she has is mine. All her nice books are mine – she offered to give me them, and her pretty birds, and her pony Minny, if I would get the key of our room, and let her out; but I told her she had nothing to give, and they were all mine. And then she cried, and took a little picture from her neck, and said I should have that; two pictures in a gold case, on one side her mother, and on the other, uncle, when they were young . . . I said *they* were mine, too; and tried to get them from her . . .'

Romantic novelists, nevertheless, generally remained content to cast men in the roles of lords and masters and, so long as they were touched with chivalry and blessed with good looks and large incomes, their dominance was seen as a positive attribute. Of course, the classic last-paragraph cliché of the leading lady melting into the robust embrace of Mr Right begged the question of what happened afterwards. We rarely discover whether he remained adoring or turned oafish; whether he was generous or on the stingy side; whether he was adept or awful in bed – and so on.

To play safe, several female authors drastically curbed their heroes' powers before committing their heroines to the matrimonial state. Male sexuality, in particular, was viewed with a wary eye, and in consequence many a macho character had to be cut down to size by becoming crippled, blind or disfigured – and sometimes even all three at once!

Jane Eyre's Rochester is a case in point. (See Chapter 1.) As a result of his frantic but vain efforts to save his mad wife from perishing in the fire which consumes Thornfield, Rochester loses his sight and has to have his left hand amputated. Although he had never been a conventionally handsome man, Jane had delighted in the dark intensity and integration of his appearance – 'all energy, decision, will'. When she is psychically recalled to her 'sightless Samson', rapture is 'kept well in check by pain' as she observes his groping gait and the change in his 'countenance ... that looked desperate and brooding – that reminded me of some wronged and fettered wild beast or bird, dangerous to approach in his sullen woe'.

Jane, the mousy ex-governess who had previously and somewhat masochistically referred to her employer and potential future husband as 'my master', now aproaches Edward Fairfax Rochester as an equal – or, indeed, as his superior; she has not only become a woman of independent financial means but, in contrast with this mutilated male, is sound in wind and limb, and looks and confidence. The Byronic lord of creation has been tamed, but it is to Jane's (and Charlotte Brontë's) eternal credit that she knows just how to cope with him and to make their union into a real meeting of minds and bodies. Jane continues the process (at which she

excelled when *he* was 'master') of 'vexing and soothing him by turns
... a sure instinct always prevented me from going too far ...' She
loves him even more now that he is dependent on her; the role of
protector has switched from him to her, but she has sufficient
insight and integrity to know that this is a quirk of fate, that in a
partnership love and trust are more important than power, and, of
course, that a man who has suffered such onslaughts on his virility
has to have his confidence restored:

> 'You are no ruin, sir – no lightning-struck tree; you are green and
> vigorous. Plants will grow about your roots, whether you ask them
> or not, because they take delight in your bountiful shadow; and as
> they grow they will lean towards you and wind around you, because
> your strength offers them so safe a prop.'

Jane, in fact, deals with the problem of a disabled lover more
sensitively and practically than many more modern fictional
heroines.

Charlotte Brontë certainly started something here. After *Jane
Eyre* a succession of apparently fragile but actually very determined
heroines were able to accept romantic union only after the heroes
had suffered permanent or long-term physical handicap. True to
this tradition, Ethel M. Dell favoured the dilution of male dominance by disability (see Chapter 3). In *The Way of an Eagle* (1912),
Nick Ratcliffe's courtship of Muriel Roscoe suffers many vicissitudes. Ugly but attractive, he is 'the sort of chap who always comes
out on top', invested, according to a brother officer, with 'personal
magnetism' and 'black magic', and in the view of one of the
memsahibs, with 'something uncanny, abnormal ... almost super-
human'. Nevertheless, it is only when he has lost an arm and spent
some time disguised as a filthy, crippled, native beggar at Muriel's
gate that she realizes how much he needs her, and allows herself
the ecstasy of final surrender. Male masterfulness then reasserts
itself:

> 'Let us be married soon then, Nick.'
> 'At once,' said Nick promptly.

And, although his voice cracks with emotion as his one arm draws the 'passionately quivering' Muriel close, he warns:

> 'You are putting yourself irrevocably in my power, and you will never break away again. You may come to loathe me with your whole soul, but I shall never let you go. Have you realized that? If I take you now, I take you for all time.'

Florence Barclay settled on blindness rather than maiming as a way of evening things up between her plain, hefty heroine, Jane Champion, and her handsome, idealistic and artistic hero, Garth Dalmain, in *The Rosary*, which, published in 1909, had been reprinted eleven times by the middle of the following year, and heaven knows how often since. In romantic fiction, a partner's or a lover's loss of sight usually enhances a girl's loyalty and brings out the best in her, while paraplegia, for pretty obvious reasons, produces a more negative response, as in the cases of Constance Chatterley and Stella Tabret, which are described later. (Rochester and Nick Ratcliffe were fortunate that mutilation only affected their upper regions.) Garth, of course (see Chapter 2), has discovered and fallen in love with the Honourable Jane Champion's beauty of character long before he is blinded. Because of her doubts about her plainness Jane can only come to him wholeheartedly when he lies 'sightless, helpless and disfigured'. Her devotion then becomes unquenchable. Some time earlier when, fully sighted, he had proposed, she acknowledged that her 'soul arose and proclaimed him mate and master' but she also saw him as 'a tiger who had tasted blood', and was distinctly cautious about physical entanglement with him. Blindness, it seems, has conveniently clipped his claws; he has also undergone a great deal of religious purification by accepting his dual 'cross' (her rejection of him, and his loss of sight).

In the end, however, he is rewarded by his closeness to Jane as they sit together 'in the still, sweet darkness', playing and singing 'The Rosary' and other pseudo-spiritual, sentimental ditties. Most of all Garth relishes the fact that Jane, who despite her massive build and inner strength now frequently succumbs to bouts of womanly weeping, 'must lean on him . . . for the great essentials . . . Even in his blindness he was the stronger . . . The sense of manhood and mastery: the right of control, the joy of possession, arose within him . . .' Fortunately, perhaps, Florence Barclay takes us no further over the threshold of their married life.

Ironically it was in a peacetime situation, because he had tried to rescue an injured rabbit, that Garth's retinas were accidentally pierced by shots from a fellow-member of a shooting party. But the two world wars were to provide book-authors with ample opportunities for blinding, crippling and castrating their heroes, though not surprisingly many such stories appeared retrospectively rather than during the period when death and disablement touched so many families in real life. Weekly pulp papers and magazines were more likely to exploit these themes while hostilities still raged because, naturally, they strived for topicality in their fiction.

The penny *Heartsease Library* ran a long series of adventures starring Mary Latimer, an impossibly serene and beautiful nun who, as well as being devoted to the Church, made it her mission in life to smooth the paths of young lovers. In 'Girlish Dreams' (28 November 1914), like so many real-life and fictional girls, Mary leaves England to nurse in battle-scarred and beleaguered Belgium. She is soon running a front-line troop hospital in Flanders. Eighteen-year-old Nora Carver, who is described as 'a little flower', has been thrown over by her lord-of-the-manor sweetheart, Jack Latham, for a glamorous gold-digger. Disoriented and disconsolate, Nora rushes off to nurse wounded soldiers in Mary's hospital, where Jack – predictably – is soon brought in. He is blinded and badly disabled, but only temporarily. He swiftly recovers, and has of course been brought to his senses by his experience of disability. He rejoices that he has rediscovered Nora, 'the little girl whom he might have lost for ever', and that she has retained her flower-like quality despite wrestling with bedpans and soiled dressings, and cleaning up vomit.

The 'sweet radiance' that Nora constantly emanates springs from her dreadful docility. She defers in determinedly 'quiet and brave feminine tones' to every male she meets. In the final paragraph of 'Girlish Dreams', when Mary Latimer is fastening the orange-blossom-trimmed veil on Nora's head, the bride-to-be is still whispering, 'Reverend Mother – I am so frightened ... I am not really good enough for him ...' She would probably have felt more confident about marrying Jack if he had not been so fully returned to health and lustiness.

By the time the Second World War began, pulp-paper heroines were made of sterner stuff. Even the mildest of them knew what she wanted and tried tenaciously to get it. In Newnes & Pearson's *Peg's Paper*, the coveted and unashamed prize was matrimony – at almost any cost. It was generally an uphill task because so many of the paper's male characters were seducers and schemers who tricked blameless working girls into extremely questionable romantic allegiances. Even when a heroine appeared to have achieved her marital goal, she was unlikely to be home and dry because her union often turned out to be bizarre (see Chapter 6): 'It was her wedding night ... she had married the man of her dreams ... too late, she found she was a BRIDE FOR SALE!'

Molly Grant's predicament in Jessica Scott's 'Her Baby Had No Name' (9 Dcember 1939) is a typical one. 'Just eighteen and facing the greatest disaster a girl can know', Molly finds herself pregnant and homeless, having been 'swept into a world of rapture' but then unceremoniously dumped by Gerald Burke, the man she had presumed to be her husband. His curt farewell note reveals that as well as trapping her into bigamy he has been supporting her on illegal earnings:

'Did you never suspect that your fascinating husband lived by his wits? Confidence trickster and jewel-crook – these were my occupations. But things have got too hot for me ... so Gerald Burke will disappear for good ... No use kicking up a fuss, Molly. Best forget me!'

Molly would 'give her soul' (an expression used frequently throughout the story) to be able to do so. Regrettably, however, the child she is carrying keeps Gerald's memory perpetually and frighteningly green.

Molly's desperate desire to legitimize her baby precipitates her into yet another strange marriage: she meets Blake Dormer, a recently blinded RAF officer, who mistakes her for his fascinating but fickle fiancée, Dolores (bitches and good-time girls in *Peg's Paper* generally have slightly exotic names: Dolores and Gloria are frequent choices). Dolores has realized that her fun days with Blake have ended with his blindness, and that she'll have a more 'wonderful time' and far better financial prospects with one or other of the many officers who respond to her well-displayed charms. Molly discovers her callous farewell note to Blake but hides it from him, partly to save his feelings and partly because a daring plan has formed in her mind. When she accidentally bursts into Blake's life he is expecting Dolores to arrive for their registry-office wedding. Molly decides – on the instant – to take her place. Fortunately for her, the ceremony seems to be carried out without the presence of a single friend or relative of Blake, who might have spotted the bridal substitution. Happily, too, in common with other *Peg's Paper* heroines, she doesn't experience any difficulty over the trivial matter of having a birth certificate which carries the wrong name.

Fortune, however, smiles only briefly on Molly, whose new and fulfilling life of cherishing her handsome hero-husband is abruptly shattered when he announces that he is going into hospital for some treatment which might restore his sight. It works, and he rushes back to their love-nest longing to clap eyes on the golden-haired Dolores, but finds instead the quiet and rather mousy Molly. His tenderness turns – not unreasonably – to tantrum: he cannot believe that Dolores has jilted him, and he condemns Molly as a nasty little schemer who has deprived him of his true love. Outraged at her deception, he tears off to France where his 'plane is again brought down and he is once more severely injured. Blinded (but this time only temporarily) by bandages staunching a head-wound, he marvels at the gentle touch of the VAD who is caring for him. It is, of course, Molly, who is nursing not only wounded servicemen but a broken heart and a lot of ambivalence about her recent miscarriage ('Molly cried for the tiny life that had slipped away . . . but he might have been like Gerry . . . crooked, cruel, because heredity is so strong . . .').

Chastened by his second experience of disabling wounds, Blake begins to realize that Molly, dubbed by the other patients as 'an angel with sad eyes', is indeed a far more worthy recipient of his affections than Dolores. They affirm their devotion to each other in 'poignantly quiet voices', husky with emotion of such intensity that even 'the sound of the roar of gunfire cannot reach them in their new paradise'.

In war and peacetime settings, and at a variety of literary levels, the theme of the self-effacing young woman nobly standing by a blinded or crippled lover has proved remarkably resilient. Sometimes, however, one has a sneaking suspicion that these heroines are motivated by power-lust rather than self-sacrifice in seeking maimed and dependent husbands. Certainly many fictional working girls have been able to move socially upwards because disability is an extraordinarily effective demolisher of class barriers.

Barbara Cartland would probably pour scorn on these unsentimental reflections but, as well as providing romantic intensity, her blind-hero novel *Open Wings* (1942) includes snatches of social comment (even though these largely come from the mouths of the bitchiest character): 'Propinquity is what happens when a man and woman see a great deal of each other. It's the reason why invalids marry their nurses and business men their typists.' Basically, the story's attraction lies in Barbara Cartland's adept manipulation of the Cinderella motif, but one relishes the engagingly caustic moments when the author seems more challenging of Cinders than in her blander narratives.

At the beginning of *Open Wings*, Squadron-Leader Jameson (Jimmy) Braith is presented as the embodiment of almost everything a girl could want. As well as having 'a very slight look of Clark Gable', this dashing fighter pilot is, we are told, the only son of one of the richest men in England – a millionaire, in fact. These assets are only slightly offset by a temporary limp and damaged arm resulting from a recent forced landing: permanent disability does not affect him until later in the story when he is blinded in an air battle.

Lorna Overton comes from a different social background. She is the unassuming daughter of the vicar of Little Walton, and Jimmy's upper-crust confidence and masculine vigour occasionally overwhelm her. Her world is a serene succession of Women's Institute whist-drives, knitting parties, Sunday School and Girl Guide activities. Living in a country village with no experience of air-raids, she is at first largely insulated from the effects of war. Jimmy sweeps his 'Cherry Ripe' (a name that springs from their first meeting when Lorna was picturesquely gathering fruit) into marriage. This, however, turns out to be far from ideal. Jimmy's self-indulgence shows up even when they are honeymooning at one of his family's large Cornish country houses. Out of harmony with the prevailing national mood of cheerful acceptance of austerity, Jimmy basely yearns for Cap d'Antibes, for Biarritz, and gambling. Lorna, who is used to the quietness of Little Walton where (astoundingly for the period) the Overton family did not even possess a wireless, is naturally disturbed by this upper-class restlessness and irresponsibility. It has further distasteful manifestations. Jimmy begins to flirt with Lorna's cousin Sally, a go-getting character who looks fetching in her ATS uniform and even better off duty, when her 'perfectly shaped legs' are encased in 'superfine silk stockings'. (It is of course too early for nylon, and generally speaking the girls who managed to get silk hose at that particular period of wartime shortages were likely to be considered 'fast'.)

Before he is blinded, Lorna has another problem with Jimmy. Despite the upheavals and challenges of war, which cut away a great deal of humbug in relationships between men and women, she has difficulty in discussing anything serious with him. Apparently he has merely to touch her or smile at her for her heart to lurch in her breast: 'she could not withstand him, could only surrender herself without reservation into his arms . . .'

This, of course, makes any kind of planning or partnership complicated. Lorna's status improves only when she is eventually able to help the broken, savagely suicidal Jimmy to come to terms with his blindness. The solution is extremely simple: his self-respect and macho strength instantly reassert themselves when Lorna informs him, somewhat genteelly, that 'so far as he [the gynaecologist] can ascertain ... there is every reason to believe that I am going to have a ... baby'. Hitherto unbookish to the point of philistinism, Jimmy suddenly discovers dormant literary gifts. He becomes a playwright for the BBC, and a stable husband and father.

Open Wings was published at a time when its exploitation of the casually heroic, sexually exciting pilot fantasy figure must have guaranteed its appeal to many women readers. Millionaire Jimmy Braith did not quite conform to the ordinary-fellow-who-taught-this-heart-of-mine-to-fly image of the immensely popular song 'Silver Wings', but his verve and charisma linked him appropriately to the real-life RAF pilots whose exploits were so widely applauded. It is more difficult to understand how the story can have appealed to readers when the book was reissued once or twice during the 1970s. It lacks the colour and explicit sexuality of more recent romantic novels and, compared with these, its dialogue might seem stilted and naïve, but presumably tales of Cinderella taming her prince never quite fade away.

In D. H. Lawrence's *Lady Chatterley's Lover* (1928) the heroine's well-known deflection from the social pattern might never have occurred if her husband, Clifford, had been blinded instead of shipped home from Flanders 'more or less in bits' towards the end of the First World War. After prolonged medical treatment it is clear that Clifford will remain permanently paralysed from 'the hips down'. He is twenty-nine and Constance twenty-three. She is, according to Lawrence, all woman: 'a soft, ruddy-looking girl, inclined to freckles, with big blue eyes, and curling, brown hair, and a soft voice, and rather strong, female loins ... a little old-fashioned and "womanly"'. Although Constance tries to remain faithful to Clifford and to live with him totally 'in their ideas and his books', those robustly built loins have to find satisfaction. However, it is not only 'the cruelty of utter impotence' in Clifford that makes Connie seek 'phallic tenderness' elsewhere. There is also disenchantment with his intellectual pretentiousness, and a repudiation of the bleakly anachronistic life she is expected to share with him in the isolation of his ugly ancestral home. Clifford is ruined rther than tamed by his terrible disability. He starts off as a fairly dull and ordinary character, but, after becoming a paraplegic, sinks deeper into superficiality and downright nastiness. His loss is, of course, the gain of Mellors, his lusty game-keeper. Once Connie's infidelity with his employee becomes known, Clifford's pettiness totally engulfs him: her behaviour seems to him the ultimate in feminine perversity and his response – to Connie, Mellors and the reader – the ultimate in 'sour grapes': '"That scum! That bumptious lout! That miserable cad! And carrying on with him all the time, while you were here and he was one of my servants! My God, my God, is there any end to the beastly lowness of women ..."' Clifford is represented as a 'perverted child-man' who is incapable of rational judgement of the usual responses between men and women. It is small wonder that Connie turns to Mellors who, if not the most imaginative of lovers, is at every level at least 'cocksure'.

Long before her marriage to Clifford, Connie had learnt to cope with the virulence of masculine desires:

> A man was like a child with his appetites. A woman had to yield him what he wanted, or like a child he would probably turn nasty and flounce away ... But a woman could take a man without really giving herself away ... Rather she could use this sex thing to have power over him ...

Lawrence is remarkably adept at tackling explicitly but without crudeness the themes of sexual fulfilment and deprivation. Somerset Maugham's play *The Sacred Flame* is another challenging comment on the predicament of a woman whose husband has become paralysed. Maurice Tabret has suffered spinal injury as the result of a post-war flying accident. He and his wife Stella are certainly more affectionate towards each other than the Chatterleys, and this warmth is expressed effusively. But it does not alter the fact that Maurice has become to Stella 'no more than a dear friend' for whom she is desperately sorry. He deplores the waste of 'all that beauty, all that superb and shining youth' in his wife: '"Oh Stella, if we'd only had a little kid. After all, it's a woman's destiny to have children. You wouldn't have felt that you had entirely wasted your life."' There is an unconscious irony in this observation: Stella and Maurice's brother Colin are having an affair and she is actually pregnant.

Maurice's mother realizes what is happening. Refusing to allow her disabled son's 'beautiful illusions' about his wife to be destroyed, she kills him by administering an overdose – an action which accords with a pact between Maurice and herself that 'if life became intolerable to him' she would help him to end it. Maugham investigates several moral issues in this play which had a special relevance in the years following the 1914–18 war. There is of course the question of the right of voluntary euthanesia; also whether accepted standards of sexual morality within marriage could reasonably be applied when one partner had become impotent.

Maurice's tragic situation moves Mrs Tabret to become more generally compassionate, but it has the opposite effect on Stella who, despite her own infidelity, thinks it 'horrible' and 'disgusting' when she finds out after Maurice's death that his nurse was in love with him. Nurse Wayland has rather petulantly exhibited the contempt that certain working women feel for the privileged idle. Stella's response is similarly vindictive: '"I've often noticed that the average woman who works for a living looks upon it as a little miracle and can never believe that any other can be clever enough to do the same thing ... I might have made hats or invented a face cream."' Stella's hypothetical choice of careers underlines her superficiality and her social milieu. Whatever difficulties Stella Tabret or Constance Chatterley had in dealing with their disabled husbands, these were not exacerbated by shortages of money or nursing and domestic help. For poorer families the problems of looking after paraplegic ex-soldier relatives, on minimal pensions, must have been appalling.

Soldiers (almost always officers) coming home to change and challenge were featured frequently in the years following the First World War in books by male writers as popular as John Buchan, Warwick Deeping and Dornford Yates. Few women tackled this tricky subject, but of those who did Evadne Price (as 'Helen Zenna Smith') horrifically described physical disability and deprivation; Rebecca West rather whimsically addressed the subject of disorientation resurrecting an old romance; while Vera Brittain provided her usual realistic and pacifist assessments.

Evadne Price's trilogy, *Not So Quiet* . . ., *Women of the Aftermath* and *Shadow Women* was written in the 1930s as a first-person, apparently real-life narrative by 'Helen Smith', who had supposedly been an ambulance driver at the front during the war. Her style is brutally expository, whether conveying the agonies of the wounded, the hypocrisies associated with jingoistic nationalism, or the incapacity of many men and women who survived active service to forge new ideals or to make lasting relationships. Helen is assailed by one grisly shock after another, so that the reader soon becomes immune to her sufferings. In the general climate of social disintegration sex is an illusory antidote to purposelessness, but there is little tenderness in the heroine's attitude towards her fiancé, a war-hero named Roy Evans-Mawnington, who has been blinded, crippled and castrated. Like Clifford Chatterley, he has been destroyed rather than tamed or mellowed: '"here's your MC – shove it down the lavatory for me"'. He commits suicide, and Helen's horrific experiences continue tenaciously.

In her first novel, *The Return of the Soldier* (1918), Rebecca West describes the homecoming of Chris Baldry, a war-hero whose wounds are mental rather than physical. Shell-shock has wiped away all memory of his ten-year marriage and, indeed, of Kitty, his wife. His thoughts and emotions are fixed on his sweetheart from long ago, Margaret Allington, whose social background is vastly inferior to that of Kitty and Chris, and who has become coarsened, at least superficially, by poverty and marriage to a dull man. To Kitty, and at first to Chris's unmarried cousin, Jenny, who narrates the story and is rather obsessively devoted to him, Margaret seems shabby, cheap and clumsy. In fact, she understands Chris far better than the elegant but insensitive Kitty can. There is a quality of fable about this story: Kitty symbolizes falsity while Margaret embodies goodness. Jenny switches her allegiances during the course of her narrative from Chris's spoilt and snobbish wife to Margaret, in whom she sees an 'inner beauty' which overrides her awkward gestures, muddy boots and unstylish clothes.

Chris seems to be living in a romantic trance: his 'body and soul were consumed with desire' for Margaret, but there is a curious innocence about his relationship with her. His mental injuries seem to have wiped away not only memory but time; he is reliving a youthful idyll, and is puzzled by the fact that those around him look so much older than they should. We see him very much through the eyes of the three women, as a love-object, extremely vulnerable and almost passive. Chris's contentment with Margaret is, despite emphasis on its spiritual quality, based on delusion. For a time Jenny hopes that Chris will be able 'to live in the interminable enjoyment of his youth and love' but, prompted by Margaret, she realizes that if he is left 'in his magic circle there would come a time when his delusion turned to senile idiocy ... when one is adult one must raise to one's lips the wine of the truth ... or else walk for ever queer and small like a dwarf'.

Margaret engineers his 'cure' and passage back to reality. This is symbolized by the fact that he stops walking 'loose-limbed like a boy' and assumes the 'hard tread' and gait of a soldier. Kitty can only suck in her breath with satisfaction and murmur that he is cured; Jenny realizes that now that illusion and malfunctioning have been removed, he will 'go back to that flooded trench in Flanders ... where bullets fall like rain'. Chris's fate is not disclosed but the restoration of his manliness carries with it the ring of death.

In *Account Rendered* (1945) Vera Brittain also examines psychological problems resulting from wartime injury which drastically affect a married relationship. In the closing months of the First World War, nineteen-year-old Francis Halkin is temporarily buried by a bomb from a trench mortar. He appears to be uninjured, except for a slight concussion, but, after his demobiliza-

tion, suffers brief, inexplicable and disturbing lapses of consciousness which prevent him from pursuing his chosen career as a
concert pianist. With some reluctance, he joins – and makes a
success of – his father's Midland paper-manufacturing business,
diverting his musical talents from performing to composing.

He marries a local girl, Sally Eldridge; they seem ideally suited
and, for many years, their marriage is happy and fulfilled (despite
the fact that the narrative suggests a certain aloofness in Francis).
However, with the declaration of the Second World War Francis
finds himself increasingly under stress. The carnage that he has
witnessed at the front in 1918 has made him reject the military
ethic but, as Hitler's forces advance through Europe and invasion
of Britain seems imminent, Francis becomes the victim of the
recurring 'maladjustments of the brain resulting from shell shock'.

Quite unconscious of his actions, he kills his much-loved wife. It
appears that for Francis, as for many another fictional leading man,
disability has brought complete distruction. But he gets a second
chance. Declared guilty of murder but insane, after an enforced
period of treatment in an 'asylum' he is released in order to try to
pull the shattered strands of his life together again. Throughout
his incarceration he has been visited by Enid Clay, a young
stenographer from his factory who has always loved him but felt
him to be unattainable. Certainly in the heyday of his running of
the family business he was arrogant enough to give her short shrift.
However, his disability has softened him and when Enid gathers all
her courage and virtually proposes to him, he responds positively,
although he is both astounded and touched that she can care for 'a
damaged piece of human wreckage ... a criminal and an ex-
lunatic'.

Cured of the fears that apparently caused his ultimate breakdown, Francis still embraces the pacifist cause but decides to
support the struggle against Fascism by volunteering for ambulance
service in North Africa. Enid is heavily pregnant when he takes off
but, as always, adoringly accepts that whatever Francis wants to do
must be right: 'her body itself carried the proof that human vitality
is indestructible and the human spirit immortal. As she turned to

go home the child stirred vigorously, and she rejoiced that out of death and sorrow, new life had come.'

Vera Brittain's conveyance of the long shadows cast by war on romantic relationships is down-to-earth, indeed often bleak in its realism. It strikes few echoes in June Deveraux's tongue-in-cheek historical romp, *The Taming* (1989), which has a fifteenth-century setting. Despite Lord Rogan's hellish arrogance, blonde and beautiful Liana Neville agrees to marry this darkly dishy suitor (who is interested in her only for her dowry). She knows that he is fearfully fetching – all over – because she's seen him sun-bathing in the nude, but she does not bargain for the fact that he is overbearing to the point of brutality and hardly even house-trained. His castle is rat-infested, filthy and decaying, and the fastidiously efficient Liana is determined to clean things up on every level, but doesn't know quite how to start. Her husband is more at home making war than making love, and it is his custom to treat all women with contempt. Even after he has entered Liana 'with all the force of a man using a battering ram to attack a locked door', he is likely to pass her by an hour or two later without remembering her name or even recognizing her. When she realizes that he intends to continue his pre-marital practice of bedding a different girl on every night of the week, Liana takes drastic action. She sets fire to the mattress on which Rogan and one of his maid-servants are sleeping off their sexual satiation. Thus begins the process of his taming!

Soldiers returning from the war in Vietnam have not yet been accorded a romantic place in fiction, as *Intimate Enemies* (1987) by Caryl Rivers makes clear. Mark Claymore went away a healthy, uncomplicated farm-boy and came back an amputee, with 'moods and anger' and frightful recurrent nightmares. Like so many returning Vietnam veterans, he provides a perpetual reminder to a confused public and establishment of an anguished and ultimately frustrated campaign which severely tarnished America's good-guy true-leadership image.

Two decades after his return to civilian life Mark seems, on the surface, to have adjusted to the killings, the heat, the drugs and 'the paranoia' which 'all conspired, in 'Nam, to destroy a man's moral radar'. However, his disability has broken up his marriage. His wife, Gerry, morbidly invested the stump of his amputated leg with a 'life of its own . . . Mark, Gerry and the leg that wasn't there' had become an outré ménage à trois; her apprehensive awareness of it during love-making made him impotent, and their sex-life had simply withered away. In contast, Helen, the girl he had dated in his post-divorce period, had 'a thing' for amputees and 'used to kiss and fondle his stump with an ardor that made him uncomfortable'. Their relationship ended when Mark realized that it was his abnormality she 'dug' and not himself: 'Helen just grooved on guys with parts missing. After him, she went on to a double amputee.'

Intimate Enemies tackles a serious subject with insight, robustness and plenty of humour. It underlines the fact that women who love mutilated men are also marked by their scars, and by stigmas which society sometimes imposes on them. The relationship between Mark and Jessie McGrath is an unlikely one – love between 'enemies', in fact (see Chapter 6). In the early days of the Vietnam conflict, Jessie was a student who sprayed inflammatory anti-war slogans on military buildings. She is established in a successful career (the youngest-ever provost of Kingsolving College in Boston) when, towards the end of the 1980s, Mark becomes one of her colleagues. He is still proud to be a 'Nam veteran, has remained in the Army and is responsible for the reserve officers' training courses at Kingsolving. Time, experience and various levels of disillusionment have nibbled away the extremes of their differing attitudes towards war and political issues; Jessie fancies Mark and, suspecting that he is inhibited by her being his boss and by his disability, makes the first sexual move by bluntly saying that she wants to go to bed with him. Mark is responsive, but insists that she sees his damaged leg first. She finds it unusual but not repulsive, and is far more interested in the 'gratifying bulge' under his jockey shorts. They begin an extremely satisfying affair but it soon becomes soured by Mark's recapitulatory nightmares and his incapacity to share his fears with Jessie, or indeed with anyone else. It is only when he has split up with her, and after his best friend –

a dreadfully disabled war veteran – has committed suicide that Mark comes deeply to terms with the fact that he has many 'Nam ghosts to lay before he can achieve real balance and harmony in his life and relationships: as he tells Jessie, 'There's a lot of shit I have to shovel.' If they resume their relationship things won't be easy; he knows he'll sometimes be hell to live with, but he won't shut her out any more. He no longer wishes to be a bystander but a participant in life, and with help from a Vietnam veterans' support group is already starting to clear his psychological decks. Jessie, on whom he has inflicted a great deal of hurt, has to consider whether or not she is ready to try again with Mark. She is tempted to take the easier path of abandoning him in favour of less intense potential lovers who would be 'witty and charming and who would ask nothing of her but a passable white wine and a reasonable fuck'. Nevertheless she settles for Mark – dreams, rages and all – and their reconciliatory discussion ends with her characteristically demanding, 'Oh, shut up and take your leg off and let's do it.'

In literature, as in life, disaster and injury can strike unexpectedly. It is difficult to accept that in *Rebecca* Maxim's totally taken-for-granted strength and confidence will be eroded by disaster and physical injury. Nevertheless Daphne du Maurier cuts the almost arrogant master of Manderley down to unheroic size. In the second chapter, which is of course of a postscriptorial nature, the ever-unnamed heroine comments that her own confidence has come to her rather 'late in the day. I suppose it is his [Maxim's] dependence upon me that has made me bold at last.' The exact nature of this dependence is not spelled out. We only know that she and Maxim have settled into self-imposed exile abroad. Yearning for the most trivial of news from home, isolated from their fellow-hotel guests, living quiet, middle-brow and middle-aged lives, they seem shadows of their former selves, despite their harmonious and affectionate relationship.

However, du Maurier's 'The Rebecca Notebook' and 'The Rebecca Epilogue', published in 1981, many decades after the original novel, leave no doubt that after the destruction of Manderley Maxim is crippled, and able to walk only 'slowly and awkwardly with the aid of sticks'. He has to be settled every day by his wife into his long, adjustable chair, with pillows and a rug arranged around him. How, one feels, are the mighty fallen. De Winter, bereft of Manderley, of an occupation and his physical impressiveness, seems indeed to be shorn of grandeur. His body is 'maimed' and his hands are 'scarred'. The 'Epilogue' stresses Maxim's weakness and the heroine's strength. She delights in looking after him, in protecting him from prying eyes and from the possible legal consequences of his murder of Rebecca. (His dependent and rather unromantic situation is somehow emphasized by the fact that in both the 'Notebook' and 'Epilogue' du Maurier refers to him as 'Henry'. She had originally intended to call him this but had decided instead on 'Maxim' at the time of *Rebecca*'s publication (1938). The change was felicitous: by no stretch of the imagination can 'Henry' be made to sound as charismatic as 'Maxim'.) It seems that only with Maxim's disablement could his wife achieve her wish, expressed half-way through *Rebecca*, not to be treated like an infant or pet but to become a full partner: 'I did not want to be a child. I wanted to be his wife, his mother.' Apparently she becomes both.

Although heroes may be tamed by severe handicap, they frequently retain romantic auras; with heroines the situation is vastly different. One-armed, one-legged or one-eyed girls are rarely love-objects in popular fiction. They are more likely to be treated with scorn and contempt, to be bullied and even indicted of witchcraft. Mary Webb's *Precious Bane* (1924) is an impassioned plea for the full integration of a disfigured heroine into society (see Chapter 2). It persuasively conveys the extremes of country life in Shropshire at the time of the Battle of Waterloo, from the beauty and expansiveness of the natural scene to the oppressiveness of bigotry and the unremitting hard labour of poverty. Like her heroine, Prue Sarn, Mary Webb had a hare-lip and, although in the 1920s the worst excesses of superstition associated with this were less evident than in Prue's time, there is little doubt that the author directly experienced prejudices that proclaimed 'if there was something wrong with a person's outward seeming there must be summat wrong with their mind as well'.

There is a terrifying build-up of suspense as the innocent and industrious Prue comes under increasing threat from the villagers' belief that she is guilty of witchcraft; they move gullibly and ruthlessly from assuming that her hare-lip is a sign that her mother was 'frightened in pregnancy by the devil in the shape of a hare' to deciding that her physical blemish sets her apart from other women as a witch. Their condemnation is also partly aroused by Prue's capacity to read and write, which was of course rare in peasant girls of her time, and by the fact that she slaves 'like a man, at men's jobs', working as unremittingly as her ambitious brother Gideon on the family farm. Such departures from accepted images of the female role place Prue in jeopardy: in particular, hostility is aroused by her innate vitality which is equated by the bigots with the eroticism that had long been attributed to women who were supposed to have practised witchcraft. Any hint of sexuality in a disfigured woman is, apparently, taboo. Prue's treatment thus sharply contrasts with that of those fictional male characters whose handicaps are used to enhance their romantic appeal. There is pathos as well as pride in Prue's confirmation, after she has fallen in love with Kester Woodseaves, the weaver, that 'even if he'd got but one leg, or one arm, or was all pitted with the small pox' she would love him 'the more for it'.

In fact, Kester is extremely handsome, although his attraction for Prue lies more in his personality than in his looks: on several occasions he courageously confronts and puts down prejudice and violence, and his enlightened behaviour distinguishes him in her eyes as a mountain of 'silent power'. She loves him from the first moment she sets eyes on him but, aware of her marred appearance, feels obliged to observe him only from the shadows: 'I sat down farther in my corner, and a faintness came over me. For here was my lover and my lord, and behold! I was hare-shotten.'

Prue's passion for Kester awakens her to the full realization of her womanhood:

Though my hands were hard and chapped and my face red and coarsened with weather, I should be, while I thought upon him I loved, a flower and the petal of a flower. For love is a May-dew . . . And though I had but the shadow of it, yes! the shadow of a shadow, as when you see the reflection of a water-lily in the mere, not still, but in ripples, so that even the reflection is all distraught and is not wholly yours, yet it had made the world all anew.

Misfortunes begin to fall upon her hard and fast. Her mother, brother and closest friend meet untimely deaths (which the villagers blame on Prue's supposedly evil powers). She is isolated and persecuted, sustained only by her as yet unfulfilled love for Kester, and her own inner strength: 'I was the witch of Sarn. I was the woman cursed of God with a hare-shotten lip . . . And now, almost the worst crime of all, I stood alone.' She goes on to describe local superstitions about lost and forgotten farms in the mountains, long and lonely winters when winds howled around buildings like wolves or witches, and the fretting of 'unhappy ghosts . . . the dreadful music of the death pack'. Despite her resilience she understands why 'nobody could choose to be alone, and nobody without good reason would condemn another to be alone. Therefore, if you were alone you were as good as damned.'

The lyrical and fairy-tale elements that lift Prue's saga from occasional near-gothic gloom to luminosity are expressed in her 'waking dream' fantasies about Kester, which eventually find fulfilment. Whenever she meets him and is subjected to 'all the strong life of the man' that is 'gathered in his eyes' blazing full upon her, she forgets her 'curse' and allows her natural warmth and sensuality to flower. Kester *is* indeed the Prince Charming or chivalrous knight who rescues Prue from the wrath of the villagers, snatching her away from the ducking-stool and riding off with her 'towards the blue and purple mountains' and their 'chosen bit of Paradise'. Prue, however, has proved herself to be no mere Cinderella or passive female shuttlecock of fate.

In spite of Mary Webb's outstanding story-telling skills, success came only after her death. Born in Shropshire in 1881, she died in 1927, dogged throughout her brief life by invalidism and poverty.

Even though *Precious Bane* had received some excellent critical notices and, in 1925, the Femina Vie Heureuse prize 'for the best work of imagination in prose or verse descriptive of English life', sales were slow until Stanley Baldwin, the then Prime Minister, discovered, publicized and eulogized the book. Baldwin, whose family had lived for generations in Shropshire, applauded not only Mary Webb's vivid conveyance of the region during a particular period but her capacity to create a human drama which was timeless in its truth and appeal. His championship was double-edged. There is no doubt that it phenomenally boosted sales of *Precous Bane* to the general public. There was, however, an opposite response from the 'intelligentsia' to whom Baldwin was not the bluff and honest man of popular image but a manoeuvring Conservative politician whose literary tastes and opinions were likely to be clichéd. Nevertheless, the book retained its best-seller status for several years, remained in print for decades and is available today, almost seventy years on from its first publication, in Virago's Modern Classics series.

Although Stefan Sweig's *Beware of Pity* was published towards the end of the 1930s, considerably later than *Precious Bane*, it also reflects society's negative attitudes about female physical handicap. Edith von Kekesfalva, the crippled young girl at the centre of the story, is a far from romantic figure. She is petulant, demanding, self-enclosed and bitter – but with some cause, having been smitten with an unspecified disease five years earlier which changed her lively, able-bodied existence into one of severe disability. She is virtually chair-bound, walking only slowly and very clumsily with the aid of crutches and calipers.

Beware of Pity's first-person narrative unfolds from the viewpoint of Anton Hofmiller, a second lieutenant in the Austro-Hungarian army who meets Edith when he is posted to a small frontier garrison town. He is invited by her extremely wealthy father to visit the 'marvellous, enchanted' Kekesfalva Villa. At first he is attracted to Edith's cousin Ilona (who turns out to be betrothed to someone else). She temporarily absorbs his full attentions so that he hardly notices the daughter of the house and is unaware of her disablement. (The period is 1913 when, of course, Edith's atrophied legs would have been covered by long, enveloping skirts.)

It is an 'ill-fated blunder' on his part which brings Anton into contact with Edith. Conscious of having neglected her at an informal dance at her home, he approaches her with a formally polite invitation to partner him. Her response is devastating. Her face and body are convulsed by spasms of anguish – or rage – and she bursts into 'wild, elemental' sobs which 'break forth again and again, like a gush of blood, like a hot agony of vomiting'. Horror at his gaffe and the realization of Edith's dreadful handicap inspire Anton with the determination to make amends by giving time, attention and sympathy to the invalid.

Touched by what he considers to be her innocent response to his friendship, he thinks he has discovered 'the creative magic of pity'. Unhappily, however, Edith falls passionately and desperately possessively in love with him, and mistakes his sympathy for a romantic response. Gradually and inexorably, Anton finds himself both the victim and the instigator of tragic events, all of which are triggered off by the immense pity he feels for the girl. This eventually changes from a tender emotion into something soured, grinding and destructive. As surely as Edith is confined by her physical disability, Anton is caged by her acute psychological dependence on him.

Pressed by Edith's father, whose once proud spirit is broken by his daughter's suffering, Anton slips into ever-closer intimacy with her and, against his own better judgement, comforts her with false hopes of the cure that some new treatment might effect. In fact her doctor has assured him that only very minimal improvement in her condition could ever be expected, but Anton lacks the courage to tell Edith the truth. The long process of his 'lies born of pity' has begun. She is frenziedly happy and optimistic, and with the revival of hope her sensuality, and passion for Anton, increase.

Kekesfalva tries to persuade him that he must offer himself in marriage to Edith 'when she's had the new treatment': otherwise she will refuse to undertake this and lapse again into bitterness, self-loathing and possibly even suicide. Responding to her new vitality but deeply resenting the trap which is closing upon him, Anton is too emotionally battered to resist. He begins to appreciate the wisdom of Edith's doctor's comment that 'it is only at first that pity, like morphia, is a solace to the invalid . . . but unless you know the correct dosage and when to stop, it becomes a virulent poison . . .'

It is only when Edith kisses him for the first time ('with a kind of drunken strength . . . never in my life had I received such a wild, despairing kiss as the one given me by the crippled girl') that Anton realizes he has never thought of her body as being able to function fully in the sexual sense. The full focus upon him of her extraordinary intensity makes him aware that being loved against one's will is a greater 'torture' than one's own experience of 'longing and desiring'.

In desperation Anton decides to resign his commission, to leave Austria and, in some sort of civilian post elsewhere, to escape from the whole horrible web of Edith's insistent and demanding adoration. However, her doctor, to whom he confides his plans, tells him bluntly that this would be a 'dastardly crime' tantamount to murder.

Anton swithers and agonizes, and lies about his intentions to Edith, her father and his fellow-officers. In the end so great is his emotional turmoil that he hardly knows whether he has decided to go on with the relationship, to end it and disregard the consequences, or to shoot himself. His commanding officer tries to sort things out by an immediate transfer of the still undecided Anton to the reserve battalion in distant Czazlau. Still wrestling with his doubts, Anton tries on his long journey to contact Edith – only to learn that the tragically disappointed girl has taken her own life.

The Great War begins and, after four years of fighting during which he is wounded and decorated as a hero, Anton is unable to forget the suffering he has caused in the name of pity: 'no guilt is forgotten so long as the conscience still knows of it'.

The story is told with sensitivity and perception: it provides some stark assessments of the images which were then often associated with a disabled female. Anton's commanding officer, for example, callously dismisses Edith as 'a crippled and deformed creature'. Anton himself feels that 'she's not a real woman', a view that is somewhat endorsed in a comment made to him by Edith's doctor. He says that 'the slightest physical abnormality in a woman produces a kind of pathological aversion' in many men which, of course, 'excludes all possibility of a sexual relationship'.

There is no doubt that disabled heroes generally get a far better deal than handicapped heroines.

CHAPTER FIVE

From Sahara Sands to Shangri-La

♡

ONE MALE 'BEAST' whom heroines found difficult to tame was the indisputedly dark, handsome but lean-and-sexually-hungry sheikh of the desert romances. From the late eighteenth century orientalism had exercised a fascination for the British public. Byron's poems had provided images of minarets, fountains and marble courts – and most potently of odalisques – which conjured visions of the alluring atmosphere of 'the East', while its popularly accepted sensuousness was further celebrated in the paintings of Delacroix. Many highly unoriental Regency homes began to be adorned with lushly evocative artefacts from Arabia, India and other Eastern locations. A fever for things oriental infected people from most ranks of society, including the Prince Regent, whose lasting expression of it was the building of the brilliant but over-the-top Brighton Pavilion. From then until the Second World War and the break-up of Empire, an unending stream of oriental ornamentation, from richly inlaid coffee tables and intricately designed carpets to mock-ebony miniature elephants and bizarre brass pseudo-Buddhas, continued to flow into a wide variety of British homes.

Throughout the nineteenth century there were, of course, countless travellers' tales from soldiers, explorers, traders and archaeologists who had savoured both the hardships and the fulfilments offered by the East. Hot on the heels of these real-life adventurers, authors began to produce heavily emotive fiction that focused particularly on the Arabian desert and the India of the Raj. Stories ranged from vaguely romantic travelogues to epics of extremely specific lust and love and/or spiritual realization. Heroes and heroines found that their inner selves as well as their sexuality functioned at full blast and in hitherto unsuspected ways beneath Indian or African skies and, especially, in or around the Sahara Desert which seemed frequently equatable with Divinity itself (albeit an extraordinarily quirky one). Those sandy stretches were to become the repository of strangely erotic and mystical dreams, a place where the past could be obliterated and where individuals were exposed for the first time in their lives to destiny with a capital D.

No one brought these elements together with more confidence (or more verbiage) than Robert Hichens, whose *The Garden of Allah* (1904) marked the creation of the desert romance as a distinct sub-genre. He was already a successful writer with nine novels to his credit: the first of these, *The Green Carnation*, published anonymously in 1894, had wittily sent up Oscar Wilde and the Aesthetic Movement. This was out of keeping, however, with the general feeling of Hichens's books which, even before they began to sink deep into desert sands, conveyed an overblown intensity about sex and spiritual redemption.

The son of a clergyman, Hichens was born in 1864, far away from Araby in the Kentish village of Speldhurst. Although imbued with many mid-Victorian values, he was soon to question his father's religious orthodoxy. In his early journalistic career he became fascinated both by the 'night-birds' (prostitutes of Piccadilly who plied their trade *al fresco* in Green Park, and inspired his 1897 novel *Flames*) and by aspects of occultism. Even though most of the contacts he made with spiritualists, faith-healers and so on were inconclusive, he maintained throughout his life the view that there was some truth underlying their beliefs and activities.

His preoccupation with the metaphysical had been sharpened by a visit to Egypt (1893–4) when he travelled up the Nile with Lord Alfred Douglas, who was, of course, soon afterwards to achieve notoriety when Wilde's trials brought their affair to public attention and outrage. The remarkable impact on Hichens of exposure to the Sahara Desert and the whole ambience of Egypt was both instant and long-lasting. Before he tackled *The Garden of Allah* he produced two other stories with North African themes, a novel called *An Imaginative Man* (1895) and a short story, 'The Charm of Snakes' (1897). Both were concerned with abandoned honeymoons, sex that had gone wildly awry, extravagant religiosity and supernaturalism.

As far as celebration of the apparent mystical qualities of the desert are concerned, these fade into insignificance when compared with *The Garden of Allah*. In this the desert can hardly be called background: as a living, untamable entity, it virtually takes over from the main narrative at times and is seen to symbolize not only the religious quest but the totality of Islamic culture and history. Hichens was, it seems, absolutely captivated by the Arabs, both collectively and as individuals. *The Garden of Allah* occupies almost 500 pages, and very many of these are taken up with his vivid word-pictures of these 'free-born sun-suckled men' who 'uncivilized or not, at least live' with a vitality that far outstrips that of the Europeans whose approach to their own religion and culture is frequently conveyed as tired and jaded.

Domini Enfilden is the daughter of an English lord and his wayward part-Hungarian spouse, from whom she has inherited dark, gipsy-like good looks. In other ways she is a no-nonsense Britisher – five foot ten, walking 'splendidly', looking disconcertingly strong, with broad shoulders and an athletic figure, and having 'never used a powder-puff in her life'. The book is concerned with her search for inner peace. Unsatisfied by upper-class English life, she has travelled to a small settlement on the edge of the Sahara Desert (the eponymous garden of the title, of course) where she meets the half-Russian, half-British, brooding and almost tortured Boris Androvsky who, despite possessing 'the most male' and 'full of sex' voice which Domini has ever heard, spends a lot of his time being very silent and withdrawing suddenly and dramatically from apparently ordinary and unchallenging situations.

Boris shows a particular aversion to the steamy religiosity which surrounds Domini and all those with whom she associates. Two lines from the 'song of the freed negroes' crop up constantly in the text, sung both in and out of the desert by servants, dancers and tribesmen:

> No one but God and I
> Knows what is in my heart.

Domini is much struck by this motif, although in her case it is not often relevant. She rarely knows what is in her heart, even if God does. For every passionate feeling which pulls her in one direction, with pages of appropriate reflection, there is a rapidly formed and equally intense reverse one dragging her in a psychologically opposite direction. She is, of course, both violently repelled by and drawn to Boris.

Attraction eventually triumphs, although Androvsky has a lot working against him. He is socially extremely awkward, hints at 'dark places that should be left dark' inside himself, and fails to respond to the beauty of a Moorish garden which has totally enchanted Domini. Most disquieting of all, he appears to have repudiated the Roman Catholicism to which Domini still somewhat tenuously clings, despite her lurking suspicion that the followers of Islam might be on to something rather more efficacious.

Domini is so disturbed by Boris's lapses from social and spiritual grace (priests dislike him on sight and crucifixes fall from the wall in his presence) that she finds herself asking 'whether he was a gentleman or not'. One has to say the answer is in the negative. Boris is a renegade member of a silent (Trappist) order of monks who has not only absconded from his Tunisian monastery but taken with him the knowledge, handed down to him alone, of the recipe for the making of Louarine, a liqueur for which the monks are famous (and which presumably brings in much of their revenue).

Domini's awareness that she has fallen for Boris comes suddenly but is described at length (as indeed are her moments of Great Pause, which represent religious fulfilment). There is a strong, slow build-up to their eventual marriage, with a proposal in which Boris sobs violently on his knees around her skirts, clasping her hand like 'a furnace pouring its fiery heart upon her' and breaking out into sweats that thrill Domini with their 'male power' which 'might make for either good or evil, but which had nothing to do with littleness'. Wallowing in her passion, Domini prays earnestly to God to put her love for Androvsky 'to the uttermost proof' (which He obligingly does, of course, later on when they are in the throes of their honeymoon).

The Catholic wedding ceremony takes place, performed reluctantly by the local priest who can't stand Boris. Seeing Domini as an 'Amazon who could have been a splendid nun', he feels that she is wasted. Even the elements express displeasure at their union: the sunset at the time of the ceremony is unusually murky, and a storm blows up when they set off into 'the great hiding place' (the desert) for their honeymoon.

The storm dies down and the ride to the oasis camp continues with the lovers' silent but rapturous anticipation of their sexual union. Domini rejoices at her hitherto unrevealed female fragility in the face of Boris's physical strength; there is the implication that she hopes his psychological capacities will match this, and that 'his nature should rise above her with eagle's wings, that when she looked up she should see him, never when she looked down'. (Like Ethel M. Dell, Robert Hichens liked to equate the masculine contribution to the sex act with the functions of the eagle. In foreplay heroes tended 'to rise with eagle's wings' and in fulfilment to swoop, dive and thrust, also in the manner of that predatory bird.)

Once Domini and Boris are safely set down and established in their tent, we begin to look for the consummation which has been so fervently anticipated, but the long, long lead-up continues in dialogues about forgetting the past, about the qualities of freedom, of good and evil, of man and woman, and, of course, God. For two people who are throbbing with physical yearning which has 'the glory of fire' and whose natures are 'galloping like an Arab horse across the sands towards the sun', they take a terribly long time to do much about it, and when, at last, Boris puts his arms around Domini while she is kneeling at prayer, and 'she did not resist him', that is all we are told about the crucial moments of the wedding night. The action jumps forward three weeks in a single bound, as it were, with the couple in a state of dreamy happiness and fulfilment.

However, this is not to last. They entertain a group of French soldiers whose officer comments at dinner that the liqueur (Louarine) which they are drinking might not be available for much longer. A little later, when during their desert travels Domini talks with a Catholic priest, she is told the whole, sad story of the monk's defection. She puts two and two together immediately and knows that her beloved Boris is the absconder. She and he talk earnestly and devoutly about the problem. Although torn by the desire to continue to be Domini's husband, Boris seems to have recovered his faith sufficiently to agree with her that he must return to the monastery and renew his vows.

They travel there with frequent acclamations of their mutual love and expressions of the hope that, in some future life, God might let them be together again – and in the desert. But Domini does not weaken an inch: physical contact between Boris and herself is not to be contemplated now that both have accepted that their destiny is to be divided. This is really very hard on Boris. He will not only soon be living chastely until the end of his days but, as his honeymoon utterance makes clear, had never known a woman until he bedded Domini: '"Don't let us miss anything to-night," he said. "All my life is to-night. I've had no life yet. To-morrow – who knows whether we shall be dead to-morrow?"' Presumably Domini will have other sexual options in the future, although the narrative implies that she is likely to remain faithful to the memory of her few nights of rapture with Boris.

Only at the moment of parting, when they reach the monastery, does Domini allow some slight physical contact: she puts her hands on Boris's shoulders and touches 'his forehead with her lips'. The final scene of the book is, in fact, a happy one, but poor, tormented Boris is excluded from it. We see Domini ensconced once again in the Moorish garden which had given her so much delight at the time when she was getting to know herself, her future husband and the mysterious satisfactions of the desert. She is not alone, however. A diminutive Boris is playing by her side, and listening with her to the song they love above all others ('No one but God and I', etc.). But far away in the fastness of the Tunisian monastery, Androvsky does not hear this haunting and compelling music. Nor, of course, does he know that he has sired a son. Alas, poor Boris!

Published towards the end of 1904, *The Garden of Allah* ran into five editions within two or three months. It retained its popularity for over a quarter of a century and was filmed three times, in 1917, 1927 and, in colour, in 1936 with Marlene Dietrich as a blondely fragile rather than a robustly brunette Domini, and Charles Boyer, whose Gallic good looks and brown-black eyes appropriately conveyed Boris's unfathomable intensities.

It is interesting to see how differently the sexual needs and taboos of a man of the cloth have been treated in a more recent romantic novel. Colleen McCullough's *The Thorn Birds* appeared in 1977, seven decades after Hichens's epic. Its setting is not Arabia but Australia; its direct tone had none of *The Garden of Allah*'s intricate and over-used allusiveness and introspection although its atmosphere is at times similarly high-key. Its central male character is Ralph de Bricassart; he is a black-haired, blue-eyed, finely featured Roman Catholic priest in a remote Irish/Australian agricultural community, who captures the affections of two women. Although they are from the same family, their circumstances and status are very different.

They are Mary Carson, a wealthy widow who owns Drogheda, an enormous sheep station, and Meggie Cleary, the young daughter of Mary's brother Paddy who, as farm manager, 'works himself ragged' to support his wife and many children, and is very much Mary's poor-relation employee. With both Mary's and Meggie's love there is a double taboo. For each, of course, Ralph as a priest who has taken vows of perpetual celibacy is a forbidden object of desire. Mary is further handicapped in finding any fulfilment with him by the fact that while he is in his twenties she, at sixty-five, is written off by him and society as 'old enough to be officially beyond the drives of the body'. (She is not, in fact, and bitterly resents her figurative assignment to the granny-shelf.) The prohibitive qualities of the gap between Meggie and Ralph are also compounded by age. He is eighteen years older than she. Her 'passionate forbidden' love for him begins when she is still virtually a child and will eventually span more than half a century. By the time she reaches her teens she has realized exactly what is involved in her responses to Ralph although, as a practising Catholic, she accepts at first that at the fundamental level their relationship has no future.

However, Ralph, whose awareness is clouded by ecclesiastical ambition, takes twenty years to recognize that the extraordinarily protective tenderness he has felt for Meggie from the moment they met is neither priestly nor paternal but sexual. Mary Carson has no illusions about the nature of Ralph's feeling for Meggie and continually goads him with his inability to face this. She has made mirror-clear her own partiality for him and, suffering the antici-pated rejection, believes that this springs as much from his repul-sion at her age as the restrictiveness of his vows. Over the seven years of their association her fancy for him develops into an explosive amalgam of convoluted passion and determination for revenge.

Mary's wealth extends far beyond ownership of Drogheda. The fortune left her by her husband amounts to some thirteen million pounds and she devises a scheme to use this to ensure that Ralph will be thrust totally out of Meggie's reach. Recognizing that there are temporal as well as spiritual elements in his reiterated aspira-tions to become 'a perfect priest', on the eve of her death Mary makes a will leaving her money to the Church on condition that it 'appreciates the worth and ability of . . . Father Ralph de Bricassart' who is to be entirely responsible for 'the administration and channelling' of all her assets, receiving a personal salary from these of £10,000 a year.

She knows, and so does Ralph, that on his acceptance of these terms his advancement in the Church will be spectacularly rapid. Just before she dies she gives him the only copy of this will, which replaces an earlier one, held by her lawyer, leaving all her estates to Meggie's family. Ralph therefore knows that he has the option of destroying the new will that deprives the Cleary family – including Meggie – of long-term affluence, but he succumbs to Mary's fiendish conniving. He inwardly acknowledges that he has become the accessory and sharer of her monstrous shame. His only consolation is that Meggie's innocence is untouched by their corruptive actions and ambitions: he berates the dead Mary: 'You disgusting old spider. You've won, but what a victory. The triumph of one disintegrating caricature of humanity over another. You can't defeat my Meggie, nor can you take from her what was never yours . . .'

Through the 'master-stroke' of her new will, Mary has been able both to express beneficence towards her 'beautiful, ambitious priest' and to direct spite against Meggie, who has long been the object of her jealousy. She does, however, have to suffer posthumous punishment and retribution, although whether this is for her presumption as an ageing woman in physically wanting a younger man, for her malice towards Meggie or her railing against religious hypocrisies is not made clear. At any rate, she dies alone in the expectation that she is en route for Hell, and as soon as her body is cold, it starts to decompose, horribly and malodorously. Contemplating her corpse after forcing himself to deliver retrospective extreme unction ('laying sacred things on Mary Carson's body was obscene'), Ralph becomes aware of 'hordes of flies buzzing, insanely clamoring as they feasted on her, mated on her, laid their eggs on her'. A little while later he revisits the foetid room and Mary's stinking carcase and 'the fly eggs were beginning to hatch maggots in all the wet parts of her face, ballooning gases puffed up her fat arms and hands to greenish blobs, her skin was breaking down'. He fears that if she is not quickly consigned to a coffin she will have to be poured into a petrol drum!

Ralph shows no compassion for his misguided and defunct benefactress. He is probably still smarting from the last, blasphemous gibe which she flung at him only hours before: 'Sham, sham, sham! That's all you are, Ralph! . . . Impotent man and impotent priest! I don't think you could get it up and keep it up for the Blessed Virgin herself! . . .'

Ralph predictably progresses from priest to bishop, archbishop, cardinal and papal aide. Meggie drifts into an unsatisfying marriage with Luke O'Neill, a 'clever . . . hard-working and hungry to enrich himself' stockman who spends most of his time away from her. It is not until Ralph (in his archbishop phase) is forty-four and Meggie twenty-six that they become lovers; then, in an away-from-it-all idyll on an island near the Great Barrier Reef, he admits at last that he has been plagued almost from the beginning of their relationship with physical want and love for her. Sex brings ecstasy that religion appears to have denied him: in acknowledging his manhood he has to question whether all that part of his life which has been spent 'in search of godhead' has been a delusion.

He and Meggie spend only a few deliriously happy days and nights together before he has to leave for Rome. Their parting is anguished but they accept the inevitable, and are, in fact, allowed considerably more fulfilment that the ill-fated Boris and Domini in *The Garden of Allah*, with further brief but passionate encounters taking place between them in the future. Unlike Boris, who returns to a life of true poverty and chastity after renouncing Domini, Ralph always has the glittering fruits of great rank within the Church to console him. He does, however, share one desolating loss with Boris: he too fathers a child without knowing it. Meggie bears Ralph's son, Dane, but pretends he is the offspring of her husband Luke (whom she divorces soon afterwards). She cannot win, however: Dane grows up to be truly devout and enters the Church, so she loses – to God – the second as well as the first man in her life whom she has adored. Ralph (by now a cardinal) helps to further Dane's career, and ironically 'sees his own son ordained' but does not know it. It is only when Dane, after heroically rescuing a woman from a turbulent sea, is drowned off Crete that Meggie confesses the truth to Ralph. Too late he realizes what wonderful fulfilments his career demands and ambitions have denied to both himself and Meggie, and at Dane's interment Ralph dies of an apparent heart-attack, closing his eyes and finding for 'that last time, forgetfulness in Meggie'.

Although there are parallels about duty, honour, destiny and the questioning of religious faiths in *The Garden of Allah* and *The Thorn Birds*, Colleen McCullough permits her protagonists to challenge the Almighty with a vigour which Boris and Domini (and most early readers of Hichens's book) would have considered blasphemous and obscene. Meggie's protests have also a vaguely feminist awareness: talking with a friend after Dane has decided to become a priest, she comments: 'You said I'd lose him. I didn't believe you . . . But there's never a woman born who could defeat God. He's a Man.' More bitterly, when Dane dies, she tells Ralph that 'We stole what you had vowed to God, and we've both had to pay.' Here there are certainly echoes of the guilt that haunted Boris and Domini's heart-searchings in and around the desert, and here too, at least temporarily, religiosity appears to have triumphed over romance.

In the canon of Edith Maude Hull, who started to write desert adventures in 1919 and continued to do so for twenty years, romance (or at any rate abduction and rape) was all that mattered. Although *The Sheik* (1919) and its successors contained amorphous references to sand-strewn spiritual awakenings, these are mere backcloths to the playing-out of the main sexual-conquest themes. When E. M. Hull created *The Sheik*, her vision of Arab mores and habitats was several stages removed from reality, but its violent, erotic escapism put an indelible stamp on the desert sub-genre from 1919 until well into the 1980s. It is difficult at times to realize that all those desperate horse- or camel-back chases to and from Bedouin tents, and the truly torrid amours that were enacted beneath their awnings flowed from the pen of a respectable Derbyshire lady who was married to a pig-breeder. The Arabia of *The Sheik* lost little in literary appeal by existing only in its author's imagination (the days of cheap flights enabling topographical and social details to be easily checked at first hand were still far away), and it was some years after its publication that Edith Maude first visited the desert to research a non-fiction work (*Camping in the Sahara*, 1926).

She was not, of course, the first female writer to exploit the amatory stimulation of North Africa's 'billowy, shifting' sands and highly charged inhabitants. Ouida had blazed the trail in the 1860s, followed by Elinor Glyn with *His Hour* (1909), and Olive Wadsley with *Payment* (1916). Kathlyn Rhodes wrote *The Will of Allah* (1908), *The Desert Dreamers* (1909) and several other desert novels. Her 'Great Romance of the East', *The Lure of the Desert*, was recycled as a long-running serial in the weekly *Girls' Own Stories* in 1921 some ten years after its first publication. Some of Rhodes's stories featured events and trappings which presaged those of *The Sheik*, although their focus is more European than Hull's celebrated saga. The man of mixed race in *The Lure of the Desert*, for example (who was to become a stereotype of future Eastern romances), is the apparently impeccably English Clive Amory, whose sudden realization that he is half-Arab stirs him to colonialist outrage: 'the cry broke from him as from a soul in torment. "I – I am the child of that – that intrigue between an Englishman and a – a *native*! ... I'm half native myself!" He stammered again in his horror ... "Good God ..."' (Even worse is to come: his wife Carol, 'who hates the East and Eastern people', is to become involved with an Arab man.)

E. M. Hull was almost certainly inspired by the exploits of a clutch of real-life European ladies who, in the words of Lesley Blanch in her intriguing factual study, *The Wilder Shores of Love* (1954), 'followed the beckoning Eastern Star'. (Lawrence of Arabia, still very much *the* cult hero in 1919 when *The Sheik* appeared, might also have had something to do with the vogue for fictional trips into the desert.) Lesley Blanch describes the extraordinary affinity for the Middle East felt by four widely diverse nineteenth-century women: Isobel Arundell and Jane Digby, from England, Isobella Eberhardt from Russia and Aimée Dubucq de Rivery from France.

Isobel Arundell became the adoring wife of Sir Richard Burton, the Anglo-Irish explorer who shared her passion for Islamic cultures. Before meeting her he had not only had a native 'wife' in India but also enjoyed a relationship with a high-born Persian beauty. His love for the East was, it seems, reflected in his appearance – his 'Arabic' physiognomy, dark, panther-like eyes and strangely un-English accent. Isobel was not always able to accompany him on his travels but, by the proxy of Richard's well-recorded activities, could share his intimate knowledge of a variety of Arab locations, and indeed of their sexual customs, which fascinated him.

The aristocratic, Amazonian and much-married Jane Digby was to become successively Lady Ellenborough, Baroness Venningen and Countess Theotoky before eventually finding lasting happiness as the wife of the Bedouin Sheik Abdul Medjuel El Mezrab. Isobella Eberhardt, a rather tortured Russian with transvestite tendencies, achieved some measure of peace by embracing Islam before meeting her early and bizarre death (she drowned in the desert at the age of twenty-seven). Aimée Dubucq de Rivery, a French convent girl captured by corsairs and sold into the Harem of the Grand Turk, literally became the power behind two thrones – first her husband's and then her son's.

It is, of course, unlikely that Diana Mayo, the haughty, pale-skinned, amber-haired, upper-class English heroine of *The Sheik* should think about these European ladies who had walked the wilder shores of Arab love when she rashly ventures into the desert. She is almost immediately abducted on horseback by the Sheik Ahmed Ben Hassan, who appears to be motivated by revenge (he hates everyone and everything English) as well as lust. Diana finds herself a prisoner in his sensuously well-appointed tent. Until they arrive there, clamped in his iron grip and almost stifled by his flowing robes, she has had little chance to examine his appearance. He turns out to be magnetic, in fact bedazzling, but distinctly sadistic: magnificently robed, 'tall and broad-shouldered', he has 'the handsomest and the cruellest face' she has ever seen. He makes no secret of why he has brought her to his tent, and by turns swaying, swooning and struggling in his strong embrace, she has soon to surrender to his 'crushing' strength. She has to endure not only 'the first kiss she has ever received' but also rape, which takes place off-stage and consequently loses something of its narrative impact. Her 'unadulterated terrors' continue day after day, night after night, as she suffers repeated sexual assault from the Sheik who, despite his evident ruthlessness, is adored by his servants who refer always to him as 'Monseigneur'.

There are long passages of reflection and analysis by Diana about the shameful humiliations he is heaping upon her. The horror of these is considerably sharpened by the knowledge that her tormentor is not only a 'beast' but an 'Oriental' one. Diana and Ahmed spend little time in conversation but when they do speak to each other it is in French, and his accent is cultured. In fact, his behaviour is rather ambivalent. On the one hand he seems determined to 'tame' (brutalize and degrade) her: on the other, he drapes her with expensive jewellery, strokes and addresses her tenderly, and swears that she will learn to love him. Curiously, too, in spite of his flagrant pride and pleasure in his sexual prowess, he has, in his own words, 'no harem and, thanks be to Allah, no wives'.

Diana is not only the direct recipient of Ahmed's cruelties but is forced to witness his barbarities to others, from the whipping of recalcitrant dogs and horses, for example, to the murder of Ibraheim Omair, who abducts her from Ahmed with the intention of subjecting her to further ghastly treatment. Slowly and savagely Ahmed throttles his enemy, with evident enjoyment of his 'last agony' as 'blood bursts from his nose and mouth, pouring over the hands that hold him like a vice'.

Appalled by his violence, Diana eventually tries to escape, only to be forcibly brought back by her insatiable lover. To stop her getting away he has to shoot Silver Star, one of his favourite horses, from under her. With typical arrogance he rubs in the fact that the animal is far more valuable than she: 'There are plenty of women' but Silver Star is 'unique'. On the ride back to his tent he viciously threatens Diana with dire but unspecified punishment, and makes it clear that she cannot escape him: 'What I have I keep, until I tire of it – and I have not tired of you yet.' Perversely, when he is at his most obnoxious on the journey back to her canvas prison, Diana's responses to Ahmed change dramatically:

Why did she not shrink from the pressure of his arms and the contact of his warm, strong body? What had happened to her?

Quite suddenly she knew – knew that she had loved him a long time, even when she thought she hated him and when she had fled from him . . .

Of course, with his usual unpredictability, as soon as Diana begins to act lovingly towards him, the Sheik appears to cool off. Despite her protests, he arranges to send her back to Europe. At first this seems to be just another expression of his determination to treat her callously – but it is not so. He has fallen for her just as passionately as she has for him, and self-sacrificingly feels that she will have a better life back in England or France than with him. (Some of E. M. Hull's more intelligent readers would surely have agreed with him!)

All, eventually, is well. Not only will Diana henceforth live rapturously with her Sheik in the desert but she learns that she need harbour no further qualms about having sex with a man of a different race. It turns out that he is actually as white-skinned as she (though, of course, a touch more sun-bronzed) and is the son of a British peer and his strikingly beautiful Spanish wife. Ahmed's pre-Diana hatred of her countrymen is explained by the fact that his father was a bullying drunkard who, when his wife was pregnant with Ahmed, treated her so appallingly that she took off into the desert, from which she was rescued by a Sheik who protected her until her premature death, and then adopted her small son.

If one takes it seriously (which is unlikely now, though not when it was written), E. M. Hull's novel can be seen not only as an anti-feminist tract in which rapist behaviour is rewarded but a justification of racism. *The Sheik* reached its pinnacle of fame and influence when it was filmed in 1921 with Rudolph Valentino playing Ahmed. It became the model for hundreds if not thousands of future desert romances, in various pulp magazines, as well as in book form. In 1922 *Betty's Paper*, for example, as well as serializing Hull's original tale of terror and abduction, throws in other stories of rapist Arab sheiks and Indian rajahs for good measure. *Peg's Paper* also frequently followed the formula of English girls being sold into white slavery. This remained popular throughout the

1920s and 1930s until 1940, when the war and its soldiers, sailors and airmen provided fresh inspiration and new heroes.

When Britain had its back to the wall, *Peg's Paper* caught the patriotic mood and its heroines donned the uniforms of the women's services, the overalls of munition factory-workers or the crisp dresses and caps of VADs. However, the paper still ran a colourful beauty feature by Barbara Broad entitled 'Desert Glamour Secrets': 'She will reveal how you can become as mysteriously lovely as the harem women of Arabia.' Madame Sunya, who gave astrologically slanted advice to the lovelorn, also provided potent whiffs of North Africa's sandy wastes in her star-spangled appearance. Garbed in a jewelled head-band, heavy veil and flowing chiffon, she offered surprisingly down-to-earth (and predictable) help in those war-torn days: 'The man you are most likely to find happiness with is a fairly slight, dark man . . . he will probably wear a uniform of some sort.'

The spate of novels that immediately followed and emulated Hull's prototype perpetuated the myth that the mere presence in the desert of fair-skinned (and preferably amber-haired) English girls was an irresistible invitation to their capture and rape by oversexed (and generally pseudo-) sheiks. (In fact, according to Lesley Blanch, Arabs consider contact with fair hair to be unlucky.) Fictional young women might therefore have been expected to give the desert a wide berth but, it seems, they were either incapable of learning from the sordid exploits of their predecessors or unwholesomely eager to copy them. Even British schoolgirl-heroines went off to the desert for their hols with surprising regularity.

Horace Phillips was one of the most prolific authors of girls' school stories during the 1920s and 1930s. Having previously written tales for popular women's magazines, he had, in accordance with his publishers' policy of not bringing sex into juvenile fiction, consciously played down his flair for producing lushly romantic exploits. However, he could not resist introducing into the saga of Morcove School, which, as 'Marjorie Stanton', he wrote for the weekly *Schoolgirls' Own* from 1921 to 1936, a mysterious Arabian girl called Rose of the Desert. Her appearances are usually the signal for highly charged stories which tremble on the brink of becoming full-blooded romances. Rose is older than Betty Barton & Co., the fifteen-year-old chummy heroines who admire her greatly. She flits in and out of their Devonshire form-rooms and hockey-fields, with adventure and intrigue clinging to her as tenaciously as the flimsy veils and draperies which she never supplements with woolly cardigans, even in the coldest moorland mists and sea breezes. For a period of fourteen years she cherishes a passion for Jack Somerfield, the explorer brother of the school's headmistress, whom she originally encountered in Arabia. During their long-running (but never completely fulfilled) relationship they exchange endearments like Rose's 'O Engleeshman with the heart that never quakes!' and Jack's 'I will never forget how, in the breast of my little brown maiden, there always beats a heart of gold.' Sadly, however, Rose's most axiomatic utterance turns out to be her Kiplingesque 'Kismet – it is fate. I know East is East, and West is West, and never the twain shall meet . . .' Despite the fact that Jack constantly implies that her 'secret longing' will one day be satisfied, and despite the number of times when, at terrible risk to herself, she has rescued him from slow and grisly death, he eventually fobs her off with 'Well done' and an extremely casual kiss on the hand. Rose bows out of the saga when he marries a European princess. It is of course possible that Horace Phillips's publishers, the Amalgamated Press, had warned him to cool Rose and Jack's relationship, because in the early 1930s even their progressive papers for juveniles could hardly encourage marriage between a white man and a 'dusky' girl.

Rose serves her story-line purpose by being instrumental in repeatedly getting a gaggle of Morcove girls into the desert where, expectedly, they undergo a variety of dramatic experiences including sandstorms, slavery, harsh imprisonment and hair's-breadth escapes from death, although amorous sheiks, either real or synthetic, were notably absent. Phillips seems to have recognized that lengthy camel-back trips into the desert were actually more likely to trigger off enteritis than to act as aphrodisiacs (which they did in several popular romances). At any rate, the Morcove girls assess their North African adventures with realism rather than rapture, as, for example, when they have to flee for their lives and are asked by Rose's beloved Jack 'with the cheery humour of a Britisher in a tight corner . . . "which of you are the most tired – the camels or yourselves?"' The attractive but slightly affected 'swell' of the Fourth Form, Paula Creel, unhesitatingly replies, 'Weally, it is cwuel!. . . Talk about being pwostwate, geals! This is worse than fifty hockey-matches wolled into one!'

So much for the romance of camel transportation. Paula's comments are echoed by the grown-up heroine of *Desert Night* by W. E. Johns, who is, of course, better known for the hair-on-the-chest exploits of his intrepid aviator Biggles than for love-stories. The cover of this early thirties' novel shows blondely beautiful Maureen O'Dell sitting on a camel with a man in full Arab garb. It goes almost without saying that he is not the seductive sheik that appearances suggest. He is Haydn Roper, a British Secret Service agent who, for complicated reasons, has had to assume the identity of the Sheik Ali Mustapha Ben-Salim. Haydn is abducting Maureen for her own safety because he has learned that her dishonourable Russian fiancé, Paul Velonsky, who works undercover for England's enemies, plans to use her, and even to sell her, for his nefarious purposes. Fairly early in their camel-ride Maureen murmurs to her apparently Arabian kidnapper: 'I'm afraid this lurching about is going to make me sick.'

In the high-adventure tradition of P. C. Wren's *Beau Geste* in 1924, W. E. Johns equates romance with chivalrous exploits more often than with tender passion. Also like Wren and other male desert raconteurs, he provides moments of woolly mysticism (his hero, for example, believes in God rather than 'accident' because of 'the love between man and woman') which are generally bound up with speculation about honour and decency.

Haydn is the typical fictional forthright Britisher abroad. However, even when he wears his well-cut 'semi-military' khaki drill suit, 'as only an Englishman can wear such garments in the tropics', he has, like the real-life Victorian traveller, Sir Richard Burton, a deep rapport with Arabs. 'He speaks the language like a Bedouin' and could, we are told, 'pass for a native'. His long-standing friend, Sheik Ali Mustapha Ben-Salim, pays him an appropriate tribute: 'Once or twice in a lifetime there is born in Europe a man who sees things as we see them. Such a one was Lawrence. He came here from College, drawn irresistibly. So it was with you.' It is perhaps surprising that Johns is pandering here to the popular Lawrence myth. In 1922 T. E. Lawrence enlisted in the RAF as Aircraftsman Ross, and Johns – who was then an Interviewing Officer for the Inspector of Recruiting – recalled Lawrence as 'a thin, pale-faced chap' with 'something so off-hand about his manner, almost amounting to insolence, that I took an instinctive dislike to him. I had got to know the type. He was "different" from the other men and he was letting me know' (*Flying*, 20 Augst 1938).

Playing for political reasons, at Ali's request, the role of his long-disappeared brother, Abdullah, Haydn finds himself falling in love with Maureen, although this spirited Irish-American girl doesn't take kindly to his protection – which makes her virtually his prisoner. The action is seen almost entirely from a male (Haydn's) viewpoint. In their camel treks and chases, he urges Maureen never to be deluded by the 'glamour' of the desert but to 'Forget about sheiks: they are an outworn theme [hardly an accurate comment] that no novelist would dare to write the truth about ...' That particular truth is not vouchsafed to the reader, and Haydn goes on, rather incongruously, to tell Maureen that the moon, the stars and 'each grain of sand' are exhorting him to kiss her. She takes his blunt 'May I make love to you?' with a pinch of salt, still convinced, of course, that he *is* a sheik or at any rate an Arab, while she remains nominally engaged to Paul Velonsky.

Haydn hides her in one of Ali's palaces which to Maureen's disgust houses a well-populated harem. Her feminist hackles rise even higher when Haydn laboriously but simplistically points out that the lot of its inmates compares favourably with that of many women in her own country. He explains that these favoured Arab ladies need never doubt 'their husband's' word, because he has no necessity to lie to them, and that, 'within reasonable limits' they can 'do as they please'. He stresses that they are free from toil as well as anxiety 'for the present or the future'. Although they are denied 'bridge clubs and gin parties' they are 'not defiled by malicious gossip' or the attentions of 'philanderers' who break up homes in America and Europe. In short, in his estimation, the women of the harem have everything. Except, of course, as Maureen caustically points out, liberty.

Haydn provides further justifications of women's subservient role in Arab society and these sit strangely on a character who is narratively applauded on many occasions for his liberalism. They sit strangely, too, on W. E. Johns who, only a few years later, was to create one of the most compelling feminist role-models in girls' fiction: 'Worrals' of the WAAFs.

Not surprisingly, Maureen is constantly baffled by Haydn's contradictory attitudes – and by the warmth of her own responses to the man whom she sees as an exploitative, macho Arab. In spite of their enforced proximity he is too honourable to force anything more stimulating than a fairly low-key kiss upon her, although there is a lot of slightly stilted romantic word-play between them. Stereotypically, it is only at the end of the story, after political power struggles have been resolved (to England's advantage) by Haydn and his loyal Arab associates in a violent shoot-out, that Maureen learns his real identity from one of his Secret Service colleagues: 'You mean that Abdullah – is really – an Englishman?' After this they need only a few moments together to clear up misunderstandings and declare their mutual love. However, in spite of the author's references at this point to the moon, the stars, the sand-dunes, the rustling palms and other romantic trappings, Haydn and Maureen's relationship seems a pallid business in comparison with the tempestuous affairs of Domini and Boris, or Diana and Ahmed.

The authors who most colourfully carried the desert romance from the inter-war years into the 1980s were generally women. From the beginning of the 1960s Violet Winspear, who wrote primarily for Mills & Boon (London) and Harlequin (Toronto) has been prominent among these. Several of her seventy-plus novels follow closely in the sand-prints of E. M. Hull's *The Sheik*.

An interesting aspect of their development is that despite their comparatively modern settings her 1960s evocations of erotic encounters strike a more restrained note than Hull's steamy 1919 original. Since then, however, Winspear's descriptions of lust and longing have hotted up and been conveyed much more specifically. In her 1969 *Blue Jasmine*, Lorna plays the respectable English girl role and Prince Kasim the sheikish seducer. The storyline of abduction, conquest and taming provides no surprises, but Kasim, although sending 'flames through her body' with his kisses and engaging in a lot of lordly and masterly sexual talk, actually treats Lorna far less violently than Ahmed did Diana.

Sixteen years after *Blue Jasmine*, in *Sun Lord's Woman* (1985), Winspear makes her heroine suffer more acutely, although the hero stops just short of rape: sexual violence takes place only after they are married – and largely because the heroine is deliberately provoking him. Linda Layne answers an advertisement in *The Lady* for a job as a companion-cum-music tutor to a young girl in a Spanish/Arabic family. She soon finds herself, instead, the wife of Karim el Khalid de Torres, the girl's uncle. Like most of Winspear's heroes, he has darkly 'pagan' good looks and an arrogant, challenging personality. In spite of his dishiness and enormous wealth, it seems surprising that Linda, who is intelligent, pretty and, of course, fair-skinned with 'smokey blonde hair', should agree so speedily to become his wife. Surely by the mid-1980s there was more awareness than in the year of *The Sheik*'s publication of the potentially conflicting elements that could be expected in a marriage between an Islamic sheik and an Englishwoman who would have to live entirely in his culture and society? In Linda's case there is an even greater than usual possibility of clashes of mores: she is half-Jewish, an important fact which, if one is contemplating marriage to a Moslem, Middle Eastern Arab should surely at least be mentioned. It does not occur to Linda to refer to this but, predictably, it turns out to be a time-bomb which very nearly wrecks her marriage.

Karim proposes unemotionally, explaining that he is a man 'who was born without any love in him', that he wants an heir and sees

Linda as a suitable wife because she has 'a look of character, coolness and the need to fulfil an obligation'. Linda asks him, with a show of spirit, why he doesn't 'buy' for the wifely role 'a girl of the East skilled in all the ways of pleasing a man'. His reply is a little surprising: 'you have three essential qualities which, to be frank, I find captivating. You are British and I have never met one who isn't courageous. I admire your ability to make music [she plays the piano and 'cello] and above all I know that you are a virgin.'

Over the almost thirty years that she wrote romantic stories, Violet Winspear's Arabian adventures remain in essence unaltered, although there have been concessions to changes brought about by improved communications and greater internationalism. Karim still sees woman only as an adjunct of man with no life apart from him: 'To hell with your career!' he snaps when Linda, thinking he has abandoned her because of her partial Jewishness, has returned to London and begun a satisfying career as a nightclub pianist. Despite his high social status and palatial residences he still likes to make love to his wife on the floor of the desert: 'They were an Arab with his woman on the sands where time stood still ... He quirked a black eyebrow, then lowered his head to her moonlit breasts where his warm lips teased her until live wires seemed to thread her body', and so on.

We can see from all this that, in the main, Violet Winspear has been content to rehash and slightly update time-honoured themes. Of the many writers who sought inspiration from the Sahara, innovators have been few, but June Knox-Mawer broke new ground with *Sandstorm* (1991). There is nothing formulaic about her plot or characters (except, perhaps, that the heroine is yet another 'copper-blonde'): the story begins in 1913 and covers several decades without anachronisms of historical fact or attitudes. Eighteen-year-old Rose, newly married to Captain Geoffrey Chetwynd, travels with him to Arabia where he is taking up a diplomatic appointment. Rose has more or less drifted into marriage because for a girl of her time and class it was the expected thing. Geoffrey – fair, blue-eyed, good-looking but rather chilling – turns out to be a violent, unimaginative lover and an extremely unsatisfactory husband. Rose realizes that for him marriage is a veneer to hide his homosexual inclinations and activities, and, degraded by his abuse and neglect, she begins to respond to Hassan Karim, the Emir of Jehal. At first their relationship is constricted by the social structure in which they have to function. Jehal is a British protectorate, so, although Hassan is the son of the Sultan, it is Rose and not he who is a member of the ruling class. The wary, patronizing friendliness which characterizes the British diplomatic circle's attitude towards Hassan and other local dignitaries is conveyed perceptively and without exaggeration. From the beginning Rose rejects this and brings a surprising openness into her relationships, with both her fellow-countrymen and the Jehalese.

After one or two run-of-the-mill encounters there is a sudden, extraordinary moment of awareness between Hassan and Rose when, in company with Eleanor, Lady Rawlinson, the British Resident's wife, Rose is visiting the Sultan's palace:

> He was staring at her with a sudden intentness. Bronze against the green of the leaves, the wide vivid face with its Tartar cheekbones and heavy-lidded eyes printed itself on her mind as something rare and precious. She could feel the moment branded on her, almost like a burn ... A radiance hummed between them, dazzling the mind. Everything else was blotted out. Only a second had gone by ...

Even when the moment is over, eclipsed by their companions' mundane comments ('Oh look! The tennis court,' Eleanor called out) a new joyousness continues to tremble on the air between them. There follows a long build-up of intensity and troubled wooing before, at last psychologically free from her repellent husband, Rose rides into the desert with Hassan and, sheltering from a heavy sandstorm in an old shack, makes love with him. Their mutuality of feeling contrasts keenly with the initially one-sided compulsions of most fictional desert unions, although their romantic fulfilment is as passionate as anything provided by E. M. Hull or Violet Winspear:

There was no such thing as shame, no consciousness of a separate self any longer, only this miraculous question and answer of his body on hers, this slow mounting pursuit of an ultimate mystery, hidden at the very core of existence.

'Together,' he whispered to her.

'Together,' she answered.

June Knox-Mawer, in common with many other contemporary women writers, has no difficulty in finding the exactly appropriate words for the expression of love and sex and all their gradations. The over-the-top vulgarities which seemed at the root of a great deal of earlier romantic fiction probably came about because women authors had not yet developed their own vocabularies of love and eroticism. (This was hardly surprising because until comparatively recently sensuality was considered a male prerogative and, if evident in females, frowned upon rather than celebrated.) They therefore rechauffé and manipulated images originally employed by male authors writing largely from their own viewpoint. These, of course, generally failed to convey the actuality of female erotic experience. Many women writers, in their efforts to fit such linguistic approximations to their heroines' amatory adventures, produced ever-wilder sexual extravaganzas.

Despite the differences in Rose's and Hassan's backgrounds, and the social and political problems which bring about their lengthy separation, the concept of their total union at all levels is convincingly sustained. In fact, contrasts in culture and religion – which are narratively explored in depth – seem to enrich rather than disrupt their relationship. For Hassan, Rose is 'the sacred flame that lightens the darkness' of his life, and she is almost equally lyrical about their love when she describes it to a sympathetic woman friend: 'It's a miracle . . . It is almost a holy thing between us . . . I can't explain it.'

When they are separated by a terrible twist of fate, Rose returns to England and, unknown to Hassan, gives birth to their son, Idris. However, Hassan is luckier than either Boris in *The Garden of Allah* or Ralph in *The Thornbirds*: he discovers after only three years that he is a father, and Rose, with many trepidations, is persuaded to allow the boy to return to Jehal with him. (Hassan is now married to someone else who, it transpires, is unable to have children.) Their affair continues, with Rose established far away from Hassan's palace in a house in Cairo, but after a year or two she can no longer accept the deceptions involved in this, or the long intervals between their meetings. She builds a new life and marriage in Britain. However, after her second (and sympathetic) husband dies in the late 1940s she is drawn back to Arabia. Meeting Hassan again she can still truly say that 'the real part of my life has always been with you'. They are both now free of marital commitments and, after a gap of nearly thirty years, resume their almost magical affair.

Rose's reunion with her son is far less tender. Now known as Aidrus, he has rebelled against his father and is determined to free Jehal from its British Protectorate status. He doesn't know that Rose is his mother, and sees her merely as 'a middle-aged woman journalist sent out from London to sum up the politics of South Arabia in a few brief sentences'. Unlike Haydn's loyal friend, Sheik Ali Mustapha Ben-Salim, in *Desert Night* (see pages 133–4) Aidrus represents the modern, independent Arab and pours scorn on ideas of natural affinity between the British and his people: 'That's a fairy story the British have invented for their own convenience. Lawrence of Arabia, Gertrude Bell and all that romantic rubbish about kindred souls . . .'

Rose leaves him in ignorance of her identity and his mixed-race origins. Soon afterwards, however, she becomes caught up in the fighting between his faction and the British. She has to appeal to him to save her life and, aware that he is unlikely to do so unless he knows who she is, reveals the truth. Even then, furious in the realization that he is half-English, it is with reluctance that he helps her. Rose has to accept the bitter fact that between mother and son there is no spark of rapport or affection. It seems also that Hassan – terribly wounded in the fighting – is now also lost to her, but happily June Knox-Mawer manages to contrive a positive ending after all.

Stories in which India was the setting for female romantic aspiration and masculine high adventure ran parallel with the Arabian desert genre for many years. Rudyard Kipling, of course, wrote perspicaciously about almost every aspect of life in and beyond the British Raj. Flora Annie Steel, who went to India in the 1860s as the young bride of a British magistrate, wrote short stories and novels with vivid Indian motifs. Her most celebrated work, *On the Face of the Waters*, whose main theme is the 1857 Indian Mutiny, features an Englishman who crosses the European/Asian social divide and takes an Indian mistress. (Kipling exploited the same theme in his *Beyond the Pale* and *Without Benefit of Clergy*.) Flora toured the country with her husband in the execution of his duties and had close contact with Indian rural life but, despite her sympathy with the villagers, she wrote from a very British viewpoint. Some critics consider that her books tended to present Indian women as unprincipled devotees of the destructive goddess, Kali, who seduced clean-living and manly Brits into alien carnalities.

Flora's most notable successor was Ethel M. Dell, whose Anglo-Indian *The Way of an Eagle* (1912) remained popular for decades (see Chapters 3 and 4). Vere Lockwood's 1920s novel, *Ramazan the Rajah* (described by Barbara Cartland as 'the most exciting tale of passionate abduction since *The Sheik*'), brings utterly English and somewhat assertive Valerie Ransome to India, where she falls into the amorous clutches of the even more arrogant Reuel Ramazan, Rajah of Kashmine. Echoes of *The Sheik* certainly abound: similarities between Lockwood's and Hull's novels include the abduction, the heroine's anguished, reluctant but eventually passionate response to the hero, her final self-realization in a strange culture, and desire to spend the rest of her life there at the side of her exotic lover, along with the felicitous (in the context of its time) discovery that he is not, after all, a 'native' but 'a white man'. Also in common with Diana Mayo's ruthless captor in *The Sheik*, once Reuel has managed to make Valerie respond to 'the flame of pure passion, primitive, irresistible', he feels that he should send her away from his depraving influence, back to respectable Europe:

'When you scorned me I determined to take you and make you suffer. Knowing how civilized you were, I forced you to see all the indolent, passionate sensuality of the East ... By my own actions I have given up all hope of you. I was a brute to you. I acted as no honourable Englishman would have done ...'

Valerie, of course, persuades him that her place is in 'the warm, beautiful ardent life' that they can share in Kashmine: 'He felt his control gone then. He felt himself defeated. Love mastered him, not he love. Love triumphed, as love will over all reason and the most determined wills of men.'

Greater challenge and realism are conveyed in M. M. Kaye's 1957 romance of the Indian Mutiny, *Shadow of the Moon*, and her 1978 *The Far Pavilions*, also set in nineteenth-century India. In the latter (described in a *Times* review as 'a *Gone with the Wind* of the North-West Frontier') the author compellingly tackles the theme of a mixed-race relationship between Ashton Hilary Akbar Pelham-Martin ('Ash'), an Englishman brought up from childhood by a Hindu family, and Anjuli ('Juli'), who is an Indian princess. Hatred and conflict between East and West force Ash and Juli into desperately difficult cultural choices. The British Raj clings to many rooted prejudices and restrictions, whilst indigenous Indian religions adhere as tenaciously to their own traditions. Ash sums up their predicament:

'... people everywhere are suspicious of strangers and hostile towards anyone different from themselves, and we two are both strangers ... My people wouldn't accept you because you're both Indian and half-caste, while your people wouldn't accept me because I'm not a Hindu and therefore an outcaste. As for the Mussulmans, to them we are "Unbelievers" ...'

Their future remains uncertain even at the end of the 955-page narrative: all that is certain is that they intend to remain together. They decide to seek the 'far pavilions' of the remote valley in the shadow of the Himalayas where Ash was brought up:

They rode out together from the shadows of the trees ... and spurred away across the flat lands towards the mountains. And it may even be that they found their Kingdom ...

M. M. Kaye spent much of her life in India, and her affectionate understanding of it gives credibility to the occasional excesses of *The Far Pavilions*. Similarly, Valerie Fitzgerald's intimate knowledge of the country is punched home in her 1981 *Zemindar*. Like M. M. Kaye's novel, this has a sprawling but triumphantly executed plot. It seems at first to offer the conventional ingredients of romantic adventure in glorified *Girls's Own Paper* style, with its gritty but guileless heroine caught up in hazardous exploits, but it soon opens out into a multi-layered complex of realistic relationships and challenging action.

The author grew up in India, spending several years on an estate similar to that which is featured in her book. She left for Europe in 1947 and, writing *Zemindar* over thirty years later, consciously departed from the early 1980s literary fashion of casting the British in India as cardboard colonialist baddies. Her portrayal of the natural scene, and life in the villages and bazaars, is colourfully authentic. It is 1857, and shortly before the Mutiny begins, twenty-four-year-old Laura Hewitt visits India with friends. She meets Oliver Erskine, who falls in love with her. He owns a vast agricultural estate, has a passionate sense of responsibility for his land and his workers, and is out of sympathy with the type of British resident who has no interest in Indian life but simply wants to establish provincial England in miniature there.

At first Laura is unsure of her feelings about Oliver, who is a man of contradictory moods – by turns glinting and brooding, appealing and arrogant. He appears to combine certain characteristics of Heathcliff and Darcy, and when later in the narrative he becomes maimed but remains masculinely magnetic, Mr Rochester comes to mind! With all these Brontë- and Austen-esque echoes, it is not surprising that Laura can do a demolition job on social hypocrisies with the wit and economy of style of Elizabeth Bennet. Her deepening response to Oliver becomes evident to the reader long before it does to her, for, of course, Valerie Fitzgerald has no difficulty in conforming to the traditions of the genre by keeping the couple out of each other's arms until the later stages of the book. The first terrifying eruptions of the Mutiny curtail Laura's sojourn on Oliver's estate: his home is burned by insurgents. Laura and her friends have to take refuge in the British Residency at Lucknow just before the beginning of the five-month siege. It is only after all this that she and Oliver can find fulfilment together.

Zemindar benefits considerably from the author's hindsight in non-partisan, balanced descriptions of the Mutiny. Although unable to justify the apparently senseless brutality of some of the Indian mutineers, several of her leading British characters sympathize with their resentment of provocative and blinkered Government policies. *Zemindar* points to the fact that under sufficient pressure any individual or society can erupt into violence. During the siege, for example, when Laura is threatened with rape (against which she has forearmed herself with a revolver), the attempted assault is by a recalcitrant British soldier, not an Indian mutineer.

With the unfolding of Laura and Oliver's romance, the author knows exactly when to take the panoramic and when to take the personal view; when to use succinctness and when to let rip with lusher, sweeping images.

Similar in theme but less emotionally satisfying in treatment is Emma Drummond's *Beyond All Frontiers* (1984). Charlotte comes from a sheltered English upbringing in the 1830s to join her parents at an Indian frontier garrison. She is another heroine who has to undergo several crises of identity and relationship. Her parents, the man to whom she is originally attracted, and her eventual husband all provide her with difficult problems and choices, before the love story gets fully launched and the main characters learn to understand not only each other but themselves. They are spurred on by an abundance of native savagery and some lavish splendours of the British Raj, although they also engage in progressive questioning of the imperialistic status quo.

Kate Alexander explores mixed-race unions and love–hate responses to India during the heyday of the Raj in *The Shining Country* (1991). Caste and social distinctions in both Indian and British society give the story its cutting edge: Jessica Bullen spends her childhood in Bombay and, although she is 'the daughter of the illegitimate son of a half-caste', she shares a comfortably ruling-class life-style with her mother and father until the latter's sudden death. Events then bring home to Jessica the perilously fragile foothold which she has on a secure position in society. She realizes that she has to harness all her talents in order to survive and after lengthy struggles progresses from secretarial work to becoming one of the first female Indian movie-stars. Naturally, in the context of the 1990s when the book appeared, she is prepared to take drastic social risks, coping, for example, with the conflict of loyalty to her husband and her never-abating love for her cousin Dominic, an aggressively handsome, confident young man who has set his sights on higher matrimonial hopes than Jessica could offer in her youthful, impoverished days. Possibly *The Shining Country* provides the pattern for the Indian romance of the 1990s in which love, though not exactly low-key, never soars to the heady heights of the 'sweeping' Raj or desert fictional amours of the past.

On the whole, male writers of the twentieth century on whom India has laid its spell, focus more sharply on their leading characters' spiritual transformations than women authors do. And, if popular fiction is to be believed, heroes carry their religious inquiry further and deeper than heroines, who are liable to become side-tracked by falling in love with some handsome man, or looking after the child he fathers on her. F. Yeats Brown's *Bengal Lancer*, written by a serving British officer and published in 1930, describes military manoeuvres and tribal adventures, and the Raj-ish recreations of parties, polo and pig-sticking, but it is most concerned with individual mystical inquiry. Its romantic associations are with India itself – 'that land of vivid contrasts, the Marches of the North-West, where there is blazing heat and bitter cold, feud and friendship, loyalty and treachery' – rather than linked to the male–female relationship. It is possibly remembered today mainly because of the 1935 Hollywood film, *The Lives of a Bengal Lancer*, which, though loosely based on Yeats Brown's book, concentrates almost entirely on its army and espionage thrills and chills (as well as inspiring a whole generation of 1930s schoolboys to try to grow up looking like Gary Cooper, who played its hero).

A. E. W. Mason's *The Drum* (1937) is another vignette of

military and political life, with the archetypally British colonial administrator, Captain Frank Carruthers, helping to 'keep the rickety wheel of Administration revolving' in Peshawar in the North-West Province. With him is his young bride, Marjorie. Again, sexual romance takes second or even third place to the activities of the male-oriented military and governing groups, and again, too, it was the film which brought the story to international prominence. It starred Roger Livesey as Carruthers and Valerie Hobson as Marjorie. Looking extraordinarily fetching and quintessentially English in tailored blouses and well-cut jodhpurs, the actress convinced and captivated audiences as the wife of a British officer in a remote and constantly threatened garrison.

John Masters's fascination with India has been expressed in stories ranging through different periods of its history. His most romantic novel set there is *Bhowani Junction* (1954) which, like Paul Scott's celebrated *Raj Quartet*, deals with the declining days of British rule. The heroine is Victoria Jones, a twenty-eight-year-old Eurasian who, like her engine-driver father, works for the Delhi Deccan Railway. Her handsome 'proud as Diana' looks attract the admiration of Patrick Taylor, who is also Eurasian, of the full-blooded Indian, Ranjit Singh, and of Colonel Rodney Savage, the British officer who commands the First Battalion of the 13th Gurkha Rifles. *Bhowani Junction* provides searching insights into the frustrations of the Anglo-Indian community, balanced between British and Indian society and fully accepted by neither. In the last days of the Raj they are particularly aware of their vulnerability. As Victoria confides to Patrick, 'The English despise us but need us. We despise the Indians, but we need them . . .'

Victoria experiments with the differing strands of her identity. Projecting herself into an all-Indian future, she pursues her fondness for Ranjit but gradually realizes that the divide between their attitudes is too vast to permit marriage or any other permanent relationship. She finds that she has a kind of acerbic intellectual affinity with Rodney Savage, and forces an 'angry mating' upon him, but in the end it is to Patrick that she turns for lasting love and satisfaction: 'She'd tried becoming an Indian – but she wasn't an Indian. She'd tried becoming English – but she wasn't English.' Victoria reconciles herself to her Anglo-Indian status and looks forward to building a good life with Patrick in the new India which will emerge from the ending of the Raj. She is in almost every way the prime mover, stronger in character, far more questioning and in control of situations than he is. We feel that she will need all her guts and talents to thrive – even possibly to survive – in the shaky Anglo-Indian community which will attempt, against so many odds, to preserve its identity and some measure of economic security in the shifting, post-Raj future.

It is a far cry from the uncertainties of India, Arabia and other outposts of between-the-wars Empire to the mythical Shangri-La of James Hilton's 1933 *Lost Horizon*. Swathed in a hazily romantic aura, this preternaturally beautiful and fertile valley is a modern equivalent of Shambala, the fabled blissful lands of Buddhist lore, of Avalon or the Isles of the Blest. As a synonym for an idyllic refuge from the stresses of ordinary life, or a hostile world, Shangri-La has become part of the language. *Lost Horizon* fits into the romance genre only because the hero, Hugh Conway, follows the tradition of the man who could have everything (including, of course, the love of women) but who renounces it all in order to pursue his spiritual quest. He has progressed from 'a most exciting career' at Oxford as 'rowing Blue and a leading light at the Union, and prizeman for this, that and the other' into an even more successful career in the British consular service. It is in fact not accident but design that wrecks the aircraft in which Conway and his colleague, Mallinson, are travelling and strands them in the Tibetan Lamasery of Shangri-La. Rather surprisingly, perhaps, the High Lama, Perrault, has decided that of all the people in all the world Conway has the best qualifications to succeed him.

It is some time before Conway can be shown into the High Lama's presence, and his expectations of Perrault's spirituality are high when eventually they meet. It transpires that time stands still in Shangri-La: the High Lama is actually 250 years old, and by now rather tired of guiding his spiritual flock and anxious to hand things over to a more energetic man – to Conway, in fact. The spiritual truths which are part of the handing-over process seem far from revolutionary – a kind of moderation in all things, which is possibly a watering-down of the Buddhist doctrine of the Middle Way. Alas, Conway cannot immediately accept his new role as mystical leader of mankind: he is persuaded by the weaker and more materialist Mallinson to escape from Shangri-La and to brave the snowbound mountains which surround the ever-springlike and blossoming spiritual valley in order to return to civilization. Mallinson soon dies on the way, and so too does Lo-Tsen, who is travelling with them. She is an exquisitely beautiful Chinese girl, training to be a lama – 'there are no sex distinctions among us' – with whom Mallinson has fallen passionately and Conway 'very quietly' in love: 'His love demanded nothing, not even a reply; it was a tribute of the mind, to which his senses added only a flavour.' (There is the morbidly intriguing intimation that before she perishes in the deep and dreadful snows she gradually reverts to her actual (non-Shangri-La) age. In the Lamasery she seems about eighteen, but in real time she is nearer seventy.) After a journey of terrible privations, Conway ends up in hospital suffering from loss of memory as well as physical ailments. However, his health is restored and the closing passages of the book suggest that he then – without so much as a psychological look over his shoulder at the once lovely but now defunct Lo-Tsen – embarks on the long and lonely foot-slogging pilgrimage to rediscover the Lamasery of Shangri-La. Certainly in Conway's case the love, however amorphous, of the deity eclipses that of women.

As we have frequently seen, in the romance genre, the threads of spiritual and earthly love sometimes intertwine harmoniously and sometimes conflict. Of the authors who have been intrigued by struggles between piety and passion, Somerset Maugham most dextrously develops the theme in *The Razor's Edge* (1943). The story starts soon after the ending of the First World War in Chicago, with a group of young people looking forward excitedly to the vast and rapid expansion of business opportunities which seem to be there for the taking. Laurence Darrell ('Larry') is engaged to Isabel Bradley and they are, by any standards, an impressive couple. He has an unusual strength and sweetness of character, as well as arresting good looks, while she has a vivid, animal grace and plenty of style. Isabel is also greatly admired by Gray Maturin, whose entrepreneurial millionaire father has offered Larry an excellent job in one of his thriving businesses. The first dark spot on Isabel's bright horizon comes when Larry turns down this opportunity and announces that he needs 'to loaf' for a year or two in order to discover what he really wants to do with his life. It takes quite a lot of patience and understanding for a young, passionately in love American girl to let her fiancé off the leash for a longish period in Paris while he 'finds himself', but Isabel, despite being rather petted and spoiled, agrees to this. Her hope, of course, is that after wrestling to survive on his "tiny" private income of three thousand dollars a year (not so small in 1919, perhaps) Larry will soon be ready to return to the USA, to forget all that spiritual nonsense and settle down to the real business of earning money and making a wonderful life and home for himself, Isabel and the children whom she plans they will have.

They meet again in Paris two years later. Isabel is still wildly attracted to Larry and he warmly expresses his love for her. She is, however, disconcerted by his calm, unworldly self-containment, and his declaration that he can never return to the rat-race of big American business. She dismisses his inquiry into the truth of the great religions as 'trifling' and 'adolescent' and interprets his invitation to her to travel with him across 'vast lands of the spirit' (with a Capri honeymoon thrown in) as horrid 'second-class steamship' excursions.

They part in sadness and affection: Larry goes off literally to the ends of the earth in pursuit of spiritual understanding while Isabel succumbs to the charms and affluence of Gray Maturin, now following in his father's successful business footsteps, and becomes an apparently happy wife and mother. But Larry, who frequently comes back into her life, is still her undying love. She never begins to understand any aspects of his quest, but convinces herself that in some strange way he still belongs to her. She has, however, eventually to swallow the bitter pill of knowing that he plans to marry someone else – Sophie Macdonald, who back in 1919 was a quiet and undistinguished member of their set in Chicago.

To the outraged Isabel this is an incomprehensible relationship. Sophie, whose husband and baby daughter were killed some years earlier in a motor accident, has been almost unhinged by her personal tragedy, and has sought relief in drink and drugs. Isabel, Gray and Larry meet up with her again by accident in a sleazy Paris 'tough joint' which they visit on Isabel's insistence as she wants to see some lowlife. Garishly dressed and over-made-up, oozing alcohol but not without 'a certain vicious attractiveness', Sophie has reached rock-bottom. Larry, of course, sees through her hard-bitten and slatternly veneer to the suffering beneath, and with typical altruism is prepared to put aside his own concerns and devote himself to her.

Isabel frets and fumes about 'losing' Larry to Sophie of all people, whom she simply despises, and embarks on drastic action. Sophie, at Larry's insistence, is struggling desperately to refrain from drinking, but Isabel connives to put temptation in her way so that she succumbs again to alcoholism. Sophie then removes herself from Paris to Toulon where, fairly soon afterwards, she is found naked in the sea with her throat cut from ear to ear. However, Isabel feels no responsibility at all for her dreadful death, and is merely relieved that Larry can now never marry Sophie.

She thinks that he still 'belongs' to her, but in fact after Sophie's death his last links with the society in which he grew up have been severed, and he devotes his energies entirely to his religious quest. His encounters with mystics and sages are compellingly described and, while Isabel becomes increasingly rich and socially fulfilled, he finds the understanding and sense of universal love which he has been seeking. Maugham's narrative makes clear that this is not a negation but a joyous fulfilment of Larry's passionate and sensitive nature, and the book ends on an upbeat note which sharply contrasts with the bleaker mood of the similarly truth-seeking *Lost Horizon*. Larry's spiritual 'Shangri-La' seems built on firmer foundations than Conway's.

CHAPTER SIX

Still Smiling Through

ALTHOUGH King Edward VII reigned only until 1910, the so-called Edwardian era is generally considered to have lasted from the turn of the century until the beginning of the Great War in 1914. In retrospect it can be seen that the romantic fiction of that period had an extravagance which was in keeping with the atmosphere of glamour and opulence often associated with the Edwardians. Whether heroines were savouring the spiritual and sexual awakenings offered by trips into the Arabian desert or simply looking for Mr Right nearer to home at the house parties and weekends which were then so fashionable, their exploits had a somewhat larger-than-life quality. There was still, of course, in real life an apparent social stability and expansiveness despite the shake-ups of the Boer War and the challenges of changing scientific and political thought. Heavily restrictive Victorian ideas about respectability were being toned down; the first decade of the new century had brought a general sense of modernity and progress and a mood of knowing confidence.

This was reflected in the popular fiction of the time which, predictably, was to undergo radical change during and after the war years when public and private attitudes fluctuated between idealism and despair, elation and disenchantment. There is often a marked difference betwen the topical, ephemeral ficton which appeared in magazines between 1914 and 1918 and the more reflective stories which were to be published five or ten years after the war had finished. In particular, attitudes to women's involvement altered drastically. During the period of hostilities it was accepted, after some initial doubts, that girls as well as men had an active part to play. They were urged out of their homes to nurse, make munitions, drive ambulances, cart coal, become bus conductresses and join the newly formed women's services. In fact and in fiction the war advanced women's interests by dramatically increasing and extending their opportunities for employment. Not unnaturally, many women and girls from the middle classes wanted to continue to work outside their homes once the war was over, even though they were not economically pressured to do so. (Working-class females had no choice: before, during and after the war they would take on whatever jobs they could get – usually of the low-paid, menial variety.) In the prevailing post-war mood, however, when sadly there were few enough of the jobs for masculine heroes which had been lavishly promised, women were exhorted by every kind of propaganda, including popular and romantic fiction, to get back into their homes and to concentrate on domesticity. This pattern was to an extent repeated in and after the Second World War, but the new independence which women were then able to establish began to bring about more permanent changes in their working status.

First World War stories in magazines such as *Forget-Me-Not* and *Golden Stories* managed to celebrate the contribution of girls working in factories or on the buses while never losing sight of the perennial theme of romantic fiction – love, sometimes between unlikely partners, which was frustrated by misunderstanding and misadventure but ultimately requited. Althought the flamboyance of the Edwardian love-story had ended, the vicissitudes of war gave a special intensity to these topical stories. It is sometimes difficult to know whether they were written by women or by men because authors' bylines were often pseudonymous. What we *do* know is that popular and vaguely romantic novels of the war, written by male authors, were generally pretty dismissive and even outrageous in their attitudes to women. Post-war best-sellers with a military theme, such as Ernest Raymond's *Tell England* (1922), A. S. M. Hutchinson's *If Winter Comes* (1921) and Richard Aldington's *Death of a Hero* (1929) conveyed their female characters so contemptuously that romance between them and the heroes could hardly be believable, even though the authors sometimes bizarrely equated contact with death, as far as women were concerned, with eroticism. For example, in *Death of a Hero* we are told:

> the effect of George's death on her temperament was, strangely enough, almost wholly erotic. The war did that to lots of women. All the dying and wounds and bloodiness – at a safe distance – gave them a great kick, and excited them to an almost unbearable pitch of amorousness. Of course, in that eternity of 1914–18 they must have come to feel that men alone were mortal, and they were immortals; wherefore they tried to behave like houris with all available sheiks – hence the lure of 'war work' with its unbounded opportunities.

Obviously many soldiers suffering the hell of the trenches *did* feel bitterness against non-combatants; there was often a great barrier between them and their wives or girlfriends who might not be able to empathize with their ghastly experiences. However, the blame that is heaped upon so many women in *Death of a Hero* seems totally unreasonable when the 'safe distance' which the author so much deplores was forced on them by social conventions that kept them away from the front line. In many instances, of course, girls got very near to the trenches as ambulance drivers or nurses, but there is little evidence that the exposure to death or disablement that this involved produced the eroticism suggested by Richard Aldington.

In several magazines during the war years an author called E. Almaz Stout (sex unknown) produced a clutch of stories about girls making munitions, working in hospitals or heavy transport, sweeping chimneys or delivering coal. These enterprising heroines not only did their jobs well – and released men to go and fight – but uncovered an astounding number of enemy spies and usually managed to find romance into the bargain. More generally, however, the pulp-paper heroines tended to be home-loving young ladies who were waiting for their heroes to come back on leave, when they hoped to become engaged. Such stories followed the pattern of lovers being separated by mix-ups on the part of the War Office about the identity of soldiers who were wounded or killed. Many a heroine who had to bemoan the ill-luck that had whisked away her intended found to her delight that he would quickly turn up again to claim her affections. This could, of course, lead to complications if by then she had become involved with another man.

By 1916, when the war that was expected to end before its first Christmas had already dragged on for two years, much of the glamour had rubbed off. Almost every family in Britain had someone serving at the front, and the long casualty-lists were studied with dread in many homes. Nevertheless, the penny weekly *Forget-Me-Not* put a brave face on things: every issue sported a glowing coloured cover depicting a pair of lovers. The man would be in uniform – most often a naval one – while the girl was garbed in something soft and clinging, or bright and perky. Occasionally she might be wearing the uniform of a nurse, which seemed to provide happy inspiration for illustrators. It is noticeable that girls in heavy overalls doing dirty jobs, as 'munitionettes' or coal-heavers, for example, are never featured in these prettified vignettes of romantic bliss.

A typical *Forget-Me-Not* heroine of this period is Lys Vaudrey, the eighteen-year-old who stars in 'The House Where Nothing Ever Happened' by Mrs Alfred Praga. She lives with adoring parents and 'a jolly big brother in one of the prettiest little houses in Surbiton. They kept a fairly efficient cook-general and house-parlour-maid, so that she need not even soil her pretty hands unless she was so minded. They went to the play sometimes, up to town to a matinée ...' But Lys, like so many Edwardian young women without occupation or study, is bored. The author stresses that she is in love with love but

> not wise enough to know that the greatest romance can lie in the most commonplace things. For though it is doubtless a very fine thing to have a lover who rides away and leaves you, a lady in a moated grange, it is a far finer and better thing to marry the man you love, and who loves you, and to give him the happiest life

possible even if it be plain John Smith of Bucklersbury or Lombard Street...

Mrs Praga goes on to explain that there can be 'a great deal of romance put into even the darning of a pair of socks if every stitch is only a silent prayer for the well-being of the loved-one'. The trouble is that although Lys yearns for romance there is no suitable man around to become the repository of her affections. She has a steady admirer but 'oh, how could you ever weave anything romantic out of a name like John Halliday!'

As it is 1916 there is, of course, one way to do this. Lys's devoted but dull would-be lover joins the army, becomes a lieutenant and 'looks anything but commonplace' when he comes to say goodbye to her. Lys realizes that 'there is something about khaki ... It stands for the "thin red line of heroes" and for faith and fealty and patriotism, and the love of home, and the honour of British womenfolk', and so on.

After John has marched off to the front, Lys, who is now completely captivated by him, has nightmares about his being wounded or killed, and after the Battle of Loos she learns that Lieutenant John James Halliday, 2nd Surreys, is among the missing. Later it transpires that he is alive, wounded and blinded, just as in her nightmare, and being brought back to England. In wartime things happen quickly: at first he is too ill to see anybody, then suddenly she reads in the paper that Lieutenant Halliday, 'who so greatly distinguished himself at Loos, was married yesterday while still lying on his sick bed to Nurse Estelle Mordaunt, to whom he ... virtually owes his life'. (Incidentally this story suggests that plastic surgery was more advanced in 1916 than was generally known, for the redoubtable Estelle had given 'half a dozen pieces of skin from her own arm because his wounds wouldn't heal'.)

One is tempted to feel at this point in the story that John has got the good fortune he deserves in ensnaring Estelle rather than the somewhat vacuous Lys. However, in one of those twists of fate brought about yet again by the incompetence of the War Office's record clerks, Lys, walking desolately by the river on a grey, drizzly day, almost collides with a 'very big and bronzed and fit man, coming round the corner at the double' who turns out to he *her* John Halliday – with no trace of blindness or, even more important, of a wifely nurse. The wounded Halliday is 'someone else – ripping good sort too', so Lys's lieutenant is free to marry her. Army life has given him confidence and charisma, and the war has enabled Lys to sort out her priorities. The story ends predictably with the couple having 'a war wedding from the House Where Nothing Ever Happened ... Thank God, happiness never goes out of fashion, though it may be commonplace.'

Several First World War romance stories were built on the idea of girls corresponding with lonely soldiers. In *Forget-Me-Not* of 17 June 1916, Dorothy O'Vendon provides a variation on this theme in 'The Lonely Censor'. Answering an advertisement in the Personal column of *The Times*, Daida Wanstead starts writing to Lance-Corporal Edward Thomas Burton who, unknown of course to her, is also in correspondence with several other young women. She receives a letter from the regimental censor who explains that Edward ('Tubby') Burton is an 'unholy fraud' who, on the pretext of being lonely, has over fifty ladies writing to him. The censor asks if Daida will write to him instead. She does, and they begin to pour out their hearts to each other. He explains to her that he treated a lady friend, of whom he was extraordinarily fond, badly and stupidly some time ago. She tells him that she ended a relationship with a good man because of her silly pride over something that didn't really matter at all. The correspondence is cathartic, although he seems to have her at a disadvantage: he knows who she is, while she knows him only as 'A Lonely Censor'. He is, of course, the lover Richard Soames, with whom she has quarrelled.

He is due for home leave and arranges to meet Daida at Charing Cross station: 'How would she take it? Would she be angry? Would she be overcome by shock?' In fact she simply deepens her dimples and looks up at him 'with a smile, half-shamefaced, half tender and wholly adorable'. She admits that she has known all along that he was the censor in that regiment, and had only started writing to Tubby in order to spite him. Somewhere along the way, she stopped feeling bitter and began to love him: 'I see,' said Richard solemnly. 'It's a bit involved, but – is there a dark corner anywhere about, where I can kiss you?'

And that is just about the height of passionate fulfilment attained in the women's magazine stories of the 1914–18 period.

The prolific novelist Berta Ruck packed more intensity into her lovers' physical contacts (see Chapter 2), although her leading ladies were not allowed to overstep the bounds of decorum. Berta was an enthusiastic exponent of the genre for over fifty years. Born in India, she went to school in Wales, took an art training in London and Paris, married a man with the unromantic name of Oliver Onions, wrote love-stories with every imaginable setting – from war work and deserts to hospitals and hearth and home – and lived to be 100 years old. The first eleven of her 100-plus books were published during the wartime period and they struck an appropriately optimistic mood. In essence they reflected a statement made by the author in her 1935 memoirs, *A Story-Teller Tells the Truth*: 'It is my creed that the world was created to go merry as a marriage-bell and for the whole human race to be healthy, wealthy and wise enough to be happy on all cylinders.'

Her tales of romantic entanglements were effervescent and at times slightly mocking, but there was nothing of the social reformer, revolutionary or 'New Woman' about Berta Ruck. She adroitly blended humour and strong sentimentality to put across accepted ideas about women's docility and domesticity. Her interchangeable heroines – usually about nineteen years old – are modest (always much more pretty and endearing than they realize), high-spirited, in revolt against stuffy traditions and fearfully chatty about every aspect of themselves. Frivolous, but always ready in a crisis to do their duty for family or country, they manage to be candid and coy at the same time. They come across as engaging innocents who are sexually unawakened until taken in hand by the hero, but in the long lead-up to the eventual, blissful clinch and kiss ('Isn't it wonderful to think we are "us" at last?') there is a lot of titillating speculation about what 'love-making' will be like.

Wartime challenges sometimes make heroines insensitive to the point of brutality: ('The idea of you having the Face to speak to a lady – and you not in khaki!') but more generally act as catalysts to their discoveries about themselves and others. In *The Land-Girl's Love Story* (1918), for example, Joan Matthews, who has become a farm-worker, nearly gives up on the messy business of cleaning out a stable but is helpfully shown how to do it by a young man who has until then appeared to be unpleasantly supercilious. Antagonism quickly turns to infatuation, and, of course, Joan makes good amongst the dung and dirt. In *The Bridge of Kisses* (1917) – see Chapter 2 – when the heroine's mother rushes off to work in a soldiers' canteen in France, nineteen-year-old Joey sturdily takes on the running of the household, looks after two irrepressible small cousins and has to disentangle herself from an engagement which she has entered into through a kind of wilful innocence. In fact her naivety borders on simple-mindedness, but, helped by the manly and determined intervention and wooing of Dick, a young army officer, she is saved from a loveless marriage to Hilary, who is not only an unbearable prig but a conscientious objector. In fairness to Berta Ruck it must be said that another pacifist in the story is conveyed sympathetically but, in keeping with the unquestioningly patriotic mood of most wartime popular fiction, Joey hurls contempt at Hilary when she breaks off their engagement:

> 'you have been leaving no stone unturned to get out of serving your country. And there are ... fine men ... like my father. They are away from every comfort. They've left everything and they're toiling like baggage-horses in France! They're dying in the deserts of Mesopotamia for their country and for us – and for you, Hilary, for you! Do you think you're worth it?'

The eponymous heroine of *Arabella the Awful* (1918) is a similar amalgam of patriotism, good-heartedness and naivety. Although she is only a tradesman's daughter she is taken up by 'the quality' at the squire's house, and arouses amorous feelings in the breast of the eldest son, Eric Cattermole, who is a serving officer in the Guards. Happily, however, Arabella does not rock the social boat too violently because she fancies someone of her own class, Sidney Sharpe, an unassuming grocer's boy who – like Eric – also goes off to war. Although this novel maintains Ruck's resolutely cheery mood, there are some sharper-than-usual comments about the Germans (the war had, of course, lasted four years by the time *Arabella* appeared, and inflated ideas of heroism-in-the-abstract, which had been popular in 1914, had long since been eroded). Berta Ruck draws attention to, but does not clearly define, the fact that in the early days of the war 'the optimists among us were as little prepared for what happened in these years as were the pessimists', and acknowledges that many 'poor, splendid, insolent and attractive darlings' would never return from the carnage of the western front. Sidney Sharpe, of course, is one of the fortunate; he comes home, injured but undaunted, and marries Arabella.

In 1915 St John Ervine reflected (in 'The War and Literature', *The Englishwoman*, vol. XXVIII) that the conflict would continue to influence the content of every form of imaginative literature for the next fifty years: 'Books will begin in all sorts of ways, romantically and realistically, but somewhere in the middle of them, the war will relentlessly thrust itself, diverting the characters from the normal course of their lives.' It is now eighty years since he made this estimate, and we can see that retrospective Great War fiction, particularly in the romantic field, is alive and well. It is no longer fuelled by nostalgia or the desire of those who had participated in the war to complete or vindicate their experiences, but by the extraordinary atmosphere and intensity of all that happened between 1914 and 1918 – together, of course, with the similarly addictive moods, mores and events of the Second World War.

In 1918 there was little immediate evidence of the better and fairer world in anticipation of which so many men and women had made great sacrifices. The heightened consciousness and unifying purpose of the war years evaporated rapidly, and divisions between classes and the sexes were accentuated by a sense of lost opportunity. Many men returning to civilian life found it impossible to get work of any description, and the band of independent wage-earning women that had been established betwen 1914 and 1918 was persuaded, cajoled and bullied by newspaper and magazine articles – and in a wide range of fiction – to get back to the kitchen and the cradle. As *Woman's Life* put it in February 1920: 'The tide of progress which leaves woman with the vote in her hand and scarcely any clothes on her back is ebbing, and the sex is returning to the deep, very deep sea of femininity from which her newly acquired power can be more effectively wielded.' It was not always acknowledged that, whatever their inclinations, many women *had* to earn their own living because they were unlikely to find husbands who might support them. The 1921 census showed a 1,700,000 surplus of women over men as a result of the terrible slaughter of the war years. Circumstances had denied 'the superfluous woman' the traditional role of wife and mother, and she was also irrationally expected to give up her right to work.

All this was reflected strongly in novels, which were to become immensely popular, produced by several male authors in the 1920s and early 1930s. As writers like Vera Brittain and Winifred Holtby (who had worked with Voluntary Aid Detachments) remarked, women's contribution to the war effort was largely ignored in the stream of retrospective fiction. It was left to them, Enid Bagnold, Evadne Price – in *Not So Quiet* (see Chapter 4) – and one or two other women writers to redress the balance. A curious paperback novel entitled *WAAC: The Woman's Story of the War* appeared anonymously in 1930. Supposedly one girl's memoirs of her actual experiences, it is hardly convincing. At one level it deals colourfully with wartime stereotypes (shirkers, profiteers, spies and seducers) but its overall tone is sanctimonious, condemnatory and ambiguous. There is a strongly conservative morality throughout which contrasts with the titillation of fairly explicitly described sexual encounters. The implication is that, once in uniform, girls as well as men went 'sexually mad', and that their souls were destroyed by 'the war atmosphere which ... destroyed the bodies of others'. There is no question of romance; it is simply a matter of a young woman finding physical relief with some man or other.

Several retrospective war novels showed women at odds with the society in which they lived. Rebellious females repudiated established traditions, demanded fulfilling and remunerative careers ('men's jobs') and even the right to become mothers without being married. Possibly most disconcertingly of all, they decided to become the wives or mistresses of men who had recently fought against England. Hall Caine's 1923 *The Woman of Knockaloe* probed the problems of love between enemies in the unfolding romance between a misunderstood Manx woman (Mona) and a manic German prisoner (Oskar).

Despite the novel's farcical culmination in a joint seventy-foot death-leap (with the lovers 'eye to eye, breast to breast, heart to heart' and lustily singing 'Jesu Lover of My Soul' together in both English and German), the author takes his subject very seriously. The trouble is that he can't quite decide whether he is writing a romantic story or producing political propaganda. His language is as lurid and archaic as that of many Victorian moral tales, and the considerable depth of feeling that exists between Mona and Oskar is often swamped by their own and other people's melodramatic utterances and actions.

Hall Caine had been a distinguished and popular author for well over twenty years before he wrote *The Woman of Knockaloe*. Before the outbreak of the war he had been a pacifist, but in 1914 embraced the Allied cause, convinced that 'liberty, civilization and religion were threatened'. His patriotism was beyond question but, like the celebrated Nurse Cavell, he considered it 'not enough'. Honoured for his war service, knighted in 1918 and made Companion of Honour in 1922, he was outraged at the harshness of the peace terms which were imposed upon Germany and predicted with some accuracy that these would bring about a situation leading to further wars, and that 'the little mother rocking her baby's cradle will have to pay the interest in blood and tears some day' (shades of Churchill's 1940 never-surrender speech).

Mona is certainly pretty well engulfed by blood and tears. At first she bitterly resents the presence of German internees in a camp on her father's Isle of Man farmland: 'She becomes conscious that behind the barbed wire the men are looking at her with evil eyes and laughing like monkeys. [Not exactly surprising for she *is* the only woman among 27,000 men.] Her flesh creeps – she feels as if they were stripping her naked. The beasts! The monsters!' She also characterizes them as 'dirts', 'scoundrels' and 'scum'. The hysterical pitch of her anti-German feeling is maintained until she begins to succumb to the charms of Oskar, who comes to the farm each day to collect milk for some of his men in the compound. He is a great surprise to Mona, for as well as being unaggressively good-looking he has a voice that 'is not harsh and guttural . . . but soft, deep and *human*'.

The difficulty is that as Mona becomes more tolerant of the enemy in general and Oskar in particular, her father's hatred of them begins to assume fanatical proportions. He suffers a stroke brought on by the death in action of his son, so, with this brother's posthumous VC pinned proudly on her breast, Mona doggedly tackles the work of running the farm. Things go from bad to worse, however. When Oskar learns that his small sister in Germany has been killed in a British air-raid, Mona consoles him with a very chaste embrace. It is enough to send her semi-paralysed father into another seizure which proves fatal, but not before he has fallen on his daughter 'with fearful cries – "Harlot! Strumpet! . . . Thy brother dead in France, and thou in the arms of this German! May God punish thee!"'

God, or at any rate society, appears to carry out his curse. At the end of the war the lease of Mona's farm is not renewed and she is further crippled financially by having to make good dilapidations to the property caused through its occupation by the internees. Nevertheless she and Oskar plan a future together. Although he is refused the right to live and work in England they feel sure that the Germans will not be so 'hard and unforgiving'; but, of course, they are. Oskar's mother's response to his happy letter that he will be bringing her a daughter is dauntingly chilling: 'Tell your Englishwoman from me that if she marries you and comes to this country she will be as a leper . . . rather than hear you had married an Englishwoman I would see you dead and buried.' (It was hardly, of course, a good time to expect the defeated Germans to put aside their bitter feelings for the British. Even for some time after the

Armistice they were still being blockaded, and many were half-starved.) Eventually even that marvellous 'melting-pot of the nations, America', denies sanctuary to the lovers.

Mona, apparently unhinged by an Easter sermon about Jesus dying and saving the world 'of His own free will . . . for love' fires Oskar with her own 'great, divine, delirious project'. With a first and last passionate kiss they seal their doomed love and hurl themselves off the most westerly headlands of the Isle of Man. Hall Caine gives his readers the consolation of knowing that even though their deaths were not actually instrumental in saving the world, they 'touched the hearts' of some local mackerel fishermen who buried the lovers' bodies and built a cairn memorial over them.

In the early 1980s Sarah Harrison reached back over the decades and caught the authentic atmosphere with her blooming – and sadly bud-nipped – images of the First World War in *The Flowers of the Field*. Most memorable among love-stories of the period written in the 1990s are Jane Gurney's moving *The Green of Spring*, in which both the 'upstairs' and the 'downstairs' communities of a Home Counties mansion are affected by the harrowing and prolonged conflict on the western front, and Kate Saunders's *Night Shall Overtake Us*, which persuasively conveys the loves, unusual freedoms and mind-numbing suffering experienced in or as a result of the war by four girls who have been friends since their schooldays.

By the beginning of the 1930s many books, plays and films with war themes conveyed a mood of blandness, an implication that the conflict had been fought and won, and everything had been neatly parcelled up. Even the songs of 1914–18, in spite of their extraordinary poignancy, produced a sense of security, of travelling on well-trodden paths. The war continued to provide authors with a vivid backcloth for adventure epics or love affairs, however, and one or two popular romances still struck a challenging note. These featured heroines who, with almost messianic fervour, were prepared to sacrifice their personal happiness in order to bring about changes in the structure and attitudes of society. In G. Cornwallis-

West's *The Woman Who Stopped War*, Mary Sarn is so shocked by the deaths of her husband and brother that she starts the Women's Save the Race League, an unsympathetically named organization with the admirable objective of preventing future wars. She points out to her supporters that 'at Geneva – where another League is labouring to achieve the same results as we ourselves – no nation is represented by a woman', but the feminist view is not sustained. The main female characters have scant interest in careers and seem to resent the fact that they have been 'driven in many cases to support themselves'. At first Mary struggles to support her League with what she earns as a 'mannequin' (model), but later on determination to acquire enough money to get the League established internationally leads her to become the mistress of an armaments king. Of course, in the 1930s the voluntary abandonment of sexual respectability was one of the most significant sacrifices which any woman could make. However, Mary's nice-girl image is maintained, at least with readers, because it is made clear that she is not snatching Sir Edward Enthoven away from a happy marriage: his unfortunate wife has for several years been 'an inmate of a clinic in Amsterdam'.

He does not suspect that the money which he lavishes on Mary is being ploughed into the League or that she is its leader. He accepts her declared pacifism as the harmlessly endearing quirk of a beautiful woman until, prompted by curiosity, he strolls into one of the League's meetings and hears Mary delivering an impassioned and persuasive speech. This is too much for him to take. He disapproves of women 'dabbling in politics' and has recently sacked his kitchen-maid for attending a meeting of the League. He tries without success to smash the organization of these cussed women, which begins to seem irrelevant anyway, because the world is once again on the threshold of war. Suddenly groups of women in various countries start giving each other secret signs and knowing looks. Unless their menfolk draw back from war, they threaten them with the tactics of Lysistrata, and plan to go on strike in every other sphere of female activity as well. They walk out of their jobs wholesale, all over the world, and block the streets of London and other capital cities.

Edward has not been a munitions magnate for nothing. He fiercely exhorts the prime minister to use troops to clear the recalcitrant women from the streets. However, the PM knows when he is beaten and refuses on the grounds that modern war could not be waged successfully without the supportive efforts of female 'clerks, shop-assistants, waitresses, teachers and factory-workers'. Mary's League has won the day and international war has been averted. Edward is ruined, of course, as armaments have become useless commodities. Mary's love affair with him is over, but she offers him the reassurance that although his means of livelihood has gone 'there are heaps of things – harmless, useful things – that your works could turn out – railways wheels, golf clubs, motor cars and goodness knows what . . .'

In real life it was not quite so easy for ordinary women to wield power. As the economic depression of the 1930s intensified, there was little tolerance of those 'superfluous' women who were unmarried and still demanded a share of the jobs market. Articles in magazines and newspapers frequently urged them to consider tidying themselves away by emigrating (it was popularly thought that they would be welcomed by lonely sheep farmers in the Australian outback). On the whole romance writers did not delve too deeply into the predicament of such young women, but Netta Muskett, whose novels were popular from the late 1920s to the early 1960s, grasped the nettle. She never shirked the tackling of social problems, although she managed to confine her probing of these within the parameters of the love story. In *The Painted Heaven* (1934) Anne Weston finds herself very much alone in the world, having lost her fiancé, brother and parents, and accepts a role that seemed unusually challenging in the context of light fiction of the period. She becomes a successful businesswoman and bears an illegitimate child. This does not actually represent a conscious decision to go against the tide of public feeling and to take what she feels is her due. In fact Anne simply bungles her sexual relationships. Her fiancé John Denver, wounded in the Great War, spends a long time 'raving mad' in a German prisoner-of-war hospital. Presuming that he is dead Anne resolves to remain faithful to his memory but quickly succumbs to having a short affair with an Australian pilot, even though he has 'a wife and kiddie . . . down under', and then another with Captain the Honourable Hugh Galton RHA, who is engaged to one of the rich clients of Anne's dressmaking and millinery business. He fathers Anne's child and offers to marry her, but she refuses because her relationship with him is based on pity (he suffers from shell-shock) and 'we were not of the same social class'. Their daughter, Christine, is born, and maternal sacrifice becomes a major theme of the book. She grows up, and by a bizarre twist of fate meets, falls in love with and agrees to marry a young man called Nicky – who turns out to be the son of Anne's presumed dead fiancé, John Denver, who then comes back into her life; Anne and John are still drawn to each other and, as his wife is obligingly dying of cancer, agree to marry as soon as John is free. So far, so romantic. However, Anne cannot bring herself to explain to John that she has had affairs with other men, so, with astounding disregard for the consequences of her life, she lets him think that *he* is Christine's father. (Actually they never had sex together, or rather they never went 'on the strange journey together some day – some night', but John's period of amnesiac lunacy in Germany has left him prepared to believe anything.)

It takes a little time for the repercussions of Anne's pretence to penetrate her mind (which despite her success as a career woman seems somewhat sluggish). She has, of course, made it impossible for Christine to marry Nicky, as it now seems to everyone that they must be semi-siblings. A Stella Dallas-like renunciation of her own happiness for the sake of her daughter is called for, because Anne knows that John is so strait-laced he will reject her once he learns she has been 'despoiled' by another man. (Despite the narratively expressed scorn for women who are 'always ready with transports of cheap emotion', these excesses frequently crop up in *The Painted Heaven*.) Anne sees her crisis as a modern-day Gethsemane:

'Oh, God, don't ask this of me! Not this! Ask me to give up anything else, but not John, not my beloved come back to me after the wasted lonely years!' And yet she knew, as one greater than she had known, that she would in the end drink that cup.

Although *The Painted Heaven* is on the side of women who seem to have found little place in the society of the 1930s, it is far from being progressive in its overall attitude. The goal of its female characters is to be 'little, inconsequent, adored', while its men are generally 'big' or 'reminiscent of the Greek God'. There is a woolliness about both controversial and socially acceptable matters, and a corresponding vagueness in Netta Muskett's prose: 'his eyes were grey ... that grey which had only just missed being brown and which might equally have been blue or green', while Anne's laugh 'was neither a giggle nor a guffaw, but it had the femininity of the one and the heartiness of the other'.

A different kind of ambiguity is a feature of *Blood Relations* (1935) by Phillip Gibbs which, like Hall Caine's *The Woman of Knockaloe*, deals with the theme of love between enemies and harks back to the 1914–18 War. Its hero is Count Paul von Arnsberg who is at first an unashamed militarist ('After all, there is something heroic, don't you think, in a soldier's death for his Fatherland?') but by 1918 has decided that neither German nor British soldiers know what they are fighting for, and become a pacifist. Before the war, when Paul was an undergraduate at Oxford, he met and married utterly English Audrey Middleton from Chiddingfold. At first she resisted the formality of her Teutonic lover's wooing but, once he had persuaded her to spend a holiday in the family schloss in Bavaria she was unable to disentangle her feelings for him from romantic images of local 'deep blue lakes' and 'marvellous mountains' where 'the sun always shines and the fields are strewn with flowers'. She was also much moved by seeing the sturdy Paul in Bavarian garb – 'a little blue jacket and embroidered shirt, and leather shorts above his knees, and white socks'. Audrey's dear old English dad had sensed what the trip might lead to and tried to divert her from it: "Oh no, I don't think so, old girl!" said Colonel

Middleton. "What about Bexhill as usual? Very enjoyable, don't you think? Lots of golf. A nice band."'

But Bavaria has the edge on Bexhill, and Paul and Audrey get married in the early summer of 1914, just a few weeks before war breaks out. Paul's family incessantly discuss *kultur* and the German Soul, a brand of nationalism which initially intrigues Audrey. It seems 'mystical and mysterious' and not only conjures up shades of Siegfried for her but cosy images of gnomes and forest sprites. Cosiness goes out of the window, however, when 'Our German Destiny' begins to become synonymous with 'Our good German guns' and 'Our German God'. Audrey feels obliged to point out that this deity is actually the same one as the Almighty who never lets the English down in wartime and always allows them to win the last battle.

Suddenly everything gets out of control. Paul is sent off to the front while the bewildered and resentful Audrey is left at home with her in-laws, and a new 'German' baby on its way. Her predicament is certainly one which inspires sympathy. Very recently married and barely acclimatized to her new country, she is suddenly and completely cut off from her English family and friends. She fears – but has no way of knowing for sure, because letters and newspapers from England are stopped – that her brothers might be among the first 100,000 volunteers called for by Lord Kitchener. Paul's brother gets killed by the British at Loos; eventually news filters through of Audrey's favourite brother's death in action. She is overwhelmed by the insanity of it all but 'all hatred left her . . . she had no ill will against German boys who were killing English boys. They were all victims of the same tragedy.' Paul and Audrey, possibly because of their superior social position, are far better treated than the lugubrious lovers in *The Woman of Knockaloe*; they are not rejected by their families or by their countries, but their relationship undergoes many traumas.

Phillip Gibbs's account of the post-war breakdown of German society and of social upheavals in Britain is as lurid as his descriptions of Paul's military experiences. (He is surrounded by death and mutilation, buried alive in a trench and becomes a prisoner-of-war.) Like Hall Caine (and more serious writers of the period such as Vera Brittain and Winifred Holtby), Gibbs graphically spells out the crippling economic and psychological effects upon Germany of the humiliating peace terms. However, he illogically attributes the avoidance of social responsibilities and the growth of materialism to the *women* of Germany and England, although it was male politicians who drew up and implemented the peace agreements. He sees the succumbing to 'the negro rhythms' of jazz and its associated 'dancing mania' as particularly symbolic of the newfangled amorality and of the destructive aspects of femininity (although presumably men as well as women must have 'stupefied the senses' by gyrating around the dance-halls). One of Audrey's surviving brothers carries bitterness against women who were unable to share his ghastly fighting experiences to the point of extreme and unreasonable resentment: 'these young women with frocks up to their knees have hearts like stone – cold and hard! Where is womanly tenderness? Where is the gentle creature who'll fondle me?'

Audrey and Paul's marriage survives the war and even Paul's eventual gravitation towards Nazism, which seems to him to offer Germany its only hope for economic survival. Audrey continues to love him, but by now wisely mistrusts the nationalism which he embraces – 'all that nonsense about the Aryan race ... all that mystical rubbish about the old German gods and the tribal instincts of the German folk'. Equally she is disturbed by the utterances of an English ex-officer friend (who voices the extreme assumption that many real-life children of the 1920s and 1930s absorbed from their veteran soldier fathers): 'In England most of us believe that the only good Germans are dead Germans. After all their atrocities we regard them as Huns. Personally I think it's a pity we didn't kill all the German babies. They'll only grow up to make another war.' *Blood Relations* ends on a prophetic note when one of the sons of Paul and Audrey declares, 'I hate to think I have English blood in me' and joins the Hitlerjugend. Feeling now more desolate even than she was in 1914, Audrey cries, 'Paul! I want to die ... We're all marching towards another war. The world is going mad again.'

While the Second World War was in progress, women's magazines welcomed the boost which it gave to their romantic fiction,
although they tended to play down its more dramatic ramifications
until after the collapse of France in May and June 1940, when, of
course, Britain stood alone against the might of the Wehrmacht
and Luftwaffe and had its back very firmly to the wall. Just before
this, 'Whispers', the editorial page of *Woman's Weekly*, confided to
readers that

> because we have wanted to divert you and give you something
> different to talk about, we have not talked over much about this war
> ... It is not that we have a frivolous outlook. But we felt we were
> *helping* you more if we could beguile your minds into happier
> channels.

In fact the beguiling process continued throughout the war, with
romantic stories providing welcome temporary relief from austerity, blackouts and bombing. In *Peg's Paper* it was a long-established
tradition that heroines were fairly easy prey for schemers and
seducers, as typical story titles – 'The Thirteenth Bride', 'Night of
Shame', 'Forbidden Husband', 'Wife Without a Name' and 'Make
Believe Fiancé' – indicate. Infidelity hotted up in wartime and
authors flung their leading ladies into a maelstrom of seduction
and bigamy as the boys in khaki, navy and air-force blue marched
in and out of their vulnerable lives. These oddly passive heroines
contrasted sharply with bitchy connivers who had exotic names
such as Fleur or Gloria ('To red-headed, man-mad Gloria of the
ice-blue eyes men alone made life exciting') and who came off
distinctly better than the good girls – at least until the closing
paragraphs.

Peg's Paper folded in 1940, when publishers had drastically to
reduce their consumption of pulp paper after the German occupation of Norway cut off Britain's main supply of this. *Woman's
Weekly, Good Taste, My Home, Woman's Pictorial, Woman's Illustrated*
and other magazines kept the romantic fiction flag flying (as well,
of course, as providing helpful advice on 'Make Do and Mend',
how to make the food-rations go round, and how to remain –

despite shortages of clothes, cosmetics, toiletries, elastic and vita-
mins – nice to come home to).

As in the magazine fiction of the First World War, most heroines
could only make progress in captivating heroes during periods of
leave. (Girls in uniform who were closely supporting men on active
service and stationed in various theatres of war were featured with
surprising infrequency, probably because the domestic roots of the
weeklies had always gone extremely deep.) Men remained very
much in the driving-seat. In Lola de Laredo's 'Unknown Warrior'
(*Home Chat*, 1 May 1943), for example, it takes a handsome
Canadian soldier, Don Callagher, to achieve what no member of
the British medical profession can. When Jane's parents are killed
and her home is destroyed in an air-raid, the 'shock to her nerve
centres' is so acute that although there is 'nothing organically
wrong' with her, she is absolutely unable to walk, and confined to
a wheel-chair. Don, her Canadian soldier penfriend, does not know
about her disability until he comes to see her. Jane and her old
nanny, who is once again looking after her, pretend to him that
Jane's condition is temporary and the result of her having been
tossed by a horse. Don knows better, of course, and is determined
to put things right for 'the prettiest thing he had ever seen, with
those red-gold curls and the wide, grey eyes with those incredibly
long lashes'. He does so by the simple means of driving her to a
cliff-top picnic, then pretending to fall over the edge and calling
for help: 'Something surged in her, something dynamic – impelling
her to her feet. She stumbled, crawled, stood up and staggered on
. . .' Gasping, sobbing and praying for strength, she manages to
drag herself to the edge of the cliff, carrying a rope which she
intends to throw down to Don. Once there, however, she sees that
he is only a few feet below, 'comfortably sitting against a tree-
stump and smiling up at her with a look of triumph on his face.
Then he scrambled to the top and caught her in his arms', made
her walk again to prove that her cure was permanent, and declared
his love: 'My darling! My brave darling!' Soldiers in time of war
were, of course, expected to be resourceful.

In Margerie Scott's 'Lady in Red' (*Good Taste*, September 1940) a British soldier is at the centre of the action. On the last day of his leave Terry Delmer sees a musical show in London and falls heavily for a girl in the chorus called Paddy Rains. He takes her out to tea and at first everything seems wonderful, but there is a very substantial fly in the ointment. Before meeting Paddy, Terry had drifted into an engagement with Doris Green ('who had known him since they were both in rompers'). Realizing this, Paddy honourably refuses to have anything further to do with him, although he is prepared, in fact anxious, to break off his engagement. Terry is beside himself, especially when the London show closes a day or two later and he has no way of contacting Paddy again. Felicitously, however, in one of those often-recurring wartime coincidences, she arrives only a day or two afterwards at the camp where he is stationed to take part in an ENSA concert. His romantic cause apparently remains hopeless: Paddy sticks to her moral guns – 'I won't do anything to hurt another girl . . . I despise anyone who does that sort of thing' – till the path of true love is smoothed by the opportune arrival of a letter from Terry's fiancée which makes clear to him (and to Paddy) that she is ditching him: 'Mabel Parsons saw you having tea with that dancer the day you went back from your leave . . . Our engagement is at an end, and nothing you can say will make me change my mind . . .' Terry, who has hitherto been rather hesitant, suddenly becomes masterful; he proposes to Paddy, tells her, when she protests that they hardly know each other, 'we can't waste time nowadays on getting to know people', and pretty well sweeps her off her feet.

On the whole almost all the stories of servicemen on leave punch home to readers the fact that returning heroes are looking for unostentatious femininity (in other words, domestication) rather than glitz. In 'No! My Darling Daughter' by Gertrude Swift (*Woman's Pictorial*, 28 October 1944) soldier Jack underlines this when he calls for Candy at her home after she has spent a great deal of time and money on a slinky black dress and a sophisticated new hairdo. He barely notices these, announces that he'd rather stay in than go out 'to a posh place' and saves his ecstasies for the homely refreshments provided for him by Candy's mother:

'Wonderful, chocolate sponge cake!' His next words were slightly muffled, but he didn't sound tired now. His voice was vigorous and happy. 'This is what soldiers dream of – a nice soft sofa, a warm room, a family, a piece of their favourite cake . . .'

So now we know.

The need for girls to conform to the docile image is endorsed in a story whose heroine is more fortunately placed than most. In Leonie Mason's 'Clouds Over the Moon' (*Woman's Illustrated* 5 October 1940), Angela is a woman of means. When she marries Duncan, 'a six-pounds-a-week man', she tries to live simply within his income, but cannot resist spending the generous allowance which her parents provide on way-out luxuries. Duncan's sense of independence is affronted by her extravagances, but he hopes that when he joins up at the beginning of the war she will quieten down and learn to live modestly on a soldier's pay. She doesn't of course, but embarks on a terrific spending spree, renting a luxurious 'cottage' and furnishing it lavishly. Her intention is to make a warm, cosy nest for Duncan when he comes home on leave, but he is so disgusted by her spendthrift flamboyance that he walks out. Of course his masculine ego is severely dented by the knowledge that she will always have and spend so much more than he can ever earn. All ends well, however. Only a few weeks later they meet in a servicemen's canteen in which Angela is now working. Duncan yearns for them to be together again, although he cannot see how his extravagant wife will ever be able to adopt the suitably subdued lifestyle that will keep their marriage on what he thinks are the right lines. Unbeknown to him, she has already solved the problem: '"I asked father for all my money," she said, "the capital, I mean, that was bringing in my allowance, and it was just about enough to buy two bombers, darling, so I did that."' Duncan is thrilled that, at last, his 'dear, darling idiot' will truly be 'what they call on the Income Tax papers, a "dependent relative"' and, as they squeeze hands over the canteen counter Angela says, 'grinning at him with all the love in the world in her eyes, "Bombers are awfully cheap . . . only twenty thousand each."'

Romance in more fervent style is provided by Denise Robins in *This One Night* (1942). The heroine is a twenty-year-old city typist called Tona who, in spite of her foreign-sounding name, is as English and unspoilt as they come. She is also rather reserved, which makes it all the more surprising that when travelling on business on the night train to the Balkan state of Gardenia, she succumbs almost immediately to the allure of Valentine, a man occupying the same compartment. It transpires that he is the King of Gardenia and an ardent supporter of the Allied cause which, we gather, puts his seduction of Tona on a moral footing, although even by wartime standards things happen with astounding intensity:

> She was sealed fast in his arms ... Her last vestige of control snapped and vanished when she felt his heart beat against her own ... He was a wonderful, masterful lover ... She was aghast at the relentlessness of such love. But she was his. All of her.

Sadly the *wagon-lit* idyll is traumatically cut short for the king by the call of duty. With only a 'scorching blush' (and pregnancy) to remind her of the 'heaven' of being in Valentine's arms, Tona soon finds herself horribly and vulnerably alone in Gardenia. Typing for a living seems a bit insipid now, so she becomes a café dancer until, naively swept into politial intrigues and clad only in her chiffon dance tunic and a silver cloak, she has to face a firing squad. She must have been something of an inspiration to British wartime readers for, in an appropriately gutsy *Girl's Own Paper* mood of defiance, 'she hung on her courage desperately. She would show these foreigners how an English girl should behave.' In the end she doesn't have to, because she is rescued, becomes an Allied agent and eventually gets back to her Norwood home which she shares with her royal lover when he is driven out of Gardenia by the Nazis. Valentine and Tona's romance seems to lose its edge in this rather domestic set-up after the tempestuous times in the Balkans, but Valentine at least seems well satisfied: 'I never wanted to be a king. I wanted what I am going to have now, please God. An English home – and English wife – a son, whom [*sic*] I pray will be born on English soil.' Passion seems to have been displaced by pretty heavy propaganda!

It seems rather surprising that comparatively few heroines in the popular fiction of the Second World War were members of the women's services. It is true, of course, that conscription for women was far less comprehensive than for men, being introduced as late as December 1941 and applying only to spinsters and widows between the ages of twenty and thirty. Nevertheless, vast numbers of women volunteered, swelling the ranks of those who were conscripted, to work in hospitals, on the land, in factories and in the women's services. Newspapers and magazines of the period are plentifully adorned with photographs of girls in uniforms or overalls looking both fetching and purposeful as they go about their duties on anti-aircraft sites and assembly-lines, or driving ambulances and tractors. It is, however, possibly significant that readers of the *Daily Mail* listed 'women in uniform' as the most annoying aspect of wartime, harder to put up with, because of its suggested masculinity, than the restrictions of Government bureaucracy, the blackout and the evacuation of businesses. There is no doubt that the most popular image of girls in uniform was that of the Red Cross nurse or 'VAD' and certainly these 'angels of mercy' *were* given an important role in the romantic fiction of the period (see Chaper 11).

The contribution to the war effort of women who wore 'masculine' garb was better celebrated in adventurous tales for adolescent girls than in the conventional love-story genre. When they did qualify as romantic heroines, their treatment varied considerably. In *This Above All* (1941), for example, Eric Knight (who is better known for his *Lassie Comes Home*) is pretty tough on Prudence Cathaway, an upper-class WAAF who becomes involved in an improbable and unsatisfying affair with a soldier, Clive Briggs. He is aggressively working-class and doesn't let her forget that she has lived in a world of privilege. In fact she is only too conscious of her own limitations and battles constantly with the snobbishness of an upbringing that makes her think in terms of 'common private soldiers', 'workingmen's public houses', and so on. Her main purpose in the story seems to be as a sounding-board for Clive's criticisms of the established order of things. After serving with the British Expeditionary Force in France he is totally disillusioned about the progress and purpose of the war. He deserts, and Prudence tries intently to persuade him to return to his unit, but his decision about this is never made because he dies when rescuing a woman and child from a blitzed building. Prudence believes that the war must be fought and won by the Allies but has to cope throughout the story with Clive's challenging attacks on democratic societies. At one point Clive defends Hitler and attacks British decadence; it is always his conviction that politicians are callous and blundering, and that senior military men are prepared to sacrifice soldiers' lives for a general's reputation. Although Prudence is in the WAAF, we gain little insight into her life in the service; the primary object of *This Above All* is the addressing of socio-political issues, but the book has acquired a reputation as a romance, largely, perhaps, because when it was filmed in 1942 with Joan Fontaine and Tyrone Power in the leading roles the love interest overrode everything else (and the actress looked great in her WAAF uniform).

Ursula Bloom attempted a promotional job for the women's services in her 1944 *Jenny WREN* which was unashamedly romantic and appealed to the average Englishman's and woman's fantasies of belonging to a race of sea-goers. Ursula Bloom was not the first to use this title for a popular novel: in 1920 Brenda Girvin, who wrote for girls rather than women, had used it for a book about a First World War WRNS decoder. (This was on the surface a plea for the approval of girls being employed in positions of responsibility in wartime, but it could well have achieved the reverse effect because Jenny was hardly suitable for her particular job in which, of course, confidentiality was paramount: 'Quick and impulsive, on the spur of the moment, she would burst out with some remark and regret it the second after she had said it.' Nevertheless she manages to make good, but eventually puts aside her 'jolly nice' three-cornered hat and smart uniform to become the wife of the naval officer who has most deeply resented her having a position of responsibility in the service.) The tone of Ursula Bloom's Second World War *Jenny WREN* is, like that of Brenda Girvin's book, chatty and lively, but despite its dashing nautical setting the heroine's service life is not exactly adventurous: 'She had adored the life in the officers' mess, serving meals, pottering to and fro with this and that, handing potatoes, handing brussels sprouts, handing cheese.' Jenny finds that the first object of her affections, 'Cock Robin', is as fickle as he is fascinating, so she settles for marriage to an unglamorous but immensely reassuring naval doctor who at least 'wore his cap at the Beatty angle'.

As we have seen, during the 1920s and 1930s problem-ridden fictional romances between British women and German men were understandable expressions of disenchantment about the rebuilding of post-war society. It is more surprising that the thorny theme of love between enemies should also be compellingly dealt with while the Second World War was in progress when popular books, plays and films nearly always cast Germans as villains who were far beyond the romantic pale. A slim novella, *Le Silence de La Mer*, by 'Vercors', published in 1942, described the reluctant beginnings of love between a German soldier and the Frenchwoman in whose home he is billeted. The heroine of the story is never named and is simply any woman in occupied France who has to keep the everyday activities of life going in spite of disruption and tragedy. Her passivity and her resilience are conveyed as being symbolic of defeated but undying France. The idealistic young German, Werner von Ebrennac, becomes disillusioned as he begins to realize that the 'marriage of equals' which he has envisaged between Germany and France will never materialize because the policy of the Third Reich is to subjugate the French people. Wanting no part in this degrading process, he escapes by volunteering for active service at the Russian front – for death, in fact. 'Vercors' was the pseudonym of Jean Bruller, who was involved in the underground publishing organization *Les Editions de Minuit*, and a measure of the sensitivity of his book is that it was read appreciatively by German, French and English people alike during a period when animosities between enemies (and Allies) were at their most acute.

Anne Duffield's *Beloved Enemy*, published in 1950, dealt with love between enemies in the almost immediate aftermath of war. It is an altogether lusher affair than Bruller's tentative and touching narrative. Clive Moray, who works for British Intelligence, finds himself waylaid in the dark alleyways and rubble of Berlin by Lisel Orhler, a flaxen-haired waif who is not trying to sell her body, as he suspects, but an ancient Egyptian scarab ring. (She desperately needs money to buy a decent woollen frock in which she can present herself to a Scandinavian lady who wants to employ a governess.) Clive is one of those upright but unimaginative Englishmen who have little time or sympathy for foreigners even if they are half-starving:

> He knew little about Egyptian antiques and could think of nothing he desired less than this absurd object, but she thrust it into his hand and, as he held it under the lamp, she stood gazing up at him with that terrible intensity of expression so utterly un-English, so typically Continental. Continentals neither could nor would control either their emotions or the outward manifestation of them; they simply let themselves go, and people who let themselves go made Moray's flesh creep.

There is an irony here which is soon pointed out to readers, though not to Clive. Lisel is in fact not racially German but an English orphan who was adopted in very early childhood by a German family. Clive does, however, note that Lisel's eyes 'were very unlike the usual run of German eyes . . . they seemed to be blue, certainly, but not the prevailing light-china shade . . . he thought that in daylight their colour would be the deep, dark blue of sapphires'. Reluctantly, he buys the ring and determinedly shakes off speculation about Lisel, who disappears into the frozen rain like an insubstantial wraith. However, her 'round, so dark-blue eyes' and 'pale wavering face' haunt his dreams that night:

> Poor little devil – but what was the use? There were thousands like her and you couldn't do anything about it. And God knew, they –

or their parents rather – had asked for it. Why sentimentalize over the Germans? Better to save such emotion for those who had been Germany's victims.

With still-fresh memories of concentration camps and the holocaust, readers saw his point, of course. However, when Clive meets up again with Lisel in Sweden, he warms to her. She has landed the governessing job and is under considerable pressure from her aggressively political brother and others to serve the Communist powers as a secret agent. Clive eventually manages to redirect her political allegiances and reluctantly realizes that he is falling for her. For some time she cannot countenance any involvement with an Englishman, whom she sees as the enemy (her German family are still 'Heil Hitlering' every time they enter or leave a room and resolutely refusing to accept that their charismatic but frightful führer is dead. This makes her antipathy to Clive understandable, but not her apparent acceptance of the Russians' political, social and economic creed). However, Clive's British grit and guts eventually triumph over all odds and Lisel not only abandons the Communist cause but falls – or at least nestles – into his arms at the end of the story. In fairness to Anne Duffield, her Brits are not all stereotypically blameless: Gloria Spence, an English girl who has thrown Clive over for an American soldier but subsequently regrets it, is 'utterly lovely, long-limbed, firm-breasted, beautifully tanned' but, alas, fearfully bitchy. She takes every opportunity of being grotesquesly rude to Lisel, that 'wretched little Hun governess', as well as to all other Germans who cross her path, and Russians too, whom she 'can't stick at any price'.

Like many novels that endeavour to combine romance with espionage, *Beloved Enemy* creates an atmosphere so unreal and overblown that even the totalitarianism which it condemns loses much of its sting. By contrast, Evelyn Anthony's suspense stories incisively and accurately recapitulate the mood of a particular period and perceptively explore the relationships of the participants. Her critically acclaimed novels ('in a class of their own for stylish writing, romance and sense of danger') seem almost perpetually in print and have been translated into eighteen languages. During the 1950s she produced a string of historical novels and biographies, but then, despite their success, followed an urge to move into a different area of writing. Her long-standing taste for adventure was sharpened and channelled into the creation of thrillers when she met and got to know people who had worked in the Special Operations Executive and MI5 during the war, and there is no doubt that with the romantic suspense story – especially when set in the world of espionage – she had found her niche.

Her first story of international intrigue, *The Rendezvous* (1967) set both the mood and the standard. It looks back to the Second World War and provides all the trappings of the undercover story: the courage of members of a resistance movement, the terror of discovery, the brutality of the secret police, the hideous interrogations – with even the degradations of a concentration camp included for good measure. From all this she draws not only horror, suspense, extraordinary twists and turns of plot and relationship, but vivid romance. It is a story of love between enemies; in her own words, 'an attempt to create a sympathetic German as a change from the then popular stereotypes'. Evelyn Anthony's leading ladies are sensitive, intelligent and rather modest about their own capacities and attractions, but also self-aware, resilient and endowed with strength which their impeccable, often fragile, exteriors belie.

For much of the action of *The Rendezvous* Terese Masson is of necessity rather more passive than the general run of the author's heroines. When the US Army liberates Buchenwald in 1945 she has been an inmate for ten months. Only nineteen, she has been driven beserk by interrogation at the hands of the Gestapo and a sense of guilt that she has betrayed her friends. (In fact she has not. She held out under questioning but, eventually driven mad by pain and fear, never knew the outcome.) The American officer-in-charge, Major Robert Bradford, tries to comfort her when she is taken by ambulance to an improvised hospital but she can only moan and cry, and repeat again and again that she will never tell. Bradford 'hadn't allowed himself the luxury of personal feelings since he had first driven into Buchenwald; he had done his job with his mind tight closed against sentiment or hate, but the pitiful cry of defiance and the miserable rag-doll body struggling against her rescuers haunted him ...' He sees her again several times and, as her mental state begins to improve, realizes that he has fallen in love with her. The only complete cure for Terese is 'therapeutic amnesia' which wipes away her feelings of guilt and memories not only of the interrogation but of the events which led up to it. She virtually assumes a new identity, marries Bradford and goes to live in America with him. Her psychiatrist assures Terese and her husband that nothing can unlock the agonizing memories.

They are, however, unleashed with a vengeance when fifteen years later she meets a supposed Swiss architect, Karl Amstat, who, in hiding in America, is actually Colonel Alfred Brunnerman of the Gestapo who had been one of her interrogators. In fact he was not her torturer, but had tried desperately to persuade her to give him the information which would spare her the agony that others later inflicted on her. In spite of the awful circumstances of their encounter at Gestapo headquarters, there had been an instant and almost overwhelming attraction between them – which, though obviously doomed, had haunted Brunnerman ever since.

He recognizes Terese immediately but she has no recollection of him. The original attraction between them not only still exists but intensifies and, inevitably, they decide to become lovers. When they first have sex together they are perfectly and rapturously attuned, but suddenly Terese's 'indescribably joyous cry of satisfied female love' changes to a penetrating scream of conscious terror 'and emerging from it came the single word repeated over and over as she began to fight and beat her fists against him. "You! You!"'

Although the agonizing memories flood back, the extraordinary love between them remains intact and unshakeable. They go away together, but forces beyond their control bring about their eventual separation. Brunnerman realizes that he is being hunted by the Israelis as a war criminal and to protect Terese from the disgrace of being linked with him he sacrifices his own life.

Evelyn Anthony followed *The Rendezvous* with several other novels focusing on unexpected romantic relationships as well as espionage, notably *The Occupying Power* (1973) and *No Ememy But Time* (1987). *The Tamarind Seed* (1971) is perhaps, after *The Rendezvous*, the most passionate of her novels. Its action takes place well after the 1940s, during the Cold War, and it deals with the love affair between Judith Farrow, an Englishwoman who works as personal assistant to the Director of UNO's International Secretariat, and Feodor Sverdlov, who is a military attaché at the Russian embassy in Washington. As a study in the overcoming of almost impossible obstacles to the fulfilment of love between enemies it is masterly and enthralling.

There are resonances between Evelyn Anthony's stories of the Second World War and Elizabeth Buchan's *Light of the Moon* (1991) which, though written some forty years after the period when the action took place, adroitly re-creates the authentic mood and scene. It is a truly gripping story of the fraught and intrepid activities of members of the Special Operations Executive in Nazi-occupied France, but, as its opening lines indicate, it is also the story of an unlikely love and a strange alliance:

> I thought that loving someone was simple. It isn't. Glorious, yes. Painful, yes. Unforgettable, yes. Simple, no. It took a war for me to find out.

There are several romantic threads to the story but the essential one is of love between an Anglo-French girl and a German Intelligence officer.

It is 1941 and Evelyn St John, denied both higher education and a career by her stuffy, over-protective, anti-feminist father, is buried deep in the English countryside, bored out of her mind and wanting to do some war work. With her intimate knolwedge of France and its language, she applies for what she thinks will be translation work, and finds herself recruited by the SOE. After a gruelling training course at Beaulieu, which is described in compelling detail, she is parachuted into the Périgord region to link up with the Resistance. She quickly learns that war, like love, is also waged at many levels and is far from simple. Her intelligence and alertness are stretched almost to breaking-point, with the threat of terror and anguish never far away as she has to learn whom she can trust, and who is likely to betray, either consciously or unguardedly, herself and her comrades. There is an incisive sense of reality about the author's descriptions of the basic loneliness of undercover work, and in her conveyance of the divided loyalties of a small French community which is often under terrible stress.

Evelyn has to endure the worst horror that she can envisage – questioning by the Gestapo – which she survives because of the intervention of Paul von Hoch, a German army officer working in Intelligence, who, though working earnestly for his country's interests, never loses sight of common humanity. He and Evelyn fall in love, but their relationship, fragile from the start, becomes increasingly set in the 'star-crossed lovers' mould. Both know from the beginning that their passionate feelings for each other will almost certainly never be fully expressed or lastingly fulfilled: 'Muddled with exhaustion, uncertain of Paul, loving him ... [Evelyn] was sure only of one thing: wherever she went he would come with her, like night following day, like the heartbeat pumping the life round her body ...'

As well as intense romanticism and a welcome stress on reconciliation between enemies, *Light of the Moon* has its full share of horrors, some of which stay almost – but not quite – as long with the reader as the story's lambent inspirational touches.

Retrospective novels with Second World War settings flow more rapidly now from authors of romances than in the decade or so which immediately followed it. Like the Great War, it has become a symbol of lost innocence and idealism, of heightened intensity in contacts between the sexes, of vigour and conviction. Because it is nearer in time it can be more easily accessed through its popular music, its films and plays, and a host of artefacts from comics and magazines, skimpy 'Utility' clothes, slogan-riddled leaflets and posters, regimental 'sweetheart' brooches, records, canned radio programmes, and even old ration-books and identity cards. The 1940s Home Front has become a particularly popular background for emotional stories and family sagas. Many of these also span the period between the two world wars and focus on the shadows cast forward from one war to the next. Authors of the 1980s and 1990s who have skilfully harnessed all this Second World War romantic potential include Marie Joseph (*The Listening Silence*), Joan Dial (*Roses in Winter*), Sarah Harrison (*A Flower That's Free*) and Jessie Kesson (*Another Time, Another Place*).

One of the most detailed and atmospheric retrospective accounts of life on the Home Front is provided in Elizabeth Jane Howard's novels of the Cazalet family (see also Chapter 10). Three titles of what is to be a quartet of books have appeared so far: *The Light Years* (1990), *Marking Time* (1991) and *Confusion* (1993). These cover the period from the run-up to the war to the end of hostilities in Europe, and the action takes place mainly at Home Place, the Cazalets' sprawling estate in a safe-from-bombing area of Sussex, and in London. The author focuses on the lives and loves of two generations and manages satisfyingly to strike the authentic mood of the war's vicissitudes, from the despondency of hearing about defeats and disasters to the general lifting of hearts when victories – all too few in the early years – were announced.

There is an unusually incisive recapitulation of the forced optimism of the late 1930s that war could still somehow be averted, followed by sickened awareness that it had to happen. With equal vividness Elizabeth Jane Howard describes the curious amalgam of relief and apprehension during the apparent inaction of the 'Phoney War', the horror of the British army's evacuation from Dunkirk after the fall of France, the suspenseful days of the Battle of Britain, the long anguishes of the Blitz, and the dogged determination to hang on to the end, hoping against all odds for victory, and blessed peace.

The Cazalet family is headed by William ('the Brig') and his wife Kitty ('the Duchy') who are septuagenarians at the outbreak of the war. The Brig has built up a London-based timber firm in which two of his sons, Hugh and Edward, also work. Their younger brother Rupert would like to be a full-time painter but has to depend on teaching for his livelihood until, early in the war, he accepts his father's invitation to join the business. His decision to do so is prompted by the need for greater financial security in providing for Clary and Neville (his offspring by his first wife, Isobel, who died in childbirth) and his young, beautiful but spoilt second wife, Zoë.

Hugh and Edward were in the armed forces during the 1914–18 war, but Rupert is young enough to volunteer for Second World War service in the Royal Navy. Hugh's marriage to Sybil is one of mutual felicity and understanding. They have three children, Polly, Simon and William. Edward is shorter on stability than Hugh but more generously endowed with magnetism and sex appeal. He maintains a kind of semi-detached marriage with Viola ('Villy') while frequently indulging in affairs. By the end of *Confusion* his relationship with Diana Mackintosh has lasted for several years and he has fathered a child with her (she is by then widowed because her husband has been killed in action). Edward and Villy have four children, Louise, Teddy, Lydia and Roland.

The Brig, the Duchy and their daughter Rachel convert their country home and two nearby houses into a wartime retreat for the three brothers, their immediate families, various other relatives and domestic servants. Some of the boys are away at boarding-schools but Louise, Polly and Clary are educated privately at Home Place.

Events unfold from the viewpoint of the adults and also that of the pubescent or teenage female characters. In fact the Cazalet books provide rare insights into the aspirations and frustrations of young girls growing up in a major war, longing to burst out and 'do their bit' but confined at home by parents who are anxious to protect them. Clary in particular chronicles their hopes and fears. She is a budding author and, as well as confiding her version of private and public happenings to a journal, writes a long series of extremely descriptive (but unposted) letters to her father, Rupert, who fails to return from Dunkirk in 1940. Clary is the only member of the family who really never gives up hope that he is somehow and somewhere still alive, and that one day he will be able to return and read her letters.

The war is especially bitter for Hugh who lost a hand and

suffered other severe wounds in the previous 'war to end wars'. His and Sybil's is in many ways a low-key romance, characterized more evidently by meticulous consideration for each other than by passion or excitement. Even when Sybil – in 1942 – is undergoing the psychological challenges and physical agonies of terminal cancer, her main anxiety is that Hugh should not learn how desperately ill she is, because such knowledge would devastate him. Of course he *does* know but, aware of her concern for him, will not admit this to her. Their steadfast but sometimes apparently dull relationship actually glows more brightly than Edward's flashy affairs and his stop–go love for Villy, or the compelling but edgy attraction between Rupert and Zoë.

During the third book of the saga, female members of the second generation are also being swept up into the adult world of careers and those highly charged romances which so often quickly burgeon (and as rapidly fade) in the intensities of wartime. Some find partners among the Yanks who invade, invigorate and occupy Britain from 1943, during the period of preparation for the Second Front in Europe.

Rupert's wife Zoë, who begins as a superficial and selfish character, becomes mellowed by events into an awareness of her own emotional shortcomings and evasions of responsibility. She is helped in this by motherhood (Juliet, her daughter by Rupert, is born soon after he has been posted as 'missing') and by a friendship which develops into an affair with Jack Greenfeldt, an extremely vital Jewish American war correspondent. She achieves a deeper relationship with him than she had ever known with Rupert, but, until she can be absolutely sure of her husband's death, is unable to promise Jack the lasting relationship that he longs for.

The mood of the Cazalet novels varies appropriately from the bleakness of death, loss and disillusionment to the languorous sweetness of new – and also of well-worn – love. Elizabeth Jane Howard makes excellent use of Home Front sights, sounds and symbols, from London's sandbagged, shrapnel-pitted and bomb-stricken famous buildings to people's constant struggles to eke out dwindling rations of food, toiletries, clothes, petrol, and even bathwater. In happy contrast we are given descriptions of the heady escapism of West End shows such as Ivor Novello's alpine extravaganza, *The Dancing Years*, and the dramatization of Daphne du Maurier's mysterious *Rebecca*, starring Celia Johnson and Owen Nares. There are also, for good measure, evocations of regular and inspiriting visits to the haven of the cinema, and of some of the popular songs that so tenaciously gripped everyone under their necessarily tough and hard-boiled wartime skins . . .

CHAPTER SEVEN

Regency Romps

D ESPITE THE EXTRAVAGANZA of vivid locations offered by the desert and the outposts of Empire, many top-of-the-tree popular writers left them strictly alone, preferring to set their stories of amatory adventure in the England of the Regency period. At first, perhaps, one wonders why, when Jane Austen had been there before, brilliantly exploiting all its trappings and immortalizing its manners and mores in her enduringly satisfying heroes and heroines. Give or take a few years before and after, her novels provided supremely authentic vignettes of the time (1801–11) when George III was too mad to occupy the throne and his son became Prince Regent. The definitive atmosphere of the late eighteenth and early nineteenth centuries was effortlessly created by Austen's pen, and, with all this and D'Arcy too, the last word in Regency romance had surely been written.

The period has nevertheless proved a magnet for a string of twentieth-century raconteurs, from Georgette Heyer, whose meticulously observed novels are in a class of their own, to writers for whom the Regency was simply an amorphously romantic background for frothy but formula-ridden stories.

Viewed retrospectively, the reigns of George III and George IV offered dramatic national events (the disastrous loss of our American colonies, the Napoleonic Wars with the triumphs at Waterloo and Trafalgar) as well as a social scene whose verve and colour seemed in striking contrast to twentieth-century mundaneness. Romantic writers have, of course, focused mainly on the glitter and glamour of the court and society life and discreetly bypassed the poverty, injustices and brutalities of the period. Horrors such as the press gangs or chimney-sweep 'slaves', if noted at all, are, one feels, thrown in only in passing for atmospheric effect, just as over-the-shoulder references to the guillotining of Louis XVI and Marie Antoinette, and other excesses of the French Revolution, provide spuriously sombre touches in order to highlight the romantic accretions of the Regency which have become traditional in the genre. One of its advantages as a setting is that of being sufficiently far back in time to seem exotically different while still being close enough to the present day to spawn heroines whose aspirations and achievements can strike empathic chords in twentieth-century readers. It also insures authors somewhat against their novels becoming outdated: lovingly lingering descriptions of early-nine-teenth-century sartorial splendours, for example, continue to be effective years after they are written.

Georgette Heyer produced some forty historical romances, most of which have Regency backgrounds. Surprisingly, this was not her favourite period. She preferred – indeed, had a passion for – the Middle Ages which she researched with diligence and wrote about with relish in *My Lord John*. However, medievalism as a literary theme lost out because readers and publishers incessantly demanded the Regency novels which Heyer produced so stylishly. Her immersion in the period, recorded in extraordinarily detailed notebooks and sketches, embraced everything from ephemeral fashions and fripperies to the military strategy of Wellington's campaigns. In fact, her persuasive accounts of early-nineteenth-century modes and morals provided not only escapist fantasies for her readers but a retreat for herself from twentieth-century life. Although strikingly handsome and successful in her own right, and happily married to an eminent Queen's Counsel, Georgette Heyer hated the period in which she lived (she was born in 1902 and died in 1974) and referred to it as 'this disgusting era'.

Her books were best-sellers for almost half a century. Now, twenty years after her death, her name remains a symbol of the romantic historical genre, although she saw herself essentially as a realist, firmly declaring, 'Romantic I am not', as reported in Jane

Aiken Hodge's excellent biography, *The Private World of Georgette Heyer*. As a shrewdly down-to-earth commentator who could nevertheless create potent love-stories, she has affinities with Jane Austen, distinct echoes of whom abound in Heyer's prose when she decides to subject grand passion, girlish innocence or parental manipulation to ironic scrutiny.

Her stories are fairly simplistic, with heroes and heroines meeting in situations that trigger off initial misunderstanding and mutual antagonism. These are naturally soon overcome, with antipathy transformed into appreciation and resentment into rapture. Skeletally straightforward plots are deftly fleshed out with good humour and gripping dialogue which frequently occupies several pages at a stretch but always maintains its spark and style. Her leading ladies are husband-hunters (even when they do not admit this to themselves) because, living at a time when society denied most unmarried females status or financial security, they had to be. Within these parameters they are enterprising and independent, and of course engaging enough to involve readers vitally in events which unfold mainly from the heroine's viewpoint.

Nevertheless, Heyer's male characters spend less time off-stage than those in romances by many other authors. (Generally speaking it is, of course, easier to maintain the great-male-lover image when it does not have to suffer too much literary wear and tear.) She keeps them near the centre of the action, and one suspects from some of her pithier narrative comments that her sympathies often lie closer to men than to women. Her books invest them with self-knowledge, a sense of order and an unerring capacity to control situations which few of her heroines come near to emulating.

It is symbolic of the Heyer hero's masterfulness that he handles even the most challenging and high-spirited teams of horses with an adroitness which suggests that he will, eventually, make love to the heroine with similar panache. Significantly, too, as much space seems to be devoted by the author to descriptions of male elegance as to feminine attire. In *The Foundling*, for example, the young Duke of Sale's appearance is colourfully conveyed:

The Duke turned to find Borrowdale waiting to assist him to take off his long, multiple-caped driving coat. He handed his hat, and his gloves, and his cane to his personal footman, allowed Borrowdale to remove his driving-coat, and stood revealed in fawn pantaloons, well-polished Hessian boots, and a blue cloth coat of Weston's excellent tailoring. As he did not belong to the dandy-set, his shirt-collar points were not excessively high, and his neckcloth, although arranged with propriety, did not aspire to the niceties of the Mailcoach, the Osbaldestone, or the Tone d'Amour. A single fob hung at his waist; he did not carry a quizzing-glass; and except for a plain pearl pin in his tie the only other adornment he wore was the heavy sardonyx signet ring which had belonged to his father . . .

And Sale is a fairly low-key figure compared with Georgette Heyer's more charismatic male protagonists, such as Max Ravenscar in *Faro's Daughter* or Ivo, Marquis of Rotherham in *Bath Tangle* who, tall and arrogantly handsome, both cut the compelling sartorial dash demanded by the genre. Even their beautifully tailored garb, however, pales in comparison with the adornment sported by Justin, the Duke of Avon, in *These Old Shades*, whose almost effeminately elegant appearance masks his decidedly macho-strength:

He walked very mincingly, for the red heels of his shoes were very high. A long purple cloak, rose-lined, hung from his shoulders and was allowed to fall carelessly back from his dress, revealing a full-skirted coat of purple satin, heavily laced with gold; a waistcoat of flowered silk; faultless small clothes; and a lavish sprinkling of jewels on his cravat and breast. A three-cornered hat, point-edged, was set upon his powdered wig, and in his hand he carried a long beribboned cane . . .

All these well-born heroes of 'splendid height and haughty bearing' were never quite the upright young Englishmen whom properly brought-up girls of the period might have been encouraged to meet and marry. Interestingly, they were 'tainted with vice': they gambled with gusto, were inclined to live recklessly beyond their means and showed contempt for the society which looked up to them. Most daunting of all, with the experience of several sophisticated affairs behind them, they were a touch cynical about women in general.

It is no easy task, even for the most spirited of heroines, to thaw out these hardened male exteriors and reveal the streak of sensitivity beneath. The author's most successful male leads are about thirty-five years old, sometimes indeed in their early forties. Her heroines, too, are not always in the first flush of youth but, often somewhere in their mid-twenties, are old maids by the standards of their time. They may start out as gullible-and-inclined-to-be-bullied-youngish-things, but their encounters with die-hard social prejudices, and entanglements with both pseudo- and real admirers soon toughen their resilience and sharpen their wits. Some display flashes of true feminism in psychological duels with the hero which form the prelude to their ultimate union. Some have distinctly androgynous, even mannish, traits, which keep their bucks and beaux very much on their well-booted and polished toes.

Georgette Heyer's effective use of the Beatrice-and-Benedick type of romantic tussle is particularly evident in *Faro's Daughter*. Max Ravenscar is thirty-five, a confirmed bachelor and one of the richest men in London. He has successfully eluded the succession of wily match-making traps to which friends, family and ambitious mothers have exposed him. It has eventually been accepted that, apart from occasional involvement with ladies of easy virtue, he is far more interested in horses, sport and gambling than in the opposite sex.

Ravenscar is begged by his aunt, Lady Mablethorpe, to rescue her almost-of-age son Adrian from the clutches of an older female who apparently has marital designs upon him, and with whom he is wildly infatuated. The girl in question is Deborah Grantham, who actually has no particular interest in Adrian and is determined, despite the material advantages it would offer, to avoid a 'baby-snatching' marriage to him. Socially, Deborah is disadvantaged: somewhere in her twenties, she is dependent on her aunt, Lady Bellingham, who has been forced through the massive debts of her late husband to run a private gaming establishment at her St

James's Square home in order to survive financially. Deborah has no qualms in helping her to manage this, although it drastically undermines her position in polite society. The double standard is at work again here, of course. The social status of the men who pay to gamble at Lady Bellingham's is unsmeared, but the women who – quite respectably – organize their Faro-banks and wine and dine them between hands have become creatures whom 'no person of ton [style] will recognize'. As Max Ravenscar puts it with characteristically high-handed dismissiveness, 'One does not marry women out of gaming-houses.'

From the beginning, however, he has a sneaking admiration for Deborah. 'As a connoisseur of female charms he had no difficulty at all in understanding why his young relative had so lamentably lost his head.' Deb is 'built on queenly lines', has unbelievably brilliant eyes, thick and glowing chestnut curls, a 'neatly turned ankle', an attractive, low-pitched voice and 'a good deal of humour'. It is, in fact, a shared sense of humour and appreciation of wit that keeps sparking off the reluctant attraction between Max and Deborah. Resenting his interference, she does not immediately let on that she has neither hormonal nor social aspirations concerning Adrian, so Ravenscar and she skirmish continually and acerbically, in the tradition of the genre. When he contemptuously attempts to buy off her 'pretensions to his cousin's heart and hand' she gives vigorous expression to her loathing of his arrogance and stupidity. He, of course, is allowed to be ruder than she, and declares that 'women of her stamp should be whipped at the cart's tail'. As her independence increasingly frustrates him, he goes on to call her Jade, Jezebel, Harpy, Doxy and Strumpet. After all this, it is really hardly necessary for him to say, 'I do not recall when I have met any woman whom I disliked more.' Deb is stung by his insults but, instead of retaliating with verbal abuse, she takes direct action to cut him down to size. She has him kidnapped (a pleasing reversal of the abduction procedures common in Regency romances), bound and – briefly – incarcerated in her aunt's cellar. (These moments, we gather in retrospect, are when he becomes aware of his truly tender feelings for her!)

After several more intrigues, abductions and misunderstandings, Ravenscar astounds Deborah by declaring his love and proposing marriage. Convinced – like Elizabeth Bennet on receiving D'Arcy's first proposal – that he is still proud and patronizing, she refuses with spirit and eloquence: 'I am obliged to you ... but even the thought of squandering such a fortune as yours fails to tempt me. I have met many men in my time whom I thought odious, but none, believe me, whom I hated as I hate you! I trust I make myself plain, sir?'

A few pages further on, however, he proves his worth by foiling the schemes of a particularly nasty adventurer. The barriers between Max and Deborah are then fully and finally broken down so that for the first time she can succumb to tears and unromantic snuffles into her hanky while he dries her cheeks and kisses her, 'extremely roughly'. By this time it is Deb and not Max who is over-awed by social niceties as, in between his kisses and compliments ('"My beautiful idiot!" said Mr Ravenscar lovingly'), she whispers, 'You cannot marry a – a wench out of a gaming-house!' He, of course, from the security of money and power, is able to reply categorically that he is determined to marry her 'with as much pomp and ceremony' as he can contrive, so Deborah, sighing with satisfaction, abandons 'any further attempt to bring him to a sense of his own folly'.

Their rough-edged relationship and the zest with which it unfolds are repeated with variations in many of Georgette Heyer's novels. More seriously, she deals with significant historical events with military backgrounds (as in *An Infamous Army, The Spanish Bride*), but it is her romantic tangles such as *The Black Moth, Faro's Daughter, The Foundling, The Corinthian, These Old Shades, Sprig Muslin, Frederica*, and so on which remain addictive as the leading characters weave their gilded ways through 'ton' parties, dinners at White's, gaming at Brooks's and dances at Almacks, or through curricle rides around great parks, ridottos in the Vauxhall Gardens and trips to gracious country houses. The sense of period is so authentic, even in its slang, that, as the publisher's blurb for one of the books states, readers can feel that they 'are actually living among the elegant, leisured and wealthy denizens of London's West End [or Bath or any other fashionable haunt] at that time'. As well as these elitist activities, there are also glimpses of low-life pursuits in which the more reckless of Heyer's heroes occasionally engage, from the dubious pleasures of the cockpit and bare-knuckle prize fights in 'vulgar taverns' to the garish attractions of fun-fairs and freak-shows.

One popular social entertainment of the time, the masquerade, is quintessential to several of the novels. Characters frequently assume false identities, both in fun and in earnest. In particular, women have to assume the role of young men or boys. In common with Shakespeare and several other writers, Heyer sometimes uses this device to turn romantic conventions on their head and sometimes to enable heroes and heroines to gain insights into each other's hearts, minds, motivations and personalities that would be impossible in the generally accepted framework of gender-separative society.

An interesting exploitation of this theme is provided in *The Masqueraders* (1928) which has the pre-Regency setting of the aftermath of the Bonnie Prince Charlie rising. The leading protagonists are a brother and sister, Robin and Prudence. Their father's status in society is uncertain, although it is ultimately established that he is actually Lord Barham, and Prudence and Robin are therefore as blue-blooded as any of their aristocratic associates. There are murkily mischievous undertones to a masquerade, which, we are told, they have enacted on previous occasions. They swap roles: Prudence, the taller of the two, becomes a boy, and Robin a girl. This enables them to indulge in several cross-sexual amatory intrigues which, despite some comic satisfactions, work less well than in *These Old Shades*, a masquerade-novel which was published two years earlier.

In this we meet the elaborately adorned and excessively rich Justin, Duke of Avon, (see page 191) who has vast estates in both England and France. Over forty, he is cast in the mature-man-with-a-past mould and, with power, arrogance and unscrupulousness to match his fortune, is known to his friends as Satanas. In the book's opening paragraphs he encounters Léon, a terrified urchin fleeing from the wrath and violence of his supposed older brother who ill-treats him shamefully. Apparently on a whim, Justin 'buys' the boy with a diamond pin plucked casually from his cravat. He plans to turn 'this little rat' into his page ('So entertaining to possess a page, body and soul'). Léon is obviously a sensitive character, but he never takes offence at the Duke's insults and, in fact, makes 'Monseigneur' his hero. Justin appears to be intrigued by the boy's abundant Titian hair. For good measure his new acquisition also has wide, violet eyes and a somewhat girlish look. Although the fiction of Léon's masculinity is maintained for the early part of the book, Justin – and of course any mildly intelligent reader – quickly penetrates the page's disguise. 'He' is really Léonie, a young girl who knows nothing about her real parentage, although this is soon worked out (from the clue of the Titian hair) by the Duke who plans to use her in his plan of repaying an old grudge against Le Comte de St Vire.

This unappetizing and dissolute aristocrat has switched Léonie, his legitimate daughter, at birth for a peasant boy whom he claims as his son in order to keep his brother Armand from eventually succeeding to his title and estates. Having physical evidence in the shape of Léonie, Justin forces St Vire to acknowledge his infamous rejection of her – and subsequently to commit suicide.

Léonie has, of course, by this time been transformed from guttersnipe into ravishing beauty. Nevertheless, in view of her bizarre parentage and upbringing, it is perhaps surprising that Justin should propose marriage to her. Her (almost) guileless charms have punctured the armour of his world-weariness and cynicism, and he can at least reassure himself that, though spawned by a perfectly ghastly father and brought up by pretty crude peasants, Léonie *is* high-born. In fairytale waif-to-wife tradition, she is overwhelmed with rapture and gratitude (one suspects that, even when she has become a Duchess, she will continue to address Justin as 'Monseigneur').

Georgette Heyer uses the Léon/Léonie masquerade to bring her disparate lovers into unusually close pre-marital proximity. In the

Duke of Avon's relationship with his pseudo-page there are echoes of Orsino and Viola in *Twelfth Night*, although Léonie lacks the sturdiness of Shakespeare's heroine and is rather too heavily reliant on conventional flirtatious techniques: 'She peered naughtily up at him, through her lashes. It was one of her most captivating little tricks.' (This is, after all, eighteenth-century France and not Illyria.) The shrewdly calculating Justin has plenty of opportunity to assess and admire Léonie's looks and personality, and of course her legs, when she is wearing page-boy garb. She is able to observe him at close range, gambling, conniving and generally throwing his autocratic weight about in places which no respectable woman would normally be permitted to enter. However, far from becoming disillusioned by these insights into Justin's questionable behaviour, she develops a passionate protectiveness towards him, which she maintains through thick and thin.

It would be natural to assume that Regency novelists writing more recently than Georgette Heyer would create more liberated heroines. This is certainly not true of Barbara Cartland, whose stories adeptly underpin the traditional pattern of female fragility and male dominance. Her conveyance of period, place and atmosphere is more impressionistic than Heyer's, but it is, after all, only the relationships that matter in the Cartland canon. The role of the raffish hero is simply to awaken the innocent heroine to broader and deeper areas of experience and passion. Luxuriantly named leading ladies – Magnolias, Darcias and Honoras – progress from fearing to fancying the men into whose arms they have been thrust. The novels are slim, with little space for the slow stop–go arousing of mutual understanding and ardour that the genre generally demands. Action abounds; the pace never slackens as heroines are trundled through chases and abductions and forced marriages until in the final clinches the high-flown assertions of devotion can be delivered, with supreme confidence by the male characters ('you have given me your heart, and I think too your soul'), and more haltingly by the heroines ('without your love the world is . . . empty and dark, and I would rather . . . die than go on living'). One is constantly astounded at the flair with which

Cartland carries it all off and sweeps the readers, by her uniformly one-sentence paragraphs, into plot and counter-plot of passionate intensities.

Barbara Cartland's stories have been published since 1925. After the 1930s they settled into a basic pattern: the dialogues, events and characterizations of her Regency novels are pretty well interchangeable. Having discovered what her readers enjoy, the author serves it up – rechauffé but with unaltered ingredients – again and again. With sumptuous upper-crust settings and a firmly anti-feminist approach, her books are flagrantly escapist and unconcerned with social issues, in fact, the apotheosis of attitudes so often condemned by today's critics. Nevertheless, they continue to appeal to people from widely assorted age groups, classes and cultures. Novels which might be regarded as a strangely English caprice have been translated into many languages and seem as popular in countries with very different backgrounds from those of their original setting as they are in Britain.

As previously mentioned, Cartland even achieved the distinction of selling ten titles 'to the Arabs in the middle of the Gulf War'.* She suggests that her books' success springs in part from the fact that they are essentially moral and reflect her own sincerely held views: 'I've always written about myself. That's why my heroine is always a virgin. I'm still about the only writer who doesn't allow her heroine to go to bed with anyone until she's married to him.'

The author now has a tally of some 600 novels. It is difficult to be more precise; in 1991 she remarked that she wrote 'a book a fortnight', and she was then well into the 500s. Her sales in English and in translation amount to over 500 million. Across the last two decades her Regency romances have probably been the most popular of her books, and it is interesting to consider one or two of these chronologically, and to note developments, if any. (Sometimes 'Regency' spills over into early or mid-Victorian, but one has to say that the mood and scene are not strikingly different. In each case, of course, the social structure gives emphasis to men as the

* Interview with Mary Cadogan (1991) *Million* magazine.

'do-ers' and embodiments of passion, and to women as decorous shuttlecocks of fate and symbols of purity.) Both *Love Has His Way* (no. 250) and *Love for Sale* (no. 264) bring together in apparently unpropitious circumstances a darkly authoritative, rich, good-looking male and a fair-haired, wiltingly innocent young woman. Respectively the heroes are the Marquis of Sarne and the Duke of Oswestry, and the heroines are Romana Wardel and Udela Hayward. The dialogue usually follows the formula of decisive statements from the hero and quietly tremulous comments (conveyed always in dot-ridden sentences) from the heroine. Even when Romana is inflamed to ecstatic outpouring about her Marquis towards the end of *Love for Sale*, she is unable to gulp out without hesitancy to her lover just how strongly ('You are godlike ... and divine') she feels about him.

Dollars for the Duke (no. 285) is unusual in having an American take the leading female role. Magnolia Vandevilt is an heiress whom Seldon, Duke of Otterburn – as aristocratically handsome and arrogant as they come – reluctantly agrees to marry for the sake of his enormous but impoverished estates. Forced into the marriage by her over-ambitious mother, Magnolia starts off by feeling contemptuous of Seldon, although she is not as spirited in expressing this as readers might have expected (American girls in the romantic genre were generally lively and more independent than their English counterparts). At first theirs is a marriage in name only. It takes them a lot of time, languishing looks and the experience of being imprisoned by Albanian brigands to discover their true feelings for each other. Then, as 'love carries them on the waves of ecstasy into the starlit sky', Magnolia echoes Romana's wholehearted response to her noble spouse: 'I love ... you and everything you do ... will be perfect and ... also ... Divine.'

In *Wish for Love* (no. 321) the author employs plentiful trappings of the period, including the device of the masquerade. A brother and sister, Jeremy and Mariota, pretend to be highwaymen, which brings them considerably more than they bargain for (affluent partners all round, in fact, for Mariota, Jeremy and their widowed father). Because the brother-and-sister relationship is central to the story, there is less emphasis on the masterfulness of its hero or the fragility of its heroine.

Cartland has named several of the real-life models for her fictional leading men, among whom is the late Earl Mountbatten. He inspired and gave advice for her novel *Love at the Helm*, which was published in 1980, after his assassination, in aid of the Mountbatten Memorial Fund. Set in the early part of the nineteenth century, it is one of the author's most persuasive historical romances. Its main protagonists, Lady Delora and naval captain Conrad Horn, are more feistily fleshed out than the general run of Cartland's Regency characters. Delora's delicate, golden, rose-pink and pale blue appearance is deceptive: she knows exactly what she wants, goes for it and gets it. The prize she covets is the handsome Conrad, who has been ordered to convey her in his ship to the West Indies where she is, under compulsion, to marry the ageing and debauched Governor. The gallant naval officer, of course, decides to deliver her from this lurid liaison, but despite his formidable toughness it is the feminine wiles and tactics of Delora that bring the true lovers to the safe harbour of each other's arms in the novel's closing pages.

Lively nautical touches add vigour to the story-line although, not surprisingly, Cartland has a surer touch with romance than with her depictions of rumbustious British naval types. Passages that describe Conrad and Delora kissing until they are 'dizzy with passion' come across more credibly than, for example, the genteel and strangely awkward dialogue between sea-captains: 'Only you could have evaded the enemy when you were out-numbered in quite such a clever way . . .' It seems unlikely too that even such a sweet and vivid young thing as Delora could so easily infect 'the whole ship' with happiness and have all those hardened sailors whistling while they worked and dancing hornpipes on the lower decks. Nevertheless, with a little flexibility and imagination the reader can cruise pleasantly along on the tide of Dame Barbara's breathless but engaging prose and disregard the occasional moments in her sagas when there is a daunting sense that some characters are 'dressing up' for their period rather than being rooted in it.

The American romanticist, Judith McNaught, began to exploit the Regency period for stimulus and setting fairly recently, from the mid-1980s, and her books sizzle with sexually exciting incident and dialogue. There is social realism too, with heroines who are inclined to be critical of the status quo, and, on the surface at least, feminist, although their independence is eventually ground down by the determinedly masterful wooing of an assured, upper-class hero. It is hard to resist the gutsy humour of the books, even though one suspects that this leans too much towards modernity for authenticity. It is fun, too, to spot the anachronistic American-isms: surely an early-nineteenth-century English girl would not have referred to a man's bifurcated outer garments as 'pants' but as 'breeches'? Nor would she, one feels, be likely to talk of 'freshening up' her appearance. McNaught excels in verbal sexual teasing and incredibly long and lingering kisses (see Chapter 2) as the hero moulds the object of his desire 'tightly to his muscular frame'. Unlike Barbara Cartland, she does not leave readers to guess at what goes on beyond the bedroom door: however, she skilfully maintains an aura of innocence around her female leads even after – and during – their explosively intense responses to their lovers.

In *Whitney, My Love*, for example, Whitney Stone awakens to the world's wicked ways when she finds that her bankrupt father has bargained her away to the fetching but fearfully arrogant Duke of Claymore. At that time she is in love (or thinks she is) with a different – and much duller – young man. The Duke, in spite of his smouldering seductiveness, has an uphill struggle to make Whitney forget her first idealistic love and to appreciate that he (Claymore) is one of those 'reformed rakes' who 'make the best husbands'. We know that (in keeping with the traditions of the genre) his wooing is bound to succeed when, soon after buying her, he forces Whitney to lie across his lap while he mercilessly beats her with his riding crop. She submits to this because a little earlier, stung by his insults, she has inadvertently struck the horse he was riding: her blow, intended for the taunting Duke, was deflected, and now she knows that she must accept punishment.

Fortunately for Whitney the courting process is not usually so searing. Claymore uses his undoubted charm and wit to great effect and finds in her a worthy protagonist and partner. Of course, he is head-over-heels in love with her and feels fiercely protective. Nevertheless, he brutally rapes her when he thinks – erroneously – that she has eloped with her former lover. Also, after she becomes his Duchess and makes it obvious that she is now besotted with him, he listens to malicious, lying gossip and rejects her. On neither occasion does the Duke give Whitney a chance to explain her true situation before he reacts against her. Happily, however, she is eventually allowed both figuratively and physically to bring him to his knees before he can once again lead 'her to the peak of ecstasy and then join her there'.

Judith McNaught's witty stylishness makes her a natural successor to Georgette Heyer. Although her female characters suffer rougher treatment than Heyer's, they are more liberated, while her leading men, despite their assertiveness, are not so consistently in control of their own and of other people's lives. In fact McNaught's heroines are not only capable of direct, courageous and dramatic action in their own interests but are frequently called upon to save or protect their menfolk. In *Something Wonderful*, Alexandra Lawrence is prepared to sacrifice herself for her mistrustful husband, Jordan Townsende, the devilishly attractive but cynical Duke of Hawthorne. She hurls herself in front of his body when an assailant fires a gun at him, and, though she jolly nearly dies in the process, her gritty action clears up a lot of misunderstanding and enables Jordan to swallow his pride and admit that his behaviour to Alexandra has been 'unforgivable' and that she is 'goodness and gentleness and trust', 'flowers blooming on the hillsides and laughter floating through the halls'. And, of course, 'love'. *She* typifies McNaught's intelligent and intrepid heroines: *he* is one of her long string of outwardly-terribly-tough but actually slightly soft-centred heroes.

Jane Aiken Hodge sets most of her novels in the early years of the nineteenth century, and successfully combines high adventure and the love story, casting her heroines in unstereotypical roles. They grapple not only romantically with dashingly named heroes, such as Mark Mauleverer, Hart Purchis and Gair Varlow, but with pirates, political power-seekers, foreign brigands and revolutionary mobs as well. They have the wit to plan their adventurous assignments intelligently, and the zest to enjoy them. Like Georgette Heyer, to whom she says she owes a 'vast debt', Jane Aiken Hodge meticulously researches the periods and places in which the action of her books unfolds. Her plots are multi-layered, with amatory relationships developing against the background of dramatic historical events such as the Greek campaign for independence or the Napoleonic Wars. In several of her books, as in her latest, *Escapade* (1993), there are two female leads, one of whom is considerably more mature than the other, and whose friendship plays a crucial part in the plot. *Escapade* takes Beth Prior, a famous actress, in company with Charlotte Comyn, the young heiress daughter of one of her friends, on a secret mission to Sicily. Beth is inspired to participate in this partly because Forde, her diplomat lover, requests it, and she hopes that shared dangers and intrigues on the edges of the Sicilian Court will bring them closer together, and stimulate him to propose marriage. Their differing responses to challenge and change in fact drive them apart, and Beth has to suffer the humiliation of seeing the fortune-hunting Forde opportunely courting her rich young companion. Charlotte, who is as robust in character and action as Beth, unhesitatingly rejects him and, after escaping several of his nastier attempts to compromise her, reflects that 'being abducted and nearly raped concentrates the mind wonderfully . . . but not to pleasant effect'. Beth, who feels that she has been thrown over because of her past, ruefully comments, 'I should have known there are never second chances for women' – but indeed there are, because both Beth and Charlotte find and captivate true heroes, though refreshingly neither of these husbands-to-be conforms to the conventional, raffishly-handsome-and-arrogant image.

Sylvia Andrews is another contemporary author whose heroine has to have a rugged streak in order to survive and flourish. As well as sweeping passion and dramatic reversals of fortune, *Perdita* provides wit and acerbic social comment. Few young girls have to suffer the frightful hazards which the resilient Perdita has to overcome. Her horrible step-brother, Piers Carston, abducts her and sells her to an oafish and brutal pirate, Michel Legrand, hoping to inherit her stately home and sprawling acres. Perdita soon finds herself the prisoner of an Algerian Pasha who plans to put her to death along with members of the pirate gang. Filthy and bloody after a savage beating, Perdita is surprised to find that she is not, after all, to die but to be bought by an English earl. He plans to use her as a pawn in a scheme of revenge he is hatching against his arch-enemy who turns out to be – guess who! – Perdita's grisly step-brother. (Piers has, amongst other awful doings, seduced the earl's young cousin, Linette.)

After all the hideous things that have happened to her, one feels that Perdita might have felt relief and gratitude at her new role. Our proud heroine, however, refuses to succumb tamely to the schemes of the fifth Earl of Ambourne. Her passive resistance takes the form of refusing to speak, but, of course, even without verbal communication, each begins to respond to the other. The plot satisfyingly tantalizes and twists to its expected romantic ending, when the author gives credible yet mischievous answers to the questions which *Perdita* inevitably raises. How, for example, could the dishy and powerful Earl not feel repulsed at the thought of marrying a dirty pirate's and a dingy pasha's cast-off? (What about social stigma, let alone possible disease?) And isn't it strange that Ambourne's mother, a glittering and much revered Countess, approves and vigorously encourages the match? It is to Sylvia Andrews's credit that she deals with all this adroitly enough to satisfy her readers' intelligence while still managing to project a lush sense of period romance. To survive in the 1990s, Regency romps need to offer wit as well as wild escapism.

CHAPTER EIGHT

Ruritanian and
Revolutionary Romances

♡

'FANCY DRESS' is used in the Ruritanian romances of Anthony Hope and Baroness Orczy's chronicles of the Scarlet Pimpernel with far more effect than in many Regency novels. The respective adventures of Rudolf Rassendyll and Sir Percy Blakeney are as unashamedly escapist as the Heyer and McNaught historicals but, as well as providing generous dollops of romance, they deal with powerful political intrigues and desperate life or death struggles. Each saga is shot through with idealism, strong concepts of honour and chivalry, and triumphantly swashbuckling high adventure which is matched by compelling characterization. Rassendyll and Blakeney both became outstandingly resilient cult figures. *The Prisoner of Zenda* was published in 1894 and *The Scarlet Pimpernel* in 1905: still in print in the 1990s; they have also been frequently staged, filmed and televised during their century of literary life.

Anthony Hope was born in 1863 and called to the Bar in 1887. He wrote *Zenda*, which was to become his ninth published book, in spare moments and completed it within four weeks (despite its vivid and long-lasting appeal it is actually a slim novel, considerably shorter than its sequel, *Rupert of Hentzau*, which was published four years afterwards). Its instant success persuaded him to give up law and devote himself to writing.

Although the action of the plot is supposed to take place in Hope's own time, the setting and props smack of historical romance, with castles, courts and palaces redolent of a distinctly antique atmosphere. The author's descriptive powers were occasionally woolly, but what his narratives lacked in precision was made up for by colour and zest. With Ruritania, he established for his own and successive generations an indelible image of a small, idyllic country nestling somewhere in the obscure heart of Middle Europe. He also, with the name of his invented country, gave the English language a new synonym for the essence and trappings of high romantic adventure.

The basic elements of the plot of *The Prisoner of Zenda* are well known: Rudolf Rassendyll, who is an upright, upper-class Englishman, visits Ruritania to sample its coronation festivities. He is prompted by curiosity to see the King (Rudolf V) who shares not only a Christian name with Rassendyll but some of his antecedents as well. The Ruritanian royals are Elphbergs and, two or three generations earlier, one of their princes dallied with an English countess who then bore his son, from whom Rassendyll claims descent.

Rassendyll is aware of having inherited the dark red hair, straight nose and blue eyes of the Elphbergs, but it is only when he is travelling through Ruritania that he realizes how startling is his resemblance to the King. Because of the treachery of the latter's half-brother, Black Michael, Rassendyll finds himself – at the request of the King's loyal followers, Colonel Sapt and Fritz von Tarlenheim – doubling for the monarch to save his throne. The real Rudolf V has been drugged so that he cannot attend his own coronation, at which Michael hopes to seize the crown and the kingdom.

When Rassendyll chivalrously agrees to become a temporary royal stand-in, he has, of course, no idea of the hazards that might ensue. The most complicated of these is the fact that he falls overwhelmingly in love with Princess Flavia, an Elphberg who is fairly closely related to the King and betrothed to him. Flavia, who in the past has felt pretty chilly towards her intended because of his dissolute ways, is not at first let into the secret of the substitution and is surprised to find herself responding warmly to the man she imagines to be the King. One feels that there is something slightly narcissistic about the mutual passion of Rassendyll and Flavia, for she too is auburn-haired, azure-eyed and astoundingly good-looking. The love that flares between them is frequently described in extravagant terms, with Rassendyll 'half-mad' for Flavia:

> Ah, if you had seen her! . . . She was a princess – and I an impostor. Do you think I remembered that? I threw myself on my knee and seized her hands in mine. I said nothing. Why should I? The soft sounds of the night set my wooing to a wordless melody, as I pressed my kisses on her lips.

However, despite the intensity that each feels for the other, Rassendyll rarely goes as far as this in physically expressing his passion. Generally speaking, he confines himself to kissing Flavia's hands rather than her lips. It is true that, when the real King has been abducted by his enemies, the Englishman basely but briefly considers hanging on to the throne and forcing Black Michael's hand so 'that he [Michael] must kill the King': then, of course, the Princess Flavia could be his for ever. But honour over-rules desire and self-interest, and Rassendyll sets out on hair-raisingly desperate stratagems to rescue the kidnapped Rudolf. He succeeds, of course, and in the process strews the story with symbols of dash and valour which have become models for more recent heroes of historical adventure in books, plays and films. In particular the duel-by-swords between him and Rupert of Hentzau, Michael's flashily daring henchman, has become legendary.

Rassendyll proves himself to Colonel Sapt and Fritz von Tarlenheim to be 'the noblest Elphberg of them all'. To Flavia, once she has been let into the secret, he is 'my lover and true knight', and they declare undying love for each other, even though duty demands that Flavia ('Honour binds a woman too . . .') must sacrifice herself for her country by marrying King Rudolf, and that she and Rassendyll will probably never meet again this side of Heaven. (Of course they do, only a few years after this touching renunciation, in the sequel!)

It is difficult to over-emphasize *The Prisoner of Zenda*'s impact on the popular imagination of its time. Even today, when its idealistic romanticism seems over the top, it still charms and inspires. We have to agree with Fritz von Tarlenheim who says in one of the book's highly quotable phrases that 'Heaven doesn't always make the right men kings!' – or, of course, husbands. Alas, poor Flavia.

The author begs many of the questions which arise when one person assumes another's identity. One wonders at first how Rassendyll communicates with the locals of Ruritania, until we gather that their language is German in which the very English hero is unusually adept. One also suspects that his voice must have differed considerably from that of his distant royal cousin – to say nothing of his teeth, his laugh, the shape and size of his hands or any other parts of his body with which the King's associates might have been familiar. As we have seen, however, Anthony Hope dealt decisively with the most difficult question of all – how to hold off sexual intimacy despite strong mutual attraction – by imposing the constrictions of honour.

The action of *Rupert of Hentzau* is supposed to take place three or four years after Rudolf Rassendyll has left Ruritania. As any reader must have guessed, Flavia's marriage to the King is far from happy. He has never recovered psychologically from his period of captivity at Zenda and has become a fretful invalid, tetchily critical of his Queen and jealous of the great regard which he suspects she still holds for Rassendyll. His insecurity is heightened by the knowledge that although Black Michael is dead, the exiled but ambitious Rupert of Hentzau is waiting in the wings to get back into Ruritania to try to topple the House of Elphberg.

It has been Flavia's secret custom to send her English lover just one communication each year on a pre-arranged date. This consists of a single red rose in a box, accompanied by a message of 'three words' (unspecified but not difficult to fathom) which Fritz von Tarlenheim carries and presents to Rassendyll whom he meets in Dresden or at some other appointed place outside Ruritania. Rassendyll then sends back to Flavia a note containing the same three words.

However, fear of the King's suspicious watchfulness forces the Queen to decide that she must abandon this annual rose ritual. Nevertheless, she dispatches von Tarlenheim for one last time with the boxed rose, and indiscreetly entrusts him also with a loving letter to Rassendyll which is her note of farewell. She begs her courier to bring back an equally loving message from her admirer.

In great distress, von Tarlenheim informs Rassendyll that Flavia's letter has been stolen from him by one of Rupert of Hentzau's men. It must, of course, be retrieved if the Queen is not to be compromised, so Rassendyll – as always, ready to do anything for Flavia – returns to Ruritania to embark upon another series of swashbuckling escapades in order to put things right. He experiences the almost ecstatic joy of meeting his beloved again. Kissing a *copy* of the notorious letter, he pledges his life to the return of the original:

'Had I as many lives as there are words, my Queen,' he said softly, 'for each word I would gladly give a life.'

'Ah, Rudolf, but you've only one life, and that more mine than yours. Did you think we should ever meet again?'

'I didn't know,' said he . . .

'But I knew,' she said, her eyes shining brightly; 'I knew always that we should meet once more. Not how nor where, but just that we should. So I lived, Rudolf . . . I lived through it all.'

He pressed her hand, knowing what that phrase meant and must mean for her.

On this high peak of intensity, and even knowing that they may well never meet again, Rudolf still manages to keep his passion on a tight rein: '"I mustn't kiss your face." said he, "but your hands I may kiss," and he kissed her hands as they were pressed against her face.' And, at the end of the interview, she graciously touches her lips to his forehead.

In the struggles against Rupert and his adherents, the King is killed, his murder is hushed up and Rudolf Rassendyll has once more to impersonate him. He meets Flavia again – and has to make a far-reaching decision. There is now no barrier to their being fully united: Rudolf could simply continue to play the King, and Colonel Sapt and von Tarlenheim make it clear that a secret marriage could be arranged so that respectability could be entirely maintained. Flavia is all set to go ahead, but Rudolf needs time to turn over in his mind the rights and wrongs of the situation in order to balance the apparently conflicting demands of desire and chivalry. In the end the decision is made neither by him nor Flavia but by circumstances. While he is pacing the Palace gardens alone to deliberate, he is shot by one of Hentzau's followers. As he lies 'near death', in their last hour together Flavia permits herself the indulgence of embracing him and kissing him on the lips '"In life and in death, my sweet Queen," he murmured. And thus he fell asleep.'

A touching exit line – but Flavia, who then rules alone as 'the last of all the Elphbergs' (she and the King had no offspring) provides Rudolf Rassendyll with an epitaph that is just as memorable. She has him laid 'to his rest in the vault of the Kings of Ruritania in the Cathedral of Strelsau' and she writes 'with her own hand' over his tomb: 'To Rudolf, who reigned lately in this city, and reigns for ever in her heart – Queen Flavia'.

Flavia inspires extraordinary devotion, not only in Rassendyll but in Colonel Sapt, Fritz von Tarlenheim and pretty well all her courtiers. She apparently captivates them by her glowing beauty rather than by her personality. In fact she plays a rather passive role in both stories, expecting all those chivalrous males who surround her to be active and intrepid in her interests. Portrayals of her on film by Madeleine Carroll and Deborah Kerr in 1937 and 1952 respectively have consolidated her shuttlecock-of-fate image, whilst the exhilarating performances of Ronald Colman and Stewart Granger as Rudolf Rassendyll have enhanced the hero's aura of invincible derring-do.

The woman at the heart of Baroness Orczy's Scarlet Pimpernel stories is made of sterner stuff than Flavia. She is Marguerite Blakeney, the wife of the Pimpernel himself. The first novel of the series, set in 1792, makes it clear that she is not only the most beautiful and fashionable of London society's great hostesses, but 'the cleverest woman in Europe'. Before her marriage, as the 'lavishly gifted' Marguerite St Just, she had achieved distinction in her own right, becoming a leading actress at the Comédie Française. With a lively interest in social and political issues, she had ardently embraced the French republican cause, before becoming aware of its excesses. Her 'charming salon' in the rue Richelieu 'was reserved for originality and intelligence, for brilliance and wit . . . and the entrance into it was looked upon . . . as the seal to an artistic career'.

Marguerite is also a woman of action who, unlike Princess Flavia, is not prepared to sit and wait while others undertake hazardous assignments on her behalf. Early in the saga the former actress demonstrates her readiness to cross the Channel and risk death or imprisonment in revolutionary France in order to save her husband and her brother along with some less charismatic potential guillotine victims. (It is interesting that the 1980s Scarlet Pimpernel sequels by C. Guy Clayton have cast Marguerite firmly in the heroic-adventuress mould, thus endorsing and enhancing Baroness Orczy's conveyance of her unusually intrepid and intelligent behaviour.)

At the beginning of *The Scarlet Pimpernel* Marguerite and her husband are estranged. He has learnt that the Marquis de St Cyr and all his family 'perished on the guillotine' and that his wife had 'helped to send them there'. Although it is literally true that some 'thoughtless words' of hers had been manipulated by St Cyr's relentless enemies, Marguerite is actually 'morally innocent' of his death. However, Percy, despite the astuteness which the narrative constantly attributes to him, fails to appreciate this. He can forgive neither her ill-judged action nor her failure to explain this to him. But, between the Blakeneys, love lies bleeding only briefly: by the middle of the first book they are once again looking langorously and longingly at each other, even though Percy's passion is still held back by pride, and Marguerite's 'unconquerable heartache' at his rejection has found only partial relief. The reader knows that all will be well because, alone on the terrace which his wife has just left, Blakeney 'in the very madness of his love . . . kissed one by one the places where her small foot had trodden, and the stone balustrade where her tiny hand had rested last'. (Such emphasis on the minuscule nature of her extremities is strange, as she has earlier been described as 'tall over the average, with magnificent presence and regal figure', but it is probably meant to highlight Sir Percy's masculine strength and power and height.)

He shows weakness only with regard to his wife. In every other respect he is more or less invincible, displaying superb expertise and confidence, whether he is implementing some devilishly cunning plan to outwit the Revolutionary mob, is fighting them physically, escaping from them on horseback at breakneck speed, or simply engaged in tying one of his exquisite cravats.

He is an Edwardian precursor of the 'intelligent ass', that popular convention in detective fiction and the theatre of the 1920s, (Dorothy L. Sayers' Lord Peter Wimsey is a classic example), who concealed a razor-sharp mind beneath an inane facade. For Blakeney, the persona of 'the lazy nincompoop and the effete fop' serves two purposes. It is a barrier behind which he can retreat during his estrangement from Marguerite, and, of course, it smokes the eyes of 'those Frenchies' who are so desperately trying to uncover the identity of the accursed Englishman who constantly thwarts their nefarious schemes. After the end of the first book, when the hero can no longer completely hide his light under the appellation of 'the little wayside flower', some of the magic and romance is stripped from the saga.

Nevertheless, throughout ten novels and two volumes of short stories, the elegant and dashingly enigmatic Sir Percy deftly and dauntlessly whisks potential victims away from the ever-devouring 'Mam'zelle Guillotine'. Emmuska Orczy originally developed the idea in 1903 as a play, in collaboration with her artist husband, Montague Barstow. She adapted it into a novel in 1905 and, ninety years on from his creation, the Scarlet Pimpernel has become part of the language, joining the ranks of characters such as Sherlock Holmes and Billy Bunter, who are known even to people who have never read the stories which feature them.

Like the relationship between Percy and Marguerite, the books are wildly romantic at several levels. The shadow of the guillotine seems an unlikely breeding-ground for the tender passion, but this is constantly and potently conveyed. Every story is highly wrought and intensely atmospheric. Particularly effective are the contrasts between the rabble-ridden, blood-running and squalid streets of revolutionary Paris and the sumptuous splendours of the court of King George III in England. Blakeney seems to have been equally at home in both, adroitly switching from being the Prince of Wales's gorgeously attired and favourite supper-party guest to disguising himself as a loathsome-looking old merchant, a smelly hag or simple fisherman in order to save some unfortunate aristo-crat from early and violent death.

Like Anthony Hope's Ruritanian novels, the Scarlet Pimpernel books were essentially escapist, moving away from contemporary, real-life issues into a fictional setting which, despite its background of violence and upheaval, was often portrayed as idyllic. When the Orczy–Barstow play was first produced, the working classes were beginning to demand more from life than gruelling, under-paid work followed by the sleep of exhaustion. Like the suffragettes who campaigned for women's franchise, and the Irish who struggled for Home Rule, the British Labour movement was challenging the oppressive and paternalistic attitudes towards the underprivileged which had existed for decades. Baroness Orczy uses her novels to express a good deal of social comment, and although much of this is idealistic and aspirational, it is elitistly flavoured. Generally speaking, artisans and even middle-class people do not show up too well in the books. In spite of the author's attraction to strongly chivalric ideas, she writes about the 'lower orders' with a distinct air of condescension, especially if they step out of line and fail to respect their 'betters'. And, of course, nothing could be more disrespectful than putting the heads of these 'betters' under the guillotine.

However, both Percy and Marguerite – who were 'more vivid and real' to the author 'than the friends of this world' – had liberal streaks. *He* falls in love with a woman from a different class, and a foreigner to boot, whose political opinions are very different from his own. *She* is honest and realistic enough to understand when and how she had been politically deluded, and sufficiently tough to demand direct participation in some of the most cliff-hanging rescues performed by her husband, although he generally prefers to draw his helpers from the all-male and all-upper-crust League of the Scarlet Pimpernel – Sir Andrew Ffoulkes, Lord Anthony Dewhurst, Lord Hastings, Lord Everingham and Sir Philip Glynde.

The colourful mood of the stories is an echo of the manner of Sir Percy's creation. Emmuska Orczy longed to produce 'a true hero who would have a romantic setting'. The latter suggested itself to her during a visit to Paris when the city's old streets still seemed to her to ring with the footsteps of Robespierre and Danton, the clatter of the tumbrils and the blood-lust of the Revolutionaries. Still without inspiration for her central character, she returned to London where, soon afterwards while she waited for a train at the Temple underground station, 'the personality of the Scarlet Pimpernel' came to her 'in a very curious way.' Emmuska records in her 1947 autobiography, *Links in the Chain of Life*:

> I first saw him standing before me . . . on the platform . . . Now, of all the dull, prosy places in the world, can you beat an underground railway station? It was foggy, too, and smelly and cold. But . . . I saw Sir Percy Blakeney . . . in his exquisite clothes, his slender hands holding up his spy-glass; I heard his lazy drawling speech, his quaint laugh.

She called this 'a mental vision', claiming that although it lasted only a few seconds the whole life-story of the Scarlet Pimpernel – twelve books-full – was there and then unfolded to her. She wrote the first of his adventures in five weeks, and felt that this was the happiest period of her life.

Despite the far-larger-than-life qualities of the impossibly handsome and incredibly valorous hero and heroine, despite frequent touches of melodrama, despite an occasional sense of 'dressing-up' and such exclamations as 'Zooks!', 'Zounds!' and even '*Sacré tonnerre!*' which pop up in the narratives, the novels have an untarnishable appeal. An aspect of the stories which ensured their attraction was their unashamed love of England, and the corresponding business of keeping 'those Frenchies' (Britain's long-standing political rivals) in their place. As Sir Percy modestly remarks to Marguerite after he has outmanoeuvred his opponents in a near-unbelievable way, 'a British head is as good as a French one any day'. The implication, of course, is that it is considerably better, as he proves time and again. Even when, with Marguerite held hostage, he is entrapped in some fortress or prison whose walls are lined by French soldiers with fixed bayonets, he will not only manage to extract his own exquisite personage from this fearfully tight corner but will contrive the rescue of his wife and probably of one or two other aristocratic prisoners who have been earmarked for the guillotine.

His arch-enemy, Chauvelin, the brooding, hate-filled intellectual agent of the Revolutionary Government, never succeeds in outwitting him, although the odds might seem to be formidably stacked against the apparently indolent but astoundingly astute and energetic Englishman. On the rare occasions when Sir Percy *appeared* to be beaten he still

> looked a picture of calm unconcern: the lace bow at his throat was tied with scrupulous care, his eye-glass upheld at quite the correct angle, and his delicate-coloured caped coat was thrown back sufficiently to afford a glimpse of the dainty cloth suit and exquisitely embroidered waistcoat beneath. He was the perfect presentation of a London dandy, and might have been entering a royal drawing-room in company with an honoured guest . . .

Having to build up and sustain romantic suspense over so many books, it is not surprising that Baroness Orczy dealt in stereotypes and formulaic situations. In fact these probably enhanced the saga's appeal. Readers relished the knowledge that privations and incarcerations were a certain prelude to breath-catching feats on the part of the Pimpernel and that he would always be rewarded for his selfless daring by romantically fulfilling moments with Marguerite whose beauty, like Percy's aplomb, survives all onslaughts and hazards:

> She stood with the full light of the lamp illumining her ruddy golden hair, the delicate blush on her cheeks, the flame of love dancing in her glorious eyes. Thus he saw her as he re-entered the room, and ... the joy of seeing her there seemed greater than he could bear.
>
> Forgotten was the agony of mind which he had endured, the humiliations and the dangers which still threatened; he only remembered that she loved him and that he worshipped her.
>
> The next moment she lay clasped in his arms ...

An intriguing aspect of the Scarlet Pimpernel novels is that despite their extreme Englishness they were written by a Hungarian. Emmuska Magdalena Rosalia Maria Josefa Orczy was born into an ancient land-owning family at Tarna-Ors in Hungary in 1865 and did not come to England until the 1880s when her family, after suffering drastic social upheavals, decided to settle in London. Although her knowledge of the English language was then minimal, Emmuska immediately felt completely at home in her adopted country. She became an ardent Anglophile, stating that 'there was nothing English' about her except her love 'which was all English'.

There is no doubt that with the character of Sir Percy she made a permanent contribution to English fictional mythology. The 1934 film version of *The Scarlet Pimpernel* not only extended the audience for her books and beefed up her hero's appeal but provided further examples of Hungarian empathy with British ideals and aspirations. The film's producer was that eminent Hungarian, Alexander Korda; it was partly scripted by his fellow-countryman, Lajos Biro, and it starred in the title-role the actor Leslie Howard who, despite his quintessentially English voice and demeanour, had been born of Hungarian immigrant parents.

With his blond and languid good looks, Howard projected a screen image which fused perfectly with the literary one. Surprisingly, however, he was not Alexander Korda's first choice. The producer had favoured Charles Laughton (whose plain and portly appearance surely made him singularly unsuitable for portraying the impeccably elegant Sir Percy) but, bombarded by protest letters from fans of the novels, he had been persuaded to engage Howard. Even after the film's success, Emmuska too remained lukewarm about this actor's interpretation of her celebrated character. She acknowledged his charm and attractiveness and that 'he knew how to make love' but, in her view, 'Fred Terry was the ideal Sir Percy.' Terry had created the part on stage in 1903 and he continued to play it, on and off, for the rest of his life, despite eventually becoming so corpulent that he had to swashbuckle and conduct his love-making from a wheel-chair.

It was not only to Britons and Hungarians that Emmuska's stories and characters appealed. Her play was performed in translation in many countries, including Germany, Spain, Italy and France. As might have been expected, the French were not entirely enthusiastic about the alien adventurer who so constantly thwarted their Revolutionary Government: the Paris production of the play was rather garbled, with an explosive, fist-clenching, expostulating Gallic hero replacing the restrained and dignified English milord. Similarly when the 1934 British film was dubbed in French, Leslie Howard was aurally transmogrified into a French émigré because it would have been anathema for the fiercely nationalistic local audiences to see an Englishman putting down so many of their compatriots. Such are the roots of literary and cinematic vandalism!

The traumas of the French Revolutionary period have of course provided potent stimuli not only for Baroness Orczy but for many other raconteurs of romantic and adventure fiction. Their outpourings in twentieth-century magazines and novels for both adults and children generally empathize enthusiastically with the deposed *aristos* and vigorously condemn the '*sans-culottes*'. Similarly, popular fiction about the seventeenth-century Civil War in Britain has, until recently, charismatically presented the Cavalier adherents of the monarchist cause and portrayed their Roundhead opponents as, at worst, brutes and, at best, bores.

Another lost cause which has acquired heavily romantic literary accretions is that of the Southern Confederate States during and in the aftermath of the American Civil War. Of the many popular novels and films which highlight individual passion against the raging backcloth of this war, Margaret Mitchell's *Gone with the Wind* remains supremely authoritative and addictive. This sweeping and labyrinthine blockbuster seems as fresh and feisty in the 1990s as when it first appeared almost sixty years ago. In fact it was written almost mid-way between the end of the North and South conflict (1865) and the present decade. Inspired by an intense love for the South, Georgian-born Margaret Mitchell began to research her one and only book ten years before its eventual publication in 1936. The war – and particularly its residual bitterness – was then still in living memory, and the saga's two very different heroines, Scarlett and Melanie, who both refused to accept defeat, compulsively affirmed the resilience of the almost ruined South. *Gone with the Wind* was launched during the Depression years and its reconstructive spirit had topical relevance, helping to restore in many Americans the national confidence and self-respect which they had lost.

The media-hyped announcement of the book's forthcoming transposition into film provided people on both sides of the Atlantic with the endlessly fascinating pastime of casting the colourful leading characters, Scarlett O'Hara and Rhett Butler. (Vivien Leigh and Clark Gable were eventually to prove themselves perfect in these coveted roles.) Just like its printed progenitor, David Selznick's cinematic extravaganza was perfectly timed to suit the public mood. Premiered in Atlanta in December 1939, soon after the outbreak in Europe of the Second World War, it opened in April 1940 in London where it achieved a record-breaking four-year run despite the hazards of air-raids, with several horrendous 'near-hits', and the tedious inconveniences of blackout travel. The movie, a triumphant symbol of defiance and resilience, struck immediate echoes of the prevailing 'backs-to-the-wall' spirit. Its appeal progressively increased as audiences in Britain – and in America after the December 1941 Japanese attack on Pearl Harbour – were to become more and more war-battered and restricted by rationing and austerity. Then, as now, *Gone with the Wind* worked wonderfully well at both escapist and realist levels.

Scarlett, the headstrong, self-centred, unscrupulously determined heroine, and Rhett, the dashing but cynical rogue-hero, are mavericks, whose actions, sometimes wilful and sometimes calculated, challenge many of the values of their society and make them dangerous to know. Nevertheless, they are totally the products of the old South: Scarlett had to use her feline fetchingness and wiles to maintain her position in the pre-war plantation society where women were supposed to be decorative and docile, with men taking all the important decisions. During the war, when old patterns of life were destroyed for ever, the economic survival of individual families depended largely upon their women, who managed farms and businesses in the absence of fathers, husbands and sons. Scarlett typifies the Southern belle-turned-boss who recognized that survival – and some semblance of eventual prosperity – demanded ruthlessness as well as grinding work and sharpened wits. Rhett, of course, made his own rules from the beginning. As he claimed with relish, he was 'no gentleman', but, quick to see and exploit his opportunities, he played a leading role in Georgian society, even though his behaviour (refusal to marry a woman he was erroneously supposed to have 'compromised') puts him in the position of not being 'received' in many respectable homes. However, his wartime blockade-running (even though this was largely inspired by profiteering motives) and his belated enlistment in the Confederate Army when defeat stared it in the face confirmed how deeply he was rooted in the society whose conventions he so coolly flouted.

Scarlett and Rhett can be classified as stereotypes of a particular society and culture rather than of just the romantic genre, and paradoxically it is Margaret Mitchell's skilful establishment of them in an extremely specific place and period which has contrived to transmogrify them into timeless, mythic characters with whom successive generations identify.

Scarlett is every-woman as well as a particularly unusual one, able to make difficult – and sometimes misjudged – choices when she and the people and things which she loves are threatened. Even while we deplore her impulsive marriages, her manipulation of her first two husbands, her obsessive desire to rebuild the O'Haras' war-ruined plantation, Tara, and her unscrupulous exploitation of convict labour to ensure the prosperity of her post-war lumber business, we can empathize with her. We admire the strength with which she reluctantly protects her hated and heavily pregnant rival, Melanie, on and after their escape from the burning Atlanta. We applaud her improvisation when, exhausted and emaciated from overwork and at the very end of her financial tether, she sets out to save Tara by borrowing money from Rhett, having adorned herself in an outfit run up from her mother's moss-green curtains and the 'gorgeous bronze and green-black tail feathers' of a rooster. Most of all, perhaps, we salute her stupendous grit in killing and burying the Yankee soldier whose intrusion into Tara during the last stages of the conflict threatened its women with robbery, rape and other unspecified horrors: 'She could have ground her heel into the gaping wound which had been his nose and taken sweet pleasure in the feel of his warm blood on her bare feet. She had struck a blow of revenge for Tara . . .'

Although *Gone with the Wind* up-ends many of the traditions of romantic fiction, it follows formula in aspects of Scarlett's relationship with Rhett: at their first meeting, and on almost all their subsequent pre-marital encounters, she is, despite her evident strength and independence of spirit, disadvantaged by him: 'God's nightgown! . . . He looks as if – as if he knew what I looked like without my shimmy,' she exclaims indignantly.

He does, too! 'Quite old' (thirty-five), with wide shoulders muscled 'almost too heavily for gentility' and endowed with swarthy, pirate-like handsomeness, 'cool recklessness' and caustic humour, he knows his way intimately around women. From the beginning of their relationship he has no difficulty in teasing and wrong footing the flirtatious, tempestuous but often unperceptive Scarlett: 'You should be kissed, and often, by someone who knows how'; 'Don't drink alone, Scarlett. People always find out and it ruins the reputation.'

Although he loves her, he treats her with considerably less cour-
tesy than the gentler Melanie, a fact which Scarlett notes with
chagrin. In spite of her physical frailty, her tolerance and determination to see the best in everyone (especially her unpredictable
sister-in-law, Scarlett), Melanie has reserves of inner strength to
which Rhett responds warmly. (Even Scarlett, who never forgives
Melanie for marrying Ashley Wilkes, her own first and long-standing love, is forced to recognize that 'beneath the gentle voice and
dovelike eyes of Melanie there was a thin flashing blade of unbreak-
able steel . . . that there were banners and bugles of courage in
Melanie's quiet blood'.) There exist between the apparently ultra-
refined and respectable Melanie and the unrepentant renegade
Rhett a mutual respect and surprising understanding of each other's
aspirations and desires. Significantly, it is Melanie who begs Scarlett
to 'be kind to Captain Butler. He loves you so', while Rhett's
frequent bowing to Melanie's balanced judgement is maddening to
Scarlett who, even when she captivates, can never tame him.

Her confusion about Rhett is, of course, compounded by her
adolescent but astoundingly dogged devotion to Ashley, the drea-
mer – escapist – intellectual who appears to die spiritually with the
end of the old Southern culture and society, and seems a surprising
hero for a girl with Scarlett's guts. Margaret Mitchell makes
marvellously dramatic use of Rhett's contempt for Ashley and his
intense frustration at Scarlett's longing for him even after she has
become his (Rhett's) wife and the mother of his adored and
beautiful daughter, Bonnie. He ultimately spells this out:

> I'm not a fool. Don't you suppose I know that you've lain in my
> arms and pretended I was Ashley Wilkes? . . . Pleasant thing, that.
> Rather ghostly in fact. Like having three in bed where there ought
> to be just two . . . But, hell, I wouldn't have grudged him your body.
> I know how little bodies mean – especially women's bodies. But I
> do grudge him your heart and your dear, hard, unscrupulous,
> stubborn mind . . .'

The classic off-stage rape-or-seduction scene then takes place, with
Rhett muttering as he swings Scarlett off her feet and begins to

climb the stairs, 'By God, this is one night when there are only going to be two in my bed.'

Scarlett's awakening to the 'joy, fear, madness, excitement' and surrender of loving Rhett comes too late and, unlike most romantic heroines, she seems doomed to live with the consequences of her blindness and stupidly wrong choices. With an almost clinical sense of realism – for which hundreds of thousands of readers have never forgiven her – Margaret Mitchell separates the enchanters, leaving only the glimmer of hope that Rhett, just before his famous exit-line, 'My dear, I don't give a damn!', promises to come back 'often enough to keep gossip down', and Scarlett, with characteristic stubbornness, swears, 'I'll think of some way to get him back. After all, tomorrow is another day.'

Rhett stands alone as one true hero of the romance story who is never tamed. Overpoweringly charged with energy, attractiveness and independence of thought, he is immune to the disapproval of his peers, unbowed by cataclysmic public events and personal tragedy, and able to remain his own man even when desperately stirred by passion and desire. Margaret Mitchell once remarked that his creation was inspired by her admiration for Charlotte Brontë's Edward Fairfax Rochester and Augusta Jane Evans Wilson's St Elmo Murray. (See Chapters 1 and 2.) It is interesting that St Elmo was given literary life in 1867, only two years after the end of the Civil War, by an author who, like Mitchell, hailed from Georgia. It seems likely, too, that 'Red' Upshaw, a ruthless charmer whom Mitchell married but quickly divorced, added elements to Rhett Butler's make-up. Nevertheless, whoever and whatever provided progenitorial stimulus, it has to be said that the redoubtable Rhett most satisfyingly adds up to far more than the sum of his parts.

Love was hardly a major ingredient of the fiction that had its roots in the 1936–9 Spanish Civil War but, despite his down-to-earth directness, Ernest Hemingway managed against this bleak and ravaged background to provide a persuasive romance between unlikely protagonists. *For Whom the Bell Tolls* (1940) punches home the author's disenchantment with society even more powerfully than his 1920 *A Farewell to Arms* which had looked back in anguish at the First World War (see Chapter 11). Its concern with ideological warfare, which has become the pattern of many recent conflicts, gives *For Whom the Bell Tolls* a topicality today despite its almost sixty-year-old setting. Published soon after the beginning of the Second World War, this story of an armed struggle which inexorably involved a civilian population could hardly fail to produce a vigorous response from British people of vastly differing political persuasions who were dealing with air-raids and the threat of invasion at that time. Prophetic of the nature of Hitler's and most future wars ('we have just seen the sky full of airplanes of a quantity to kill us back to our grandfathers and forward to all unborn grandsons including all cats, goats, and bedbugs . . .'), the book also vividly brings across the awesome intensity of wartime romances which are likely soon to be curtailed by death: 'There is only now, and if now is only two days, then two days is your life and everything in it will be in proportion.'

Robert Jordan, a left-wing American volunteer, is sent to work with a guerilla band operating behind fascist lines. He falls in love with Maria, a partisan who has suffered terribly at the hands of some of Franco's soldiers. The strong sense of political alignment which has brought Robert to Spain to fight against fascism can nevertheless accommodate doubt and unease. He questions his communist idealism, and the rigidity of 'that so mutable substitute for the apostles' creed, the party line'. Sleeping with Maria puts him once again in real relationship with another person and pulls him out of thinking in clichés 'both revolutionary and patriotic'. Although no one conveys more vividly than Hemingway the wastes and destructiveness of war, the overriding image of *For Whom the Bell Tolls* is the romantic one of Maria in the high pine forests of the Sierra running barefoot across the snow to join 'Roberto' in his sleeping-bag. The love-story elements were heightened by the distribution in 1943 of the Hollywood version of the novel, with Gary Cooper and Ingrid Bergman portraying Robert and Maria, and skilfully suggesting the lambent quality of their feelings for each other. Women in Britain and America were quick to emulate the short, bubble-curl hairstyle which set off Bergman's clean-cut good looks. Short hair was then, of course, appropriate for girls working in the services and on farms or assembly-lines but, although the Swedish actress had given glamour to cropped hair, for Maria it was actually a reminder of the rape and humiliation to which the fascist soldiers had subjected her. The shaving of her head had been the prelude to sexual degradation.

In spite of all that she has endured, Maria retains a curious innocence. For Robert she is a light in a dark world which has been pared down to concentration on survival against heavy odds: against cold and hunger; enemy snipers and scouts; doubts and fears and the possible break-up of their own guerilla group. There are few respites from fighting – and dying – for a bridge, a hill, a gun-emplacement or some other temporary vantage-point. Maria's involvement in the war has been reluctant, and passive rather than active. She is desperate to stay and die with Robert when his leg has been shattered by an enemy shell, but he sends her away, hopefully to safety, while he tries to delay the posse of Franco's troops who are pursuing the partisans.

Robert knows that he is dying, and his last words to Maria (expressed by Hemingway as translations of Spanish idiom) are almost biblical in their affirmation of the resilience of love: 'I go always with thee wherever thou goest'; 'I am with thee . . .'; 'I am thee also now . . .' Taking small comfort from his reassurances, she is forced to accept his decision and, like so many women in civil wars and revolutions, to become a bereaved, displaced and desolate survivor.

To the end, Robert holds on to his left-wing idealism: 'I have fought for what I believed in for a year now. If we win here we will win everywhere . . .' Hemingway, who had actively supported the Spanish republican cause, could write about communism with conviction in 1940. In *The White Dove* (1986), Rosie Thomas less enthusiastically describes the responses of a British volunteer in the International Brigade. She is, of course, writing with hindsight fifty years on from the Spanish conflict, when the oppressive ruthless-ness of communism had been bleakly evident during the Cold

War and *détente*. Nick Penry, a Welsh union activist, politician and ex-coal-miner, has been involved with upper-crust Amy Lovell in a passionate affair in London. They have split up, sadly recognizing that they can have no long-term future together because Nick is already married and cannot consider leaving his wife and his very vulnerable, handicapped small son. He volunteers to fight against Franco's armies and is received at Albacete, 'the marshalling-point for the International Brigades', by Jake Silverman, a friend from London, who sardonically welcomes him 'to the biggest bloody shambles in Europe'. Nick too is soon engulfed in disillusionment as he recognizes in various Party member officers and 'comrades' the same extremism that he despises in fascism and other restrictive regimes. He realizes that the democracy for which he has been fighting is, in the Brigade, 'denied every day. They were all conscripts now, even Spain itself, pawns in a struggle for power that was controlled far away in Moscow.' He has become a pacifist who can no longer support the communist cause.

The struggle ends for Nick when his arm is blasted by a shell and has to be amputated. Transported for surgery to a field hospital, he meets up again with Amy, who, despite her extremely affluent, aristocratic background, has become committed to the left, and is nursing in Spain. Almost as soon as his ruined arm has been amputated, Nick expresses his longing 'to go home', and Amy promises that she'll take him there: 'Somehow, I will.' She does, too, becoming the strong element in their partnership. With a decisiveness that Hemingway's Maria could probably never have harnessed, Amy takes the organizational initiative and guides her lover to safety through the hazards and hardships of war-stricken Spain. Her strength persists even when, after a last poignant love-making session together, she and Nick arrange that he will return to the Rhondda, to his wife and child.

Continuing the reversal of the Hemingway roles, once Nick is on the last, safe stages of his journey Amy returns to the battle zones and behind-the-lines areas to find Paloma, an abandoned orphan baby whom she is determined to adopt. When the child is eventually found, Amy's struggles with officialdom and red tape continue, but in the end she is granted the prized adoption papers, severs her service with Spanish Medical Aid and flies home to England with her baby. Although she is a heroine in a decidedly post-Hemingway mould, Amy, like Robert in *For Whom the Bell Tolls*, sees more than just loss in the separation from her lover: '"*He's with me every day*," she thought. "*Every day, all of the days . . .*"'

CHAPTER NINE

'The Great Husband Hunt'

A WAY FROM Ruritania and Revolutions, in Britain between the two world wars and into the 1970s the eternally popular theme of amatory fiction in both books and magazines was that of finding the right kind of husband. The archetypal hero owed something – but not too much – to the wild nature of Heathcliff, rather more to Darcy's quizzical hauteur and a great deal to Rochester's solid strength. Other heroes were also beginning to make their mark as Hollywood provided a variety of idols from Rudolph Valentino and Ramon Navarro in the 1920s, Ronald Colman, Gary Cooper, Robert Taylor and Clark Gable in the 1930s and 1940s, to William Holden and Gregory Peck in the 1950s. Television produced its own multifarious range of 'Mr Rights' from then until the present day, while Hollywood kept its end well up with Paul Newman, Steve McQueen, and so on.

What heroines and readers were looking for was a man who could combine enigmatic behaviour with good, hopefully-rugged-rather-than-chocolate-boxy looks and a kind of sexy arrogance (that occasionally touched on savagery). He should also have a sensitive streak or soft centre which, though heavily concealed because of some deep hurt or humiliation inflicted by women in his past, would be allowed to come into its own once he met the right girl and felt sure of her devotion. As well as all this, it was of course generally essential for him to be able to provide the heroine with a decent home and financial security. He had, in fact, to be a suitable subject for domestication.

The writers who provided such husband-hunting stories with

227

almost mind-boggling gusto and frequency could be numbered in hundreds. Some stand out for their capacities to invest their characters with charisma, others for humour, innovation, charm and sheer story-spinning skills. From the 1920s through the 1960s there was little basic change in the pattern of this kind of romantic fantasy but, as women's educational and career opportunities widened, and they, like men, became more upwardly mobile and financially secure by their own efforts, new trends began to creep into romances which became more firmly established once the 1970s were under way.

In the 1920s and 1930s romantic novels in enormous numbers were available from public or commercial lending libraries throughout the country, and the flow of such fiction continued unceasingly in a broad range of weekly and monthly women's magazines. In essence the nature of the stories varied little from those of pulp 'glamour' papers such as *Red Star*, *Betty's*, *Poppy's* and *Peg's Paper* to the more housewifely offerings of magazines like *Woman's Weekly*, *Woman and Home* or *Woman's Own*, except that these better-quality publications provided slightly more fleshed-out and intelligent characters.

Heroines were usually found in jobs or domestic situations with which readers could identify. In the main, they were shop assistants, nurses, factory-hands and office-workers. In the period following the First World War a new note of superficial emancipation was evident, with characters dancing, drinking cocktails and dining at smart hotels, going to shows and the cinema, being driven around in fast cars or taking taxis, smoking, and possibly living in service flats which were considered the height of sophistication. Of course, many nice girls still lived at home with parents and siblings while they were waiting for Mr Right to put in an appearance, so there was a situation for almost every reader to empathize with, whether she lived in a city, the country or a suburb.

Mabel Barnes Grundy wrote romantic and historical novels from 1902 until 1946. Even the earliest of these were surprisingly pacey and lively, and packed with engaging, frequently eccentric, protagonists. Some of their humour may well have been unconscious, but certainly it seems that the author sometimes liked to do a little gentle sending-up of her chosen genre. Her titles, for example *A Girl for Sale* (1920) and *An Undressed Heroine* (1916), are arresting but misleading. The leading lady of the former, strangely named Whiff Woffran, is out of work and 'sells herself' simply in the sense of advertising in the newspaper for a job (she gets it, and also a husband in the shape of her new employer), while the girl who inspires the second title is not, as might be expected, a stripper or woman of easy virtue but a wholesome heroine who dresses gracelessly, mainly because she can't afford to improve her wardrobe. Happily, one of the cranky characters in whom the author excels comes to her rescue and provides her with garb which considerably enhances her appeal for the opposite sex. Another eccentric triggers the action of *The Great Husband Hunt* (1922) by offering £1000 (nearly a fortune then) plus a large dowry to the first of his four nieces to become engaged . . .

Ruby M. Ayres wrote for a slightly shorter period, just under forty years from 1915 to 1953, but because her easy, slightly bantering style was slow to go out of fashion, some of her titles were reprinted, thus extending her period of influence. She wrote approximately 150 novels, and did a fairly long stint as a magazine 'agony aunt' in *Home Chat* in the 1950s, so she is unlikely to be forgotten. Her heroines are often 'irrepressible' and flirtatious, though never actually short on sexual morality, while her heroes, until such time as their warm, soft hearts can be revealed, tend to be 'stern', 'ruthless' – but unfailingly 'manly'. Like Mabel Barnes Grundy, Ruby M. Ayres went in for a spot of self-mockery from time to time. In *The Master Man* (1920) she cannot resist facetiously describing 'a young and romantic' housemaid who 'devoured every novel she could get held of'. Her benign outlook was evident in her answers in various magazines to readers' letters, and in comments which she made from time to time about her writing:

> Do you really believe in the romance you've written so much about?
> Do you believe it lasts? I'm frequently asked the question by people
> who are kind enough to enjoy reading my books and I can imagine

it would be very disillusioning if I were to reply – 'No, I don't believe in it. I just write love stories because they sell.' That wouldn't be true either. I most certainly believe in romance and know that it can and does last providing it is mixed with two most important ingredients – tolerance and a sense of humour . . .

Another prolific pillar of the genre was Ursula Bloom (see Chapter 6), who also wrote as Sheila Burns, Mary Essex, Rachel Harvey, Deborah Mann, Lozania Prole and Sara Sloane. She was writing from the mid-1920s to the mid-1970s and produced some 500 full-length books as well as plays, short stories, biographies, and volumes of helpful hints on knitting, cookery, beauty and how to become an author. Her romantic stories ranged from stereotypical girl-meets-and-ultimately-marries-boy themes to hospital and historical sagas. From so many titles (which have earned her a place in *The Guinness Book of Records*) it is difficult to select those of outstanding interest, but her first published novel, appropriately named *The Great Beginning* (1924), which became a best-seller, dramatically dealt with an innocent young heroine who 'passionately desired motherhood' and was for some time denied this because her conniving mother had married her off to a man of tainted, disease-ridden ancestry. (All ended felicitously, however.) Her 1964 *The Ring Tree*, another best-seller, conveyed a powerful awareness of the impact of war on various ordinary women whom it uproots from secure homes and temporarily turns into refugees. The book captures the spirit of the so-called Phoney War (from September 1939 to April 1940) and the traumatic events that immediately followed it. Ursula Bloom particularly enjoyed writing novels about gipsies, inspired by a gipsy forebear of her own, of whom she was intensely proud (*The Gipsy Vans Come Through*, 1936; *Gipsy Flower*, 1949; *The Caravan of Chance*, 1971 and *Gipsy Flame*, 1979). As well as having produced more full-length novels in the English language by 1967 than any other author, she also found time to be beauty editor on *Woman's Own* for a spell, to work on the staff of the *Sunday Pictorial*, and be a problems-page adviser.

Denise Robins was another extremely prolific writer (170 novels) who covered every romantic field from the exotic (deserts and châteaux) to the domestic (shops, offices and suburban semis). Her heroines were by no means always in the first flush of youth: ages ranged from late teens to mid-forties. Some of her stories acknowledged that even when a girl had got her man she was not necessarily home and dry. Robins tackled the trickier aspects of romance (divorce, extra-marital affairs and pregnancies) with an unusual openness for the genre. *More Than Love* (1947), for instance is a realistic account of a young girl's long-running affair with a married man, and in *O Love! O Fire!* (1966) the heroine, after sleeping with her boyfriend and becoming pregnant, has to face the realization that what she thought was overwhelming love was just infatuation. Denise Robins wrote from 1924 to the mid 1970s and, as well as ranging over the decades, her romances were geographically all-embracing, with locations from Morocco to Mayfair coming across convincingly.

Like Ethel M. Dell and Barbara Cartland, Denise Robins was to become a queen of the genre: 'Robins for Romance' was at one time a popular slogan not only in books and magazines but in advertisements on London buses. Changes in fashion and trends, great public events and alterations in the status of women all find a place in her novels. She was never afraid to take on new themes or to move with the times, although she commented (in *Contemporary Authors*, vol. 19) that in later life she found it impossible to write about innocence, humility, self-sacrifice and all the 'lilies and languors' of the 'almost impossible' love that she set out to describe in her early books. However, she admired 'modern' young people and was interested in their views: 'Their new world moves at a terrific pace so I find that I also like to write about it.' In the early 1970s she was regularly answering readers' letters about their personal problems in the magazine *She* ('It is my privilege to help and counsel'). Denise Robins also produced stories as Denise Chesterton, Ashley French, Harriet Gray, Hervey Hamilton, Julia Kane and Francesca Wright. She is one of three generations of romance writers in her family. Her mother wrote serials for *Weekly*

Welcome, and her daughter, Claire Lorrimer, is also an extremely popular novelist today.

With Alex Stuart, Denise Robins founded the Romantic Novelists Association in 1960 with the aim of protecting the love-story – and indeed love itself – from the sneerers and jeerers:

> those who turn their backs upon romance seem to become extra-ordinarily bitter. They like to sneer at and deride romantic love. Book critics try to toss aside the works of the romantic novelists . . . Alex Stuart and I decided to found the *Romantic Novelists Association* . . . because hundreds of other romantic novelists resented the recent attempt to belittle our type of work . . .

She was president of the association from 1960 to 1966.

Maysie Greig wrote under a variety of names from the mid-1920s until the end of the 1960s. In magazine short stories and novels her heroines, while managing in the main to cling to their statutory pre-marital virginity, strongly endorsed the 'good-time' mood of the 1920s and early 1930s, wearing smart clothes and cosmetics, and being entertained by lean, strong-jawed, dark and distinctive men in 'swish' West End haunts. Maysie Greig's attitudes towards life, love and literature were simplistic, and expressed in a brisk, no-nonsense way:

> Love is the most fascinating, inspiring, complete emotion in the world . . . I write happy love stories because I believe happiness is the greatest virtue in the world and misery the greatest sin . . . If I tried to write a really miserable story I think I should end up by committing suicide!

Mary Lutyens, who is now best known for her distinguished biographies, began to write romantic serials as Esther Wyndham in the late 1930s for *Woman's Weekly* and *Woman and Home*. She was invited by Winifred Johnson, one of the Amalgamated Press's editors, to contribute to these papers after her short story 'Mr Raymond Skedley and Miss Katherine N. Robinson' had been published in a compilation called *Forthcoming Marriages*. This conveyed first the current of the heroine's thoughts on her wedding morning, and then emotional incidents leading up to the ceremony later that day. Possibly without realizing it, the author had arrived at a satisfying balance of inner mood and outward expression that was extremely appropriate for the romantic genre.

Her heroines suffer the usual tremulous feelings of inadequacy that are stirred up by the challenge of relating to arrogantly handsome and enigmatic heroes such as the eponymous leading man of *Black Charles* (1952). Vivien fervently hopes that she is on the verge of becoming engaged to Peter Pendleton, but before this can be arranged she must be vetted by his 'cruel, domineering' half-brother, Charles, who is master of Coburn castle and its vast estates. She explains to her sympathetic friend Audrey that

> Peter is a typical Pendleton . . . that very fair hair with brown eyes – but once, every generation or so, a Black Charles suddenly appears, and . . . this Black Charles has always had the same sort of character. He has never had any children or got married, and he has always been arrogant and fierce. One of them, in the sixteenth century, was supposed to have committed murder – he murdered a woman who tried to marry him . . .

And, as if all this isn't enough to punch home the fact that Charles is a force to be reckoned with, we are told that he was a commando during the war and that there is a price on his head in Greece. Audrey nobly resolves that she will do battle with the daunting Charles if he tries to block her friend's happiness ('perhaps the feeling uppermost in her was the desire to show this proud, rude, arrogant man who hated women that she was not afraid of him, and could give as good as she got'). It is, of course, only a question of time and tenacity before this modern-day amalgam of Darcy and Rochester is tamed, and takes Audrey into his arms saying 'in a thick voice . . . "I love you, I worship you; you are my light, my love. . ."'

On the whole, even when overwhelmed by masculine magnetism (and the intensity of their own sexual feelings), Esther Wyndham's heroines are robust enough to uncover inner resources. Their independence and honest self-awareness mark them as forerunners of the intelligent and more individualized female protagonists who, two or three decades later, were to feature in the romantic suspense stories of Mary Stewart and Barbara Michaels (see Chapter 1).

Esther Wyndham has provided a lively account of the guidelines that *Woman's Weekly* romance authors were expected to follow, and this could have served as a blue-print for almost every magazine writer in the genre during the 1930s, 1940s and 1950s. In accordance with the formula insisted on by Winifred Johnson,

> one never penetrated the hero's mind until the end of the story, whereas every nuance of the heroine's feeling was revealed. In some stories she started by hating the hero because of his supposed arrogance until about instalment three when she began to feel drawn to him in spite of her better judgement. His behaviour was always a mystery to her. Disappointment and chagrin quickly followed those rare occasions when she felt he *cared*. There must invariably be another girl or older woman to make mischief out of jealousy, for it was only through misunderstandings on both sides that the couple could be kept apart for 70,000 words . . .
>
> The hero had to be brave, strong, rich, and frantically busy . . . The spirited heroine must not only have a wonderful way with children and old people but some previous tragedy or hardship in her life. And, of course, she had to work hard for her living.

She was also, apparently, not supposed to be absolutely beautiful except 'at rare moments . . . when the hero was looking at her without her knowing it. Naturally, she became permanently beautiful at the end when irradiated with requited love.'

Winifred Johnson would indicate the age of the heroine required for a particular story, and she never started to publish a serial until she had the complete text, although some years earlier this had not been the procedure. Esther Wyndham elaborates:

> The great Ethel M. Dell had then been writing serials for the Amalgamated Press, and in a late instalment of one story it transpired to the horror of the editor that the unwed heroine was going to have a baby. She searched frantically through previous instalments to see when this could have happened and found that the heroine had come back one day from a walk with the hero with

harebells in her hair. Thereafter the injunction ran through the office, 'No more harebells.'

... In one story when my hero was in Washington with the heroine, his secretary, and I had allowed her to sleep in the sitting-room of his hotel suite because all the hotels were full (a situation helpful to romance) Miss J. sent me a telegram, for I had gone abroad between instalments: ('Please make another effort to find Elizabeth a room of her own.') And when I was writing my first story . . . and I had made the hero say that he was feeling ill in order to get away from a party, she wrote indignantly, 'Who can have respect for a man who feels ill at a party?'

As the genre began to edge forward towards sexual explicitness, certain authors bridged the gap between old and new standards in their contributions to magazine fiction and trademark romances. Roberta Leigh (who also wrote as Rachel Lindsay, Rozella Lake and Janey Scott) produced stories for Harlequin and Mills and Boon from the early 1950s until the early 1990s. In 1954 *Woman's Own* serialized one of her romances which was subsequently published by Hutchinson and Harlequin in novel form as *And Then Came Love*. Keeping just within the respectable confines of its day, it nevertheless portrayed sexuality with a vividness that was to typify the more liberal approach that would soon be adopted by society – and authors – in the era of the Pill.

Stella Percy is a cool, aloof, Home Counties heroine: at twenty-seven she is being told by her mother that she ought to find herself a husband soon, and to be sure to marry money. Stella has never worked, except as a Wren at the tail-end of the war, and is 'bored to screaming pitch' with her aimless life. She would like to have become a professional pianist but there was insufficient money for her training. In contrast, Matthew Armstrong is a 'bluff, honest' Yorkshire industrialist who has plenty of 'brass' and is proud of the fact that this is the result of his own hard work. From the beginning Stella doesn't know how to cope with his straight-forwardness: he embarrasses her at the party where they meet by commenting that he fancies her, and by endorsing his remarks with exclamations such as 'Champion!' and 'Ba goom!' He even commits the social gaffe of trying to give her a present – which of course she refuses – of 'a packet of nylons' at their first encounter.

Matthew is determined to make Stella his wife and woos her, arrogantly but awkwardly. She is more drawn to another admirer, Charles Heyward, who, reserved and upper-crust, is unfortunately – like herself – short of financial resources. Despite her qualms about Matthew's 'crudeness', she can't help responding to his terrific masculinity, which Roberta Leigh puts across enthusiastically. When he proposes, bluntly and without preamble ('I've not led the life of a saint – I'm a man and I needn't say more – but there comes a time when that sort of thing isn't enough . . . I love you Stella. Will you marry me?') she explains that she isn't in love with him; she also hints at her general reserve about sexual matters by saying that, although Charles has been a friend for years,

'. . . there's never been anything very violent in our feelings for each other.'

'I couldn't have been friendly with you for long without it being violent,' Matthew said drily.

She flushed . . .

Stella agrees to marry Matthew partly in the hope that love may come later, but mainly because she fears that her young, easily led brother Adrian is sinking rapidly into a life of petty crime, and Matthew has promised to pay for his musical training if she becomes his wife. She *is* physically stirred by him but because he has 'a different outlook and background' despises herself for wanting him. Not, of course, the most propitious start for a marriage which sweeps her away to a rather bleak Yorkshire home, appropriately named Grey Walls, where Matthew's gaunt, 'big-boned' and generally unsympathetic sister, Jess, has been installed as housekeeper for some years. Stella insults Matthew terribly on their wedding night ('Leave me alone!' she panted. 'Don't touch me, I can't bear you!') and his response is, 'Never fear, I'll not come to you again unless you ask me.'

From then on, of course, she is tantalized by his physical proximity, longing for him – but too proud to say so. She taunts him in public and he punishes her by kissing her against her will with such passion that she is left a trembling mess – but he goes no further. Eventually, when he thinks (erroneously) that she is betraying him with Charles, he forces himself on her in a rape which takes place off-stage – striking echoes of Rhett Butler's last seduction of Scarlett in *Gone with the Wind:*

> Her protests were stifled as his lips crushed down on hers ... although she tried to force her mouth away, his lips would not leave hers, bruising the soft flesh with the insistence of his desire. Never had any man assaulted her senses like this, never had she been kissed with such naked passion. She reeled against him, half fainting as he picked her up in his arms, kicked open the door and mounted the stairs ...

This is no instant panacea for their relationship: Matthew feels he's behaved like a brute; Stella is totally confused. She saves his life in a car accident, but leaves him, and then realizing by now that she loves him deeply, returns. It is now Matthew's turn to be confused; he is still hurt and holding back from her, but unconsciously emanating macho sexuality (Roberta Leigh is really very good at conveying this). However, it is not long before all misunderstandings are cleared, and Stella is in his vigorous arms, 'tracing the line of the heavy brows and wide mouth' and whispering, 'Darling, darling, I love you! Never let me go.'

The era of unashamed husband-hunting in book and magazine fiction was given an up-to-date focus in 1967 by Berta Ruck, who had then been writing for over half a century (see Chapter 2) but tried resolutely to move with the times. Her *Shopping for a Husband* takes us into the world of marriage bureaux and dating agencies, and in the brisk, galloping style that the author adopted for her later books breathlessly reassures readers that there is as much romance in finding a spouse through a marriage bureau as in any other way: 'She turned and saw by his eyes that she did not look just like a film-star. She was a Queen. His.'

When Love was Like That, published in 1991, is a collection of romantic stories by Marie Joseph which originally appeared in magazines during the 1960s and 1970s. These are remarkably evocative of their period, and the heroines are perceptive and responsible. Love that stands the test of time and adversity is a popular theme, and so is that of looking for a husband. Girls were of course leading far more independent lives by then, with a reasonable range of career opportunities, but even at the purely financial level Mr Right could usually offer much more than the run-of-the-mill jobs available to heroines.

Story openings like that of 'What Kind of Girl Am I?' convey the mood:

> When you're twenty-five, and you've been in love four times, and each time it's come to nothing, and you live all alone and are considering acquiring a cat . . . well, it's time you admitted that you could have a problem.

Nevertheless, in some of the heroines the urge for independence is strong, as in 'Mr Fix-It': 'Being what was once called a helpless female had been no deterrent to my pipping three men at the post for my job as reporter on the local paper . . .'

Violet Winspear wrote prolifically for Mills and Boon and Harlequin from 1961 until the end of the 1980s. She was adept at providing the fast-paced, flamboyant romantic exploits that, on the surface at least, seem in keeping with the 'swinging sixties' and their transition into 'the permissive society' of the next two decades. Her forte is exotic foreign locations which emphasize the sharpness of response between heroines and heroes, who are generally so overwhelmed by the strength of their own feelings that they hide their passion for each other by engaging in intense psychological warfare or even physical violence. Her stories suggest that she is far from being a sentimentalist (see Chapter 5), and her comments about them endorse this:

> 'I don't really think that romantic novels should be called "romantic" . . . Between you and me, I think they're basically twisted sex stories. I mean, it is a bit sadistic, isn't it, to be reading about a man blowing his top with frustration because he can't get it . . .
>
> I have to make the heroine innocent and untouched. I try not to

make her too soppy . . .' (*Twentieth Century Romance and Historical Writers*)

Touches of this robust approach are evident in magazine fiction of the 1990s, which covers a far wider range of romantic and sexual experience than the conventional, domestically framed tales that were staple fare for so many years. For example, it is now by no means unusual for heroines to be unmarried mothers, as in 'The Secret' (for which no authorial by-line is shown) in the 1992 *Woman's Story Summer Special*:

'How did I, a woman bright enough to be a top-notch legal secretary, end up an unmarried mother when birth control was so easy to come by? I had discovered that thinking with your head is one thing, but feeling with your body and your heart is something altogether different.'

And, when he *does* come along at the appropriate moment, Mr Right is as likely perhaps to be a black Marxist as a British ex-Guards officer. In 'Dated' by Nikki Nielsen, *Woman's Realm Summer Fiction Special* (1992), the 'fiftysomething' widowed heroine, who is of course far more mature than would have been permitted a few decades ago, receives from a dating agency 'a questionnaire that the KGB would have been proud of' and optimistically gives the colour of her sun-tanned skin as 'golden-brown'. The agency then pairs her with a 'black gentleman' who, when he meets her, confesses that he was 'expecting a slightly darker shade of "golden-brown"'. He is gorgeous and they get along fine, but she is a little worried about introducing him to her extremely outspoken daughter, Amanda, who thinks the whole dating agency business is old hat, anyway. However, Amanda, suitably bowled over by her mother's attractive escort, says calmly, 'Welcome to the 1990s, Mum.'

CHAPTER TEN

Against the Tide

AS WE HAVE SEEN, despite its myriad variations the overwhelming flow of romantic fiction is concerned with the establishment of love and trust between women and men. Its basic theme is that of the traditional folk or fairy-tale – of boy meeting girl, of courtship and the overcoming of obstacles, of living together – hopefully – 'happily ever after'. There is, however, a small but significant stream of romantic literature which goes against the tide of popular opinion and widely accepted attitudes. Stories within this stream fall into several different categories, although passion and challenge are common to them all. Until recently the loudest and strongest voice of non-conformity within the love-story genre has been that of homosexual romance; more recently, the most ardent and articulate voice has been one of vengeance from women who have been mistreated by men. Sometimes, of course, these two strands come together.

The Well of Loneliness by Radclyffe Hall was originally published in 1928, legally banned as obscene before it could be widely distributed in this country and only once again made generally available when the ban was lifted in the more liberal postwar climate of 1948. It is the story of Stephen Gordon, a girl who feels fairly early in life that she is a misfit. The sexual ambivalence that alienates her from conventional society has been prophetically underscored by the fact that her father, wanting and indeed confidently expecting a son, has foisted a male name on her. *The Well of Loneliness* is concerned with Stephen's efforts to understand her own make-up and to achieve a satisfying romantic partnership with someone of her own sex. It has inevitably become something of a cult book, seen at one extreme as the 'bible' of lesbianism and at the other as a kind of 'jolly hockey-sticks' bad joke. Read with hindsight, it seems fraught with confusions between personal and general issues and even about the quintessential nature of the heroine's sexual identity; in many areas it is strident, unreasonable, short on humour, self-awareness and a sense of proportion. However, these failings have to be seen in the context of the mores of the period in which *The Well of Loneliness* was written: it remains an addictively gripping saga of love, frustration and limited fulfilment, and possibly still the greatest of all single-sex romance stories.

It provides no satisfactions for the prurient. Apart from kissing, which is described with varying degrees of warmth but without anatomical explicitness, sexual activity is never dwelt upon in any detail. Even when Stephen makes love for the first time with Mary Llewellyn, who is to become her first and only long-term partner, all we are told is that 'Stephen bent down and kissed Mary's hands very humbly, for now she could find no words any more – and that night they were not divided.'

Stephen has all the qualities required in a story's protagonist. She is a person of strength, intellectual capacity and discernment: also, for most readers, whatever their individual sexual inclinations, she has the undeniable physical magnetism that so often surrounds a character of vitality. It is easy to empathize with her high aspirations, her inherently trusting nature and her tragic disillusionments. What is difficult to accept is the fact that the compulsions of the story, which are so often splendidly conveyed, have to be unravelled from the polemic before the human drama can function at full throttle. Time and again the action of the plot and the integrity of relationships are jabbed at and jerked out of natural development by Radclyffe Hall's impassioned pleas for recognition by the 'normal' mainstream of society of the rights, status and basic human worth of those whose sexual orientation diverges from it. Her premise throughout is that lesbians are born, not made, and that for a homosexual to rail against his or her innate nature is a sin against God who created it: by extension, therefore, it must be a sin for those whose heterosexuality is equally pre-determined to condemn homosexuals for funtioning according to their genetic, God-given pattern.

In a sense, however, despite all the power and passion of her convictions, the author forces Stephen to apologize constantly for what she is. There is no narrative use of the words 'lesbian' or 'homosexual', and Stephen is referred to throughout as an 'invert', which of course immediately suggests something twisted and distorted. She is supposed to have a 'man's mind' (in other words, one that is more sharp and logical than a woman's!) in a female body, but we are also told that physically she is mannish with broad shoulders, narrow hips, 'thin flanks', large extremities and small breasts. Her tragedy is that she is attracted to non-lesbian women. Her love can only find fulfilment if these are bisexual, and even then it seems unlikely that they will opt for long-term liaisons with someone like Stephen whose consciousness of being an invert makes her fundamentally insecure.

Stephen is the only daughter of a rich and devoted couple who live in Morton, a great house with a large estate. Even in childhood she seems more mannish than girls who go through the fairly common period of tomboyishness. Ill at ease in skirts and at home in breeches, she enjoys vigorous outdoor occupations, most of all riding, and loves her horse, Raftery, with a fierce passion. Presumably this is symbolic of the fact that animals respond to humans without having any sense of gender-based divisions. Rather surprisingly for someone of her sensitivity she hunts with energy and enthusiasm until one fateful day when, soon after the death of her much-loved father, she is out with the chase and is overwhelmed by her sudden sight of the agonised and ruthlessly pursued fox. Stephen opts, instantaneously and for ever, out of the hunt and resolves never again to 'inflict wanton destruction or pain upon any poor hapless creature'. Later on, she is again to see that hunted look on the despairing faces of 'inverts' frequenting bleak Parisien bars when they have reached their bitterest ebb of rejection. By implication we know too that it is a look which one day will be seen in Stephen's own eyes . . .

She falls passionately but pitiably in love with a vain and shallow woman who, trapped in an unsatisfying marriage to a pretentious bigot, is at first flattered by Stephen's attentions but then most cruelly rejects these and exposes her to social stigma and humiliation. In the ensuing confrontation with her deeply shocked mother, Stephen realizes that as they will never be able to resolve their conflict, one of them has to go away and give up Morton. Chivalrously, although her home represents the only fulfilling and positive element in her life, she takes off for Paris and leaves her mother in possession.

In Paris she finds a few slightly kindred spirits but leads an emotionally aimless existence. She does, however, start with some success to pursue a career as a writer. The First World War engulfs her in a wave of bitterness as men rush off to fight, and women to nurse, while she feels that she can offer nothing. However, her patriotism does find an outlet when she joins a unit of women ambulance-drivers working on the western front. It is through this that she meets Mary, for whom at first she feels protectiveness, then a passionate longing which she thinks is destined to be frustrated. Mary decides otherwise. Young and vulnerable, she is sure that she wants above everything else to stay with Stephen after the war has ended. Stephen realizes that she must reveal the nature of her sexual identity which she has kept hidden:

> With Mary's kisses still hot on her lips, she must pay and pay unto the uttermost farthing. And because of an anguish that seemed past endurance, she spoke roughly; the words when they came were cruel. She spared neither the girl who must listen to them, nor herself who must force her to stand there and listen.

(Radclyffe Hall's language always has a tendency to become biblically archaic at moments of significance in the plot.) Mary's response to Stephen's impassioned revelation is simple and whole-hearted: 'What do I care for anything but you, and you just as you are . . . I love you! Can't you understand that all that I am belongs to you, Stephen?'

They settle in Paris where Stephen enjoys the stimulating company of 'fellow-inverts' with artistic tendencies of one kind or another, while Mary, feeling rather left out, looks after ·the domestic arrangements. One has a sneaking feeling that it is just a hiccup of fate that has made Mary become Stephen's lover, and that she would be more at ease as a conventional wife in an English suburban 'semi' than as the partner of a lesbian frequenter of the Paris *salons*. This, at any rate, is the view of Martin Hallam who, years earlier, had been attracted to, but rejected by, Stephen. He has come to Paris for medical treatment following severe war-wounds and contacts her again. He falls in love with Mary and presses home to Stephen his argument that what he has to offer the girl is far better than all that she, Stephen, can provide. For Mary's sake she decides to sacrifice the relationship by pretending that she is involved in an affair with another lesbian. Then predictably, her docile and discarded companion dashes away and into Martin's waiting arms.

Feeling utterly bereft, in a strange, nightmarish sequence Stephen hears the tortured cries and sees the 'marred and reproachful faces' of the 'inverts' who have abandoned their fragile hold on life through suicide or starvation because society has so callously rejected them:

> She raised her arms, trying to ward them off, but they closed in and in: 'You dare not disown us!'
>
> They possessed her. Her barren womb became fruitful – it ached with its fearful and sterile burden . . .
>
> 'God,' she gasped, '. . . rise up and defend us. Acknowledge us, oh God, before the whole world. Give us also the right to our existence!'

The story ends with that sentence, so we never learn what becomes of her. At one point, when the author shows Stephen in a moment of terrible anger, she describes her as 'grotesque and splendid, like some primitive thing conceived in a turbulent period of transition'. This phrase could, to a certain extent, be applied to the book itself.

Several periods of transition have in fact gone by since 1928 when *The Well of Loneliness* was written, and homosexual romances have strikingly changed. This is clearly shown in Joanna Trollope's *A Village Affair* (1989), which deals with a very different love affair between two women. Here we are no longer in the world of the 'born lesbian' of *The Well of Loneliness* but of women who are bisexual and have chosen lesbianism as an extension of their feminism, as the expression of strong affection for a particular person, or in some more haphazard way.

Alice Jordan, the central character of *A Village Affair*, seems happily married to Martin, who is well off if slightly dull. They have three children, Natasha, James and Charlie, and live in the Grey House, their dream home, in a picturesque village. Alice has everything to make her happy but she is restless and dissatisfied, out of sorts sexually with Martin and out of touch with the brightness of her early married life. She meets Clodagh, the lively but challenging daughter of a neighbouring family. At first Alice feels antagonistic towards her, but gradually she is intrigued: there is a quality about Clodagh which she cannot define but which gives her a sense of well-being. One idyllic day, when they are picnicking with the children, she listens to Clodagh's account of her recent love affair in America. Alice has already heard from her family that she had been living with a millionaire lawyer; she is fascinated to learn that 'he' was a woman. Clodagh goes on to explain that she has slept 'with boys and girls' and likes girls better: 'I don't like being dominated. If I did, I'd probably like sex with men more.'

She tells Alice about her 'New York job, amazing apartment and this besotted woman', and how she had eventually to leave her because she felt stifled by her possessivenees. Their confidences continue, endearingly interrupted by the children:

> Natasha came stumbling up the field to say that James had got river *in*side his wellingtons.

'Tell him to take them off and play in bare feet.' Alice was astonished her voice should sound so ordinary . . .

Joanna Trollope beautifully conveys the growing rapport and affection between the two women, and the richness of their individual personalities. Soon after the day of the picnic, when they are in the kitchen and have just finished the lunch-time washing-up, Clodagh tells Alice that she loves her, that meeting her really was a case of love at first sight. Alice is thrilled but unsure of her own responses, although she knows that she hates it when Clodagh goes out of the room, that everything she does with her is more fun, and that through her presence she somehow likes herself better. Clodagh suggests – but Alice at first rejects – bed: then

> Clodagh knelt and undid Alice's shirt and put her hands inside and then, after a few seconds, her mouth. Alice sat with her eyes closed. Relief flooded slowly, heavily through her, relief and release and a sensation of glorious blossoming, like a Japanese paper flower dropped into water and swelling out to become a huge, rich, beautiful bloom . . .

Clodagh makes it very clear that there is no question of one of them being the woman and the other playing the man: 'it's so great for us because we know what the other wants because we want it ourselves'.

The flowering of their relationship at every level, and the sheer joyousness of it, comes across very convincingly. It is how love between any two people should be, whether they are hetero or homosexual, or any gradation between. But difficulties creep in; Alice has to work out her future, and that of Martin and the children. Solutions are not easy, and she realizes eventually that she can live with neither Martin nor Clodagh because it would mean having to tow too many 'emotional leftovers' into whichever relationship she might chose. She needs a period of real freedom from them both . . .

Love between women is also sensitively probed in Elizabeth Jane Howard's Cazalet books (see Chapter 6) which, written in the 1990s, look back to the period of the Second World War and the year or so which preceded it. It is, of course, possible for authors writing retrospectively of the 1940s to discuss lesbianism far more frankly than any novelist could have done at the time. Although the upheavals of war blasted away many restrictions and prejudices, taboos on single-sex love retained their tenacity.

The saga begins with *The Light Years* when, in 1937, Rachel Cazalet is thirty-eight years old. She is unmarried, still lives at Home Place, the Sussex home of her well-to-do parents, and does not pursue a career of her own. However, she engages in charitable work, helping to organize a home for orphaned babies, and increasingly becomes the prop of her ageing parents and lynch-pin of the Cazalets' large country house and estate, which provides a refuge for several sprigs of the family during the war.

Rachel's unselfishness is constantly demonstrated. Apart from working to the point of exhaustion for her parents' well-being, she finds time for the psychological and physical concerns of the numerous young nephews and nieces who are esconced at Home Place 'for the duration'. The trouble is that in the process she neglects not only her own emotional needs but those of her long-devoted friend, Margot Sidney ('Sid').

Rachel cherishes her strong and special meeting-of-minds relationship with Sid but, despite her intelligence and sensitivity, is unaware of its full implications. Sid is a lesbian with a passionate nature who longs to share her life completely with Rachel. However, in previous heterosexual relationships Rachel has found 'that any kind of sexual intimacy revolted her', so Sid has to be content with occasional loving but chaste kisses and embraces – and the bitter knowledge that Rachel will never put her first until her filial duties come to an end. This, of course, will not be until her parents die. By the end of *Confusion*, the third novel in the series, Rachel is forty-six and still based in Sussex, whilst Sid is in London where she has spent the war years as an ambulance-driver. She is still disconsolately, and with waning hopes, waiting for Rachel to leave Home Place and come and live with her.

Not surprisingly, Sid has drifted into an affair with someone else in the meantime. Thelma, a young girl and a former music pupil of

Sid's, has what at first seems to be a schoolgirlish crush on her. But her feelings go far deeper. She shows her devotion by helping Sid domestically, always being supportive, understanding the nature of Sid and Rachel's relationship, and making herself scarce when Rachel is temporarily around.

Sid knows that she really loves Rachel and, although their chequered relationship offers little promise of deep fulfilment, is in conflict about what she sees as her disloyalty to Rachel in accepting Thelma as a lover. (It will be interesting to see if and how Sid's dilemma is resolved when the fourth and last volume of the Cazalet chronicle appears in 1995.)

'On the Verge', a story by Susanna Bowyer in Rosemary Stones's compilation, *Some Day My Prince Will Not Come* (1988), is an interesting exploration of sexual identity by two young girls, Anna and Carol, as its opening indicates:

> 'Carol, d'you ever wonder if you might be a lesbian?'
> I chucked the words over my shoulder, concentrating the heat that rose in my body into pedalling my bike harder down the busy country road. We rode in single file because of the traffic, so I couldn't see her face. Neither could she see mine, I was glad about that.

They hear from more knowing girlfriends that after they have had sex 'the world looks different and everything is utterly changed'. Anna is determined to find out if this is true – it is not, of course, because her first experimentation with a boy, who means virtually nothing to her, is fumbling and hurried, and interrupted by her mother. Carol, meanwhile, 'looks lovely' and glowing because she has met Cath, who is a lesbian, and has really enjoyed kissing her. At the end of the story Anna and Carol realize that they are beginning to sound rather like their mothers urging caution, as they warn each other to take the sexual business 'a bit easier now, not feel so desperate', as they have some idea of what it is like.

Lesbian Love Stories, edited by Irene Zahava (1989) deals with many facets of love between women. Few of these are 'happily ever after' tales, although several are about trust, faithfulness and fulfilment. There is also in-depth exploration of the sense of betrayal, loneliness and pain that comes in quarrels and break-ups. Some of the protagonists are closet lesbians; most are quite open about their sexual orientation; indeed, some are flamboyantly aggressive in their determination to display this to the world. One aim of the book is to show that 'we [lesbians] are everywhere', and according to the conditioning of the various individuals involved they call themselves dykes, feminists, butches or femmes.

There are stories of women being frightened off when another has declared her love; of older, menopausal women taking intense pleasure from the fact that they can relate to young females; of lesbians who despite intense affairs with women like to be married because they find this 'safe' and 'liberating'; of one girl making love to another in a Meditation Room of Clear Light under the unseeing gaze of a Buddha, their vibrations keeping in constant rhythm with the prayer-wheel, and so on. Most of the stories are by American writers and put across vitality and compassion, which is more than can be said for another homosexually inspired book from America, *Flesh and the Word: An Anthology of Erotic Writing* (1992), edited by John Preston. As he makes clear in his introduction, in his view 'pornography and erotica are the same thing'. Be that as it may, the moods of these stories, mostly about and aimed at gay men, differ markedly from those of the *Lesbian Love Stories* and certainly have little to do with love. Presumably the raw and frequently exploitative attitudes of the fictional protagonists in *Flesh and the Word* do have the intended effect of enriching some readers' sexual experience.

Oscar Moore's *A Matter of Life and Sex* (1991) has love interest spattered through its brutally candid, fatalistic text. It traces the story of Hugo, from adolescence, when he discovers his homosexual libido, until his eventual death from AIDS. For him sex is both an addiction and an absurdity; he knows that 'the sweets are poisoned' but, unable to change his promiscuous lifestyle, he becomes his own victim. Like an express train running into hell, he goes through syphilis and gonorrhea, then becomes HIV-positive. He has watched friends die from AIDS and knows what to expect when he develops it:

> this was a disease designed for gays ... playing confidence tricks before hitting below the belt. It was like being queer-bashed in the park after dark. Each blow came from somewhere new, and eventually, alone and crumpled, bloodied and bowed, you cried.

Not apparently from pain, shock or humiliation but from 'the exhaustion of keeping up the front' – a smiling face to friends – as another disease and another discomfort developed. It is just bearable to read about Hugo's suffering because the book's parabolic style removes the sense of immediacy and shifts thoughts and events from the individual to the general.

The tone of *After Delores* (1988) by Sarah Schulman is in complete contrast. Raunchy and sizzling with self-awareness even while she is broken up by the defection of her lover, Delores, the unnamed heroine goes out looking agressively for love. She finds it in some fashion with a Priscilla Presley look-alike and then with Punkette, a naively appealing go-go dancer who becomes a murder victim. There is some sex without tenderness in her encounters with more beautiful and more brutal lovers. Her search for Delores is an atmospheric journey into the underground clubs and back-alleys of New York's Lower East Side 'lesbian subculture'. It is witty, caustic and perceptive, and whatever the heroine might be unsure about, it certainly is not her sexual identity. As an acclamation of lesbianism, *After Delores*, sixty years on from *The Well of Loneliness*, vividly illustrates how attitudes have changed since the time when Stephen suffered such anguish about her then frustrated love.

It could be argued that some of the girls who become lesbians by choice (and not, as Radclyffe Hall indicated, by genetic inheritance) do so from romantic disillusionments with men. In fiction, of course, many women have been put in jeopardy by marriage or an adulterous affair: the eponymous nineteenth-century protagonists of Gustave Flaubert's *Madame Bovary*, Leo Tolstoy's *Anna Karenina* and Thomas Hardy's *Tess of the D'Urbervilles* come to mind as archetypal heroines who suffered the disastrous results of their own indiscretions and lack of judgement regarding men. They were judged and punished not for making tragic mistakes but for being 'sinful'. Such were the pressures of the societies they lived in that at a certain point even the strongest-minded woman could no longer stand against the tide of condemnation and retribution. A usual resource of the nineteenth-century heroine was to sink into grave or fatal illness; if she survived, it was as a broken woman, and very few were able to harness sufficient strength and inner resource to avenge themselves on the men who were responsible for their destruction.

As we have seen, gothic romances occasionally provided the exception to the rule, with tough – and sometimes crazed – females going about the business of planning and taking revenge with astounding ferocity and resolution. At the boundaries where pure gothics merged with romantic suspense stories, Louisa M. Alcott, and some other Victorian writers who were mainly notable for tales of sweetness and light, relished the creation of women avengers (see Chapter 1). At this distance it is hard to know whether these were motivated by suppressed feminism, by frustration or just explorative fantasy. What we do know is that over the last seven or eight years novels of female vengeance and retribution have become very much in demand.

Nancy Price's *Sleeping with the Enemy* (1986) is a chilling account of the extreme measures which a woman in jeopardy has to take to escape from a brutish and obsessional husband. Sara Burney is trapped in a nightmarish marriage to Martin, who beats, bullies and sexually humiliates her. His bouts of remorse when he is 'drunk enough to be sorry' are almost as awful as his violence: ' "I hit you," he crooned in her ear. "But you know I love you, don't you?" ' Peace offerings, predictably, are flowers and fetish underwear which she is expected to put on and parade around in immediately for his benefit:

> Sara got her legs through the teddy pants and pulled the top up; it
> stretched to fit her and was made to show her nipples through the

top lace and her pubic hair through the bottom ... Sara stood in
the kitchen doorway and turned slowly to show the teddy's lace and
black silk and the red-blue bruises on her hand and down the backs
of her legs, the yellow-green ones on her arms and breasts.

'Great!' Martin said, and went to get a glass for his wine ...

She has to concoct and carry out a desperate plan to get away
from him, because he has threatened to catch and kill her if she
ever tries to leave him. There is a macabre satisfaction in the
calculation and courage with which she does this; it involves her
own mock-death and then the assumption of a completely new and
disguised identity in another, distant town. The fact that she has to
give up everything – home, friends, financial security, even her
driver's licence and social security number – stresses the starkness
of her situation. She begins to build a new life and slowly her
natural liveliness reasserts itself. She even finds a man whom she
can love and trust.

Then the horror begins again. Martin's suspicions are aroused,
he realizes that he has been the victim of a clever ruse and, mad
with fury, tries to track her down. He is determined to carry out
his threat of killing her. The pursuit is dramatic and suspenseful:
Sara hears that a prowler is in the neighbourhood and senses that
it must be Martin. Once again she seems to be trapped, but
fortunately a twist of fate makes Martin his own killer, so he is
removed from Sara's world for ever.

Sleeping with the Enemy derives some of its power from our
knowledge that it is all too true to life. Some other recent novels
about women who are in danger or who are suffering marital
exploitation strike notes which alternate between realism and
fantasy. In *Nice Girls* (1993) by Claudia Crawford, three friends,
Georgina, Mona and Amy, live together in London during the
'swinging sixties'. Rich, dishy and completely faithless Nick Albert
is supposed to be engaged to Georgina, but he makes love in secret
to all three girls, each of whom is completely captivated by him.
Thereafter their friendship seems to be cemented by a shared wish
to make him suffer for his sexual betrayals. He escapes retribution

by marrying a millionaire's daughter and taking himself right out of their orbit. Mona and Amy find new lovers, but twenty years later Nick returns and, now free again, tries to persuade Georgina to marry him. It doesn't happen, of course, but we do learn the secret of his romantic success:

> 'Let me look at you.' That was Nick's secret. He loved women, and let them know it. Women recognized that intuitively. They wanted more from him than he could give, things like honesty and responsibility, when what he had to give was rarer than both.

Throughout the book, Nick's extraordinary charm frequently deflects the girls from their retributive purposes.

Female solidarity against the male is more effective in Hilary Bailey's *In Search of Love, Money and Revenge* (1990). Annie Vane, who starts out ambitious and affluent, suddenly finds herself in the same boat as Vanessa Doyle, a struggling working-class woman, who is the mother of two small children. Each is unexpectedly deserted by her husband. Annie has helped Julian to build up his business, but, contemplating divorce and a second marriage, he has connived to deprive her of both her company directorship and her half-share of their money, home and possessions. Vanessa is threatened with violence by her philandering husband, Geoff, if she sues for divorce and a fair settlement. Annie and Vanessa link up and, although they have no money, manage to take over a run-down café and built it into a thriving concern. They eventually graduate to running a smart West End restaurant and take into their partnership a teenager, Melanie Pickering, who has been sleeping rough after escaping from her father's abuse. Together they achieve their three goals of love, money and revenge – and, of course, something more: their own strong friendship.

Another vigorous gang of girls who make their husbands wish they had behaved more caringly is at the centre of Olivia Gold-smith's *The First Wives Club* (1992). When their friend Cynthia commits suicide because her husband Gil wants a divorce, Elise, Brenda and Annie decide to take drastic action:

Brenda asked, 'Are we talking about revenge, I mean Death Wish III here, or what?'

'Not exactly revenge. Something more sophisticated, I thought. Like justice,' Elise said.

They are acting in their own interests as well as Cynthia's. Each woman has been a loving wife, and although crucial to her husband's business achievements, has been discarded in favour of the 'newer, taller, blonder second wife' recognized by 'corporate culture' as 'more than an asset', a necessity in fact, 'the trophy of the fifty- and sixty-year-old businessman's success'. To add insult to injury, the men are lavishing money on their ego-boosting glamorous second wives but giving their first wives and families only parsimonious allowances.

Elise, Brenda and Annie decide to form a First Wives Club to bring about the downfall of 'the jerks'. The question is, *how*. Brenda suggests castration but this is dismissed as 'too messy' until Elise decides that there may be a way of effecting it without shedding any blood: 'Let's find each man's soft spot. They're certainly not invulnerable. And then let's go for it.'

They plan to make the punishment fit the crime in each case: they want to see Gil (the dead Cynthia's callous, entrepreneurial husband) stripped of power, Morty 'dead broke', Aaron 'abandoned and betrayed', and Bill 'put to pasture. *Finito* as a lover boy'. Needless to say, all their goals are achieved with panache.

Sally Beauman's *Destiny* (1987) is a darkly glittering tangle of sex, money, exploitation and power. Helen Craig, at sixteen, sees both her mother and her young boyfriend, Billy, ruined and indirectly killed by Ned Calvert, a local big-shot who lives on his wife's money in a large and landed house. Helen leaves her American home town for Europe, embarks upon a fairy-tale romance with Edouard de Chavigny, whom she meets by chance in Paris, but suddenly leaves him when she finds herself pregnant, thinking that the baby must be Billy's. (However, her arithmetic is incorrect! Her daughter turns out to be Edouard's but Helen does not realize this until the child is older and has developed a startling resemblance to her father.)

Edouard does not know Helen's real name but is determined to find her again. Meanwhile, she builds up a career as a movie-actress, eventually becoming a star, which of course helps her French lover to locate her. She is in part goaded to success by her desperate desire to be revenged upon the perfidious Calvert. Five years after leaving America she returns. By secretly buying his mortgages and foreclosing, she dispossesses him of his estate (his well-off wife has now left him) and gives herself the pleasure of going to see him and telling him why. She and Edouard are re-united and their love seems like something out of this world.

It is of course made even more lustrous than in Helen's wildest imaginings, partly because each partner is fabulously rich. Edouard runs an internationally celebrated jewellery and accessory business and they live amongst lush decor with brilliant trappings such as Givenchy gowns and Rolls Royce cars which are lovingly described in the text. They marry and have more children, but Edouard's huge bubble of happiness bursts when he discovers from old family papers that his relationship with Helen is incestuous. To protect her, he destroys the evidence and then kills himself in a motor crash – which all goes to show that even the incredibly beautiful and extremely talented Helen cannot have everything she wants. As well as vengeance and the unfolding of Helen's and Edouard's romance, there is a lot of torrid passion from other couples with more than usual emphasis, perhaps, on cock-sucking and semen-swallowing to titillate readers' taste-buds.

Sally Beauman's other block-buster is *Dark Angel* (1990). Though not primarily a vengeance novel, it is a three generational saga of passion, deceit and intrigue, with power and enmities projected from one generation to the next.

At one time during the early 1980s Janet Dailey, in common with Barbara Cartland, was one of the five best-selling novelists in the world, and not just of the romance genre. Her popularity continues into the 1990s with most of her books being published by Mills & Boon, Harlequin and Silhouette. These are the standard ten-chapter, fast-paced trademark romances (with the secondary details about characters and settings necessarily cut to the bone), bursting with 'physical chemistry', 'ardent fires' and stop-go relationships between strong men and – at first – slightly reluctant women.

Her longer books are far richer in character and atmosphere, especially those with ranching backgrounds such as her four-volume Calder saga. With *Rivals* (1989), she probes the very different world of big business and the relationship of an arrestingly good-looking and highly talented couple, Flame Bennett and Chance Stuart. They fully live up to the back-cover blurb: Flame is 'as fiery as her copper-red hair, yet as cool as her clear green eyes', while Chance's 'dark good looks, electric blue eyes and devastating charm have made him supremely sure of himself'. He is also a 'multi-millionaire real estate magnate' who has 'come a long way from an unhappy, poverty-stricken childhood'. Both are 'ambitious, successful and sought-after' in glittering and glamorous circles.

The by-products of their and other characters' business successes are indicated by the quality of the artefacts which adorn the text: 'sleek limousines, Rolls Royces and Mercedes' for example, and lots of designer-label clothes and accessories; Saint Laurent, de Ribes, Ungaro, Valentino, Blass, Fendi and Bulgari are represented, while it is obvious from the opulent wraps Flame sidles into and out of so sensuously that the anti-fur lobby has made little progress so far in San Francisco.

When Flame and Chance first meet, the attraction between them is breathtaking: he assesses her as 'a woman all the way through – all lace and legs', and her 'overall impression' of him is 'that of a lean and rangy black panther, coiled energy held in check, ready to spring at a second's warning'. They quickly become lovers in a fervent session which Janet Dailey describes with her customary verve and explicitness, from the first 'finger-tip gliding down the slender arc of her throat' to the final consummation when there is 'an illusion of the world spinning' as he wraps his arms around her, 'not letting her go anywhere without him'. Their romance

256

stays on course and they marry, but ecstasy then becomes clouded with suspicion. Flame inherits Morgans Walk, a vast estate which Chance has been after for development, but which Flame's family, because of an old feud, never want to fall into the clutches of a Stuart. She becomes convinced that Chance has married her only in order to acquire Morgans Walk; bitter misunderstandings, rivalries and personal vendettas build up between them, and they separate. In the end, when their relationship has reached its nadir (and she thinks he is trying to kill her), he saves her life, at great risk to his own. Happily, both survive the experience with only superficial damage to their fetching features and physiques; they agree that Morgans Walk should be deeded to the State – 'maybe for a park' (Flame and Chance are so rich that they can easily ditch it), and their romance seems all set to rise phoenix-like from the ashes of their rivalry, as he reassures her that 'It's never too late, Flame, if we don't want it to be.'

As its title suggests, Frances Edmonds's *Samson and Delilah* (1993) is a tale of deeper and darker suspicion between husband and wife. Sir Roger Samson, the head of the ever-extending business empire, Samson International, woos and weds the beautiful and intelligent Delilah Dooley ('Lilah'). She adores her handsome, suave, enigmatic, power-house husband but suspects murky goings-on in his business and private dealings. Gradually her suspicions are confirmed; she finds out about his ruthless destruction of people and organizations in shady financial deals, his betrayal of her by having affairs and the fact that he was responsible for the death of his brutal father. Carefully and systematically helped by one or two associates and a past and would-be future lover, she builds up the evidence which will destroy Roger (and incidentally put her in charge of his companies), but undergoes great torment in the process. She cannot stop loving him and is torn almost until the end between a passionate desire to save him and the urge to avenge herself and others who have suffered at his hands. The climax comes convincingly at a shareholders' meeting when her vote is crucial – and men from the Serious Fraud Office, alerted by her, are waiting in the wings to arrest Samson . . .

Fay Weldon's *The Life and Loves of a She Devil* (1983) can hardly be categorized as a romantic novel but should be commented on in passing as it is surely the ultimate in female vengeance fantasies. Mordant, implacable and blackly comic, it examines the interplay of power, identity and wealth between sexual partners who are breaking up. Ruth, the protagonist – she can hardly be called a heroine – has a rough deal from her petty but ambitious accountant husband, Bobbo. She is huge, plain and clumsy, physically and psychologically. He married her only because she was expecting their child, and made it clear to her by the fourth month of her pregnancy that theirs was to be 'an open marriage' ('We must see it as a starting point, not a finishing line'); in other words, he intends to play around whenever and with whomsoever he likes. Ruth tries despairingly and fails lamentably to conform to the conventional domesticated wifely image, and, of course, Bobbo blames her for everything that is off-key in their marriage. She takes comfort from licks of her babies' ice lollies and in reading romantic novels, 'amongst them those by Mary Fisher'. Ironically this author, who like the heroines of her books is small, fair and fluffily pretty, meets Bobbo at a party, asks him to take over her accounts – and becomes his mistress.

After a disastrous evening when, entertaining his parents, Ruth appears to mishandle everything, Bobbo takes off to stay with Mary for what he pretends will be a brief period, but the next day he tells Ruth he wants a divorce. He also says just before he goes, 'You are a bad mother, a worse wife and a dreadful cook. In fact I don't think you are a woman at all. I think what you are is a she-devil!'

At this point the story shifts from satire to sheer fantasy: Ruth really does seem to be taken over by demonic and ferociously potent forces and, as a she-devil, lets loose all hell and embarks on fulfilling all the malevolent aspirations of her lengthy build-up of hate. By bizarrely foul means she eventually succeeds in ruining her rotten, complacently adulterous spouse and his inamorata, and turns herself into a woman of confidence and power. Her transformation is not only psychological but physical; when she opts for a new face and body she re-creates herself as a Mary Fisher look-alike (the conventional concept of the 'blond bimbo'), using facial and bodily surgery as well, presumably, as supernatural methods. (There seems a strange contradiction here between her wielding of aggressively feminist powers and her behaving like a woman who is conditioned by commercial pressures to have nose-jobs, cosmetic dentistry, breast and buttocks remoulding, and so on.) Ruth has become just about the most successful avenging bad angel in fiction, but somewhere along the line of her intensifyingly diabolical retribution we become fearful about laughing with her while she so viciously turns the tables on Bobbo and Mary, and we begin to sneak over to their side.

CHAPTER ELEVEN

Nursing Angels from the Nineteenth Century to the NHS

THE HOSPITAL story as a branch of the romance genre did not come fully into its own until the 1950s. This, presumably, was because only after the establishment of the National Health Service in 1948 did regular medical and hospital treatment become part of most people's lives. Before then, visits to doctors and dentists were, at least for the working classes, restricted to the absolute minimum for financial reasons. From the 1950s on, nurses and doctors became more accessible in both fact and fiction than they had been to the general public in the pre-Second World War years. By the early 1970s, no fewer than eight British publishers were producing hospital romance series, and in the early 1990s, there is no noticeable reduction of the number of titles issued which have the simplistic nurse-meets-and-eventually-ensnares-doctor theme. It is significant that in popular hospital romances doctors are nearly always male, and nurses female. There are the occasional women doctors – many of whom, from the nurse-heroine's viewpoint, are 'baddies' – but generally speaking, emotional tales with a medical background are more firmly rooted in the domestic husband-hunting ethos than in the feminist approach to careers.

Long before hospital stories became so much in demand there were, of course, highly charged fictional vignettes of girls and young women dedicatedly nursing their husbands, fiancés, fathers, brothers or cousins back to health and strength after they had suffered severe illness or accident. Their ministering-angel roles, however, were temporary (and unpaid) rather than vocational. In the early and extremely influential romantic novel, *The Heir of Redclyffe* by Charlotte M. Yonge, (see Chapter 2) the modest, soft-natured heroine Amabel ('Amy') becomes nurse not only to a wayward cousin, Philip, who as a result of her tender attentions recovers from an intense bout of malaria, but also to her new and beloved husband, Guy, who succumbs to the fever and dies with a beautiful smile and a religious adage on his lips, while Amy wipes his brow and, at the appropriate moment, closes 'the dark fringed eyelids'. *The Heir of Redclyffe* was published in 1853, and only a year or so later images of the noble and dedicated female nurse were further enhanced by popular fantasies about the 'Lady with the Lamp' of the Crimean War. In fiction at least the girls who soothed fevered masculine brows were sweet and pretty young things, and for decades their real-life role model, Florence Nightingale, was fancifully fitted into this mould. As late as 1939, in Helen Dore Boylston's *Sue Barton – Student Nurse*, a nonagenarian patient who had been a drummer-boy at the Battle of Balaclava recalls, 'I seen her ... dressin' our wounds – hours at a stretch – lovely young thing – she was – slim – an' gentle ...' In fact the redoubtable Florence was over thirty when she went to the Crimea, and somewhat on the stout side.

Thirty-five years after Amy had wrung the hearts of thousands by her ministrations to her doomed husband, another fictional nurse began to acquire a large following. Hilda Wade was created by Grant Allen in a serial for the *Strand Magazine* of March 1899, and she achieved celebrity partly because, after the untimely death of her originator, the last chapters of her story were written for the *Strand* by Arthur Conan Doyle (whose Sherlock Holmes had been launched only eighteen months earlier but was already well on the way to cult status). Hilda was not only unusual in being a *professional* nurse but seems to have been the very first minstering-angel-sleuth in popular fiction. While attending conscientiously to her many and varied medical cases, she is also striving to prove the innocence of her dead father who has been wrongly condemned as a murderer.

This process frequently takes her out of London hospital wards into remote regions of Tibet, India and South Africa; it also involves her in a fulfilling love affair and eventual marriage with Hubert, the steadfastly admiring young man who narrates the story. Fortunately Hilda approaches her nursing more systematically than her sleuthing: she measures out medicines and prepares injections strictly according to the book, but in the business of detection despises the police force for relying on 'clumsy clues', and works through 'the deepest feminine gift – intuition', plus a photographic memory and 'a mesmeric kind of glance' that throws criminal connivers instantly off-course.

After the hypnotic, hunch-pursuing Hilda, the next fictional heroine to stir readers profoundly with her nursing dedication was the Honourable Jane Champion in Florence Barclay's *The Rosary* which was published in 1909. Jane becomes a full-time nurse-companion to the man she loves, the handsome artist Garth Dalmain, after he has been blinded in a shooting accident (see Chapters 2 and 4). It transpires that she is not the lady of leisure we have previously imagined her to be but a 'trained nurse' who acquired her professional skills 'during the [Boer] war'.

Another Edwardian young woman who was prompted to take up nursing for emotional reasons (to overcome the anguishes of a broken heart) was Emily in Mary E. Mann's *The Parish Nurse* (1905). Her experiences as visiting nurse to the poor and needy are generally unsavoury and often unintentionally comic. It is bad enough to have to treat the villagers' boils, sores and blisters in a positively wholesale way, but far worse to have to cope with a senile old gent who dons his dead spouse's frothy nightcap and tries to commit suicide by hitting himself on the head with a hammer. Not surprisingly, Emma soon loses sympathy with these representatives of 'the undeserving poor' ('I hate the smell of them, the touch of them') and abandons nursing for matrimony when the local squire proposes.

Nursing stereotypes were to crop up in magazine stories and novels of the First World War when, of course, the country needed every trained – or unskilled but enthusiastic – nurse that it could get. Even adventurous and undomesticated heroines such as the eponymous *Beryl of the Biplane* by William Le Queux (1917) had temporarily to abandon exciting exploits and turn their hands to nursing when wounded fiancés or husbands needed their soothing touch.

The most famous fictional Great War nursing heroine was created retrospectively by Ernest Hemingway in *A Farewell to Arms* (1929). Frederic Henry, a tough-living, hard-drinking American volunteer ambulance-driver with the Italian army, meets Catherine Barkley when she is working at a British hospital fairly near the front line. She is tall, blonde and beautiful, with 'a tawny skin and grey eyes'. Her fiancé was killed at the Battle of the Somme, and she feels that she was 'a fool' not to have married or had sex with him before he died. She and Henry are mutually attracted from the moment they first see each other, and their instant rapport permits mutual confidences which are unusually frank for the time. They quickly become lovers (although he is in a hospital bed suffering from severe trench mortar-shell wounds), and there is an extraordinary completeness about their relationship, in spite of the fact that he is jaded and world-weary while she almost glows with unaffected innocence.

Catherine is, of course, exactly the sort of woman that Hemingway's macho heroes want – passionate but serenely submissive: as she tells him very soon after they meet, 'I want what you want. There isn't any me any more ... You're my religion. You're all I've got.' Her nursing is relegated to the background of her life; she discovers that she is pregnant, and when Henry is threatened with arrest by the Italian 'battle police' for taking part in a retreat, the lovers escape and live in idyllic isolation in a simple Swiss lakeside chalet, surrounded by forests, mountains, terraced vine-yards and meadows. As well as sitting around and talking endlessly, they do a lot of drinking (unwise for Henry who has only recently had an acute and very painful bout of jaundice brought on by excessive intake of alcohol, and surely irresponsible of Catherine who will soon be giving birth).

The extraordinary thing about *A Farewell to Arms* is that romance flows constantly from its heart and pores, although Hemingway describes everything in apparently terse and certainly unsentimental language. Catherine does call Henry 'darling' but he tells her so earthily and so often that she is 'a grand' and 'a fine' girl that one almost expects his next endearment to be that she is a good bitch or a great filly. Their relationship unfolds from a very male-oriented viewpoint: her calm passivity is unruffled even when she learns that he has had gonorrhea, and, when she is suffering really hellish labour pains, she still tries to conform to the image of being 'a good wife' and having 'this child without any foolishness'.

In the end, all their passion and power comes to nothing: their child – a boy – is stillborn, and Catherine survives him only briefly. She knows that she is dying but characteristically accepts this in a very low-key way ('I'm not afraid. I just hate it') although, with an unusual show of spirit she urges, 'You won't do our things with another girl, or say the same things, will you?'

For a few moments before she dies, Henry prays despairingly to the God in whom he does not believe to save her. When she is gone, all emotion drains away. He goes back into her room, but it is 'like saying goodbye to a statue', and soon afterwards he leaves the hospital and walks away 'in the rain'.

It seems bleakly ironic that a nurse who so often helps to save life should die young and in childbirth, as Catherine does. It is certainly extremely unusual in the love-story genre. The romanticism of Catherine and Henry's relationship has retained its impact over the decades: it was enhanced by Hollywood's two filmed versions of the novel, starring Helen Hayes and Gary Cooper in 1933, and Jennifer Jones and Rock Hudson in 1957. There are fascinating resonances between *A Farewell to Arms*, Hemingway's First World War romance, and his saga of the Spanish Civil War, *For Whom the Bell Tolls* (see Chapter 8).

Predictably, nursing stories achieved prominence during the period of the Second World War. In *Peg's Paper* the nursing image ('Darling, you look an angel in that VAD kit') seemed distinctly more popular than that of the women's services with their undertones of masculinity. True to the paper's melodramatic traditions, even down-to-earth nurses encounter daunting emotional upsets. In Kitty Lorraine's 1939 serial, *War-Bride*, for example, Ann Fenner goes to work in a French military hospital, marries Charles Miller, a handsome, wounded soldier, but finds that he not only flirts on their wedding night with a local girl of dubious reputation but is then arrested as Carl Müller, a Nazi spy. In quieter vein, *Woman's Weekly* started a series in 1940 entitled *The Cases of Nurse Kay*, by Margaret Baumann. The heroine is a golden-haired district nurse called Stella Kay, and each week's story is a domestic episode in which the sunny-natured nurse helps patients not only with their physical difficulties but also with knotty problems of a personal nature. A typical story features Leila Dayre who, just past the first flush of youth, lives alone in a large house left to her by her parents. She often thinks of getting a job, as money is tight and she is in need of some outside interests: she feels lonely rattling around in the old home. She fancies Gordon, the bachelor who lives next door but he gives her little encouragement, mainly because he thinks she is besotted by her pet Pekinese, Princess Cham-Su of Greenhill, and doesn't quite see where he would fit into the *ménage*. Stella Kay solves Leila's problems when, treating her for a bruised shoulder and lacerated ankle after she has been knocked over by a car, she persuades her to let the village girls' keep-fit class use one of her large empty rooms. Cocoa and girlish chat afterwards do much to make the lonely Leila feel that she really does have a place in village life:

> Each day her progress continued. She was learning to *look outwards*, and the world upon which her newly opened eyes now gazed was a place of beauty and adventure. How it would be without Nurse Kay's regular visit to inspire her, she dare not think . . .

In fact Nurse Kay has worked out the next therapeutic steps: without Leila's knowledge, she and Gordon have been looking after Princess Cham-Su, who ran away when her mistress had her accident. This manoeuvre serves a double purpose: it enables Leila, who is at first distraught with worry, to learn that life goes on even without an imperious Peke at its centre, and it makes Gordon get to know – and love – her pet. He secretly grooms and enters Cham-Su for a show, in which she carries off the most coveted prizes. Armed with these and accompanied by the proudly strutting Peke, he walks into Leila's house and proposes. Nurse Kay knows the deep satisfaction of a job well done. All the stories in which she stars are in this homely vein and they are actually very short on medical detail, even when Stella pays occasional visits to the big hospital in which she took her training. From fairly early on in the saga she responds wistfully but without any immodest show of physical passion to Michael Cheston, the local GP, whose interest in her appears to be purely professional. It is a trifle hard to know what she sees in this 'bearish and impatient' young man, although he does sometimes soften his caustic comments by 'teasingly twinkling' his eyes. Fully humanized, eventually, by proximity to Nurse Kay, he makes her his wife and helpmeet, and together, in those pre-National Health Service days, they greatly improve the physical and psychological lot of almost every member of their little country community. Other nursing stories in *Woman's Weekly*, *Woman's Sphere*, *Woman's Illustrated* and *Woman* during the 1930s and 1940s were similarly cosy in their orientation, whether the heroine was a mature and apparently dragonish ward sister or a pretty and eager young probationer.

In contrast, the hospital romances which began to flourish in the 1950s, while still concerned with the sweetening of the nursing ethic and the whitewashing of the most distasteful aspects of life on the wards, introduced a sense of realism. They inundated readers with medical detail, jargon and daunting strings of initials. Even the least hospital-oriented of us can cope imaginatively with props like kidney bowls and bandages and suddenly erected bed-screens, but we are likely to remain mystified by references to pre-eclamptic toxaemia or aortic aneurysm, ETA, PTS, EMS, d.o.t., OPD, SSO, and so on.

Lucilla Andrews did not exactly create the modern nurse and doctor romantic drama but she has done a great deal to shape and influence it. Her first books appeared in the mid-1950s and they continued into the 1980s. She trained as a nurse in London during the Second World War and writes from the benefit of considerable and diverse practical experience, keeping scrupulously up to date with new medical techniques and treatments and pulling few punches about the grislier aspects of hospital life – blood, guts, vomit, incontinence – and the process of dying. Most of her stories are set in large military or teaching hospitals (*After a Famous Victory* (1984) and *One Night in London* (1979) are typical examples), but she also likes to use remote or unlikely backgrounds (*In Storm and Calm* (1974), for instance, features North Sea oil rigs).

In *After a Famous Victory*, a year after the Battle of El Alamein has been won by the Allies, its effects are still being felt in the male orthopaedic ward of a hospital in southern England. The dramas of death and doctoring are seen from the viewpoint of Nurse Rose Weston, a young war-widow, and VAD Sue Kirby, who lives with the insecurity of her bomber-pilot husband being on regular night ops. Like their dreadfully wounded patients, they are also victims of the war. Lucilla Andrews's own experiences of nursing duties during the 1940s give authenticity and atmosphere to their struggles against appalling overwork and weariness, lashings of red tape and, of course, wartime shortages. Unlike the more light-hearted hospital romances which were being issued at the time in series by Mills and Boon, romantic moments in *After a Famous Victory* are restrained, with no snatched kisses in the sluice or amorous innuendo in the operating theatre. It is only at the end of Lucilla Andrews's novel that love between Rose and Joe Arden, a firmly middle-aged and unglamorous-looking surgeon, flowers. Both are still anxious to retain their professional dignity and their hospital's reputation, though the demands of passion can no longer be denied:

'I must – ' he added with a tremor in his deep voice, 'get us away from this damned public place before I lose what's left of my sanity and provide an item for tomorrow's papers that'll give MO I a field-day . . .'

The author points out on several occasions that nurses and doctors frequently marry each other because they are too busy and bound up with their work to meet any appropriate partner from outside it. (She herself married a doctor!) She suggests that in the tightly enclosed, hot-house atmosphere of a teaching hospital, where '90 per cent of the medical and nursing staff will be under thirty and single, sex will flourish openly'. She goes on to say that conflict will also be inevitable, and that this is the essence of drama and 'good copy'.

There is no doubt that the vicarious experience of traumas such as shattered limbs, exposure to chemical poisoning, brain injuries and agonising abdominal upsets provides readers with thrills and chills which they can enjoy in the cosy security of feeling well, warm and unthreatened in their own homes. As well as books, long-running TV soaps and semi-documentaries from *Dr Kildare* and *Emergency Ward 10* to *Casualty*, and *'Jimmy's'* have dramatized, sanitized and glamorized the whole business, while also stressing the 'it-could-happen-to-you' element which makes for strong identification. (It will be interesting to see whether the tongue-in-cheek nature of recent TV series such as *Surgical Spirit* and *Health and Efficiency* will have any impact on the hospital novel.)

In the various Mills and Boon, Hurst and Blackett, Robert Hale, Arrow and Fontana series, there are common themes in the essential elements of the nurse and doctor love-story: the misunderstandings that dog their personal relationships (which are in the main simplistic echoes of the whole husband-hunting ethos of the romance genre in general), dramas of dire accident or illness, the skill and team-work of the surgical team, and the basic 'ordinariness' of the nurses and patients (though not of the doctors, who have to be lean, long-fingered, alert, intelligent, adept, sensitive, craggy, sexy – and, of course, male).

During the 1950s and 1960s the kiss was still the pinnacle of the expression of sexual passion in the hospital romance. Nurse heroines waited longingly for doctor heroes to make the appropriate moves – it was not, of course, up to the females whose roles were supportive of the males both in and out of the hospital framework to take the initiative here. When it eventually came, the kiss between medicos was well worth waiting for:

Then he ran his long, sure fingers into my hair and began to kiss me ... It was a long kiss ... It began with a gentle brush of his lips, and then the current steadily surged until there were drum rolls and flashes of scarlet and gold, and somewhere, I could have sworn, there was a full orchestra poised ready to play the Ravel *Bolero* ...

At a less inflated level, one should mention that in hospital novels the care and trust between nurse and patient also often results in romance and matrimony. In fiction if not always in fact to become an SRN or a SEN is a guarantee of ensnaring a good husband.

There has been little development in the hospital romance from the 1960s to the 1990s. In Jane Arbor's *Desert Nurse* (1963), Martha Shore, a trained nurse and midwife, takes a job in an 'up-country outpost' of Saudi Arabia primarily because she wants to forget Greg Ryder, as their affair has traumatically broken up. Her new employer, Dr Jude Tarleton, who runs his own hospital piloting schemes for fighting 'killers' such as malnutrition, malaria, bilharzia and cholera, makes it a pre-condition of Martha's job that she should have no romantic ties. This turns out to be awkward because she quickly becomes desperately attracted to Jude. She has to cope with the rivalry of Naomi, who, also from England, turns out to be the traditional bitchy vamp of the genre and has her claws well into Jude by the time Martha arrives. All, in the end, is well; it transpires that Jude's extreme arrogance and rudeness towards Martha are simply a cover-up for his vulnerability (in the past he has been duped and betrayed by women) and the fact that he responded sexually to her from the moment when he interviewed her in London for the job. Even so, for someone who occupies a position of such responsibility and status, he does seem to behave uncaringly. Without much warning he takes Martha in his arms; they cling 'together in a kind of drowning urgency', and his hands are 'rough about her hair, the line of her jaw, her throat', and her back, as he presses the 'unyielding curve of her body to the tautness of his own'. She doesn't want to check 'the torrent of passion ... in his searching lips and in the response of her own, answering kiss for kiss ... she could not count the cost of surrendering to it, of giving ... with every fibre in her'. But brutally and anti-climactically, he then suddenly thrusts her aside and tells her dismissively that she is in no 'danger' from him: 'It happened, but it's finished . . . it never even began in any way either of us need remember.' At this point, despite being tremendously attracted to Martha, he thinks she is as hard and scheming as all those frightful females he has previously had the misfortune to tangle with. However, Martha's marvellously dedicated medical work eventually convinces him that she is a worthy partner, both professionally and romantically.

Desert Nurse was published by Mills & Boon, who in the 1990s are running a 'Medical Romance' series that is very similar in mood and mores to much earlier books, although, happily, the heroines have a little more spirit than in the fairly early days of the National Health Service. In *Labour of Love* (1991) Janet Ferguson describes the tribulations of Kit Greenham who gives up hospital work to become a midwife in a thriving GP partnership. She is soon taking a romantic interest in Dr Richard Anstey who has 'the sort of good looks that would make Kit move mountains if he asked her to'. The happy ending is predictable and in essence identical with that of *Desert Nurse* which was published thirty years before. However, *Labour of Love* certainly provides rather more chat about specific medical conditions than the *Woman's Weekly* stories of the 1940s and 1950s ever provided. Janet gives her patients and their spouses good advice about everything from staphylococcal chest infections to stress incontinence.

The heroine of Caroline Anderson's *Just What the Doctor Ordered* (1993) is Cathy Harris, a young widow and a fully qualified and experienced doctor, who joins a practice in the Cotswolds which will give her more time for her small son Stephen than she could snatch from hospital employment. During her first moments in her new job Cathy has a strange encounter with one of the partners, Dr Max Armstrong, who is blond and blue-eyed and, from the cover illustration, an apparent look-alike of *LA Law*'s Corben Bernstein. For a medical man, he is singularly clumsy: when he has to relieve Cathy of some toys she is carrying his hands brush accidentially 'against the fullness of her breasts', which makes her heart very jerky. He has difficulty in coming to terms with a woman having to work for a living (which seems a bit odd in the 1990s), is horribly rude to Cathy and, when he reduces her to tears, tells her off for using 'that childish trick'. Like Dr Jude Tarleton in *Desert Nurse* he seems a bit of a bounder, fixing his eyes on her cleavage, kissing her roughly, then walking away, and so on. It is only at the very end of the story that each is able to declare love for the other – but before that, about halfway through, when Max is 'dressed only in the skimpiest pair of cut-off shorts she had ever seen', Cathy has the satisfaction of feasting her eyes and sexual fantasy on the 'acres of smooth, tanned skin with a faint sheen of sweat, and soft golden curls arrowing down across his board-flat stomach and disappearing enticingly under the gaping top button of the shorts'. She also notices that these ride low 'on his narrow hips' and that his 'long, bare legs' are 'firm and straight'.

Robert Hale have published several contemporary hospital romances, and with *Nurse's Love Affair* (1990) by Louie Williams we recapitulate all the heightened intensities of hospital life. Debbie, the nurse-heroine, seems a rather sedate character when the story begins. She is easily passed over, having had her fiancé filched by a scheming sister, and feels unsure of her own charms when she sets her starched cap at Alistair, the dashing new doctor on the wards. He is nothing if not masculine, with broad shoulders, a 'deep, bass voice' that tugs at Debbie's tender heart-strings, and sturdy emanations that owe nothing to sissy after-shave lotions or anti-perspirants: 'Snuggling into the warm maleness of [his] jacket, Debbie could detect the faint smell of Dettol ... A comforting smell it was, reminding her of far-off nursery days, when the disinfectant had been dabbed onto grazed knees.'

It is small wonder, with all this going for him, that Debbie felt an 'exquisitely strange throb, deep inside her' when their fingers touched inadvertently as she handed him the proverbial scalpel. Things hot up for Debbie, from throbs to 'ardent kisses', 'burning desire' and 'tumid' longings in her breasts. Fortunately, after frequent interruptions when physical developments seem particularly promising, and after clearing up some misunderstandings (she thinks that he thinks she's an alcoholic; he's afraid to propose because she's inherited 'a small fortune' and he has his pride) they end up, 'eyes shining', on the threshold of marriage.

One of the most original contributions to the medical romance in recent years is Colleen McCullough's *An Indecent Obsession* (1981) which, as its title suggests, offers compulsive reading. Sister Honour Langtry is in charge of the mental ward of a military hospital in the Pacific during the Second World War. Caring for soldiers who have gone berserk or are battle-fatigued, she finds that the sometimes violent cross-tensions between them are echoed in her own personal conflict between her love for an individual patient and her duty towards all of them. Duty, of course, is hardly an overworked word in today's literature and society, but the author's tough yet tender probing of its ramifications is gripping and persuasive.

Wartime pressures have thrust Honour into the rigours of psychiatric nursing without specialized training. She copes by instinct, compassion and intelligent improvisation. The eventual resolution of her conflicts highlights not only some problematical aspects of psychiatric treatment but questions of the individual's relationship with society:

> She was thirty-two years old, and what did she have to show for it?
> A few scraps of official paper, a few ribbons, a couple of medals. No husband, no babies, no life of her own. Just service to others, a memory, and a dead man. Nowhere near enough.

She is tempted to walk out and look up the man who 'said he would wait for her'. But he may have forgotten her – and anyway, when it comes to the point of decision she knows that she can't abandon her patients who, with their slender hold on reality, need all the help they can get: 'Who else have they got, if people like me go rushing off blindly chasing a dream?' She realizes that she has the stamina and 'the *love*. This wasn't just a job – her heart was in it, fathoms deep in it ... her duty lay here among those the world had forgotten, or couldn't use, or sometimes just plain couldn't bear to look at.'

She understands that duty, 'the most indecent of all obsessions', is 'only another name for love'.

272

CHAPTER TWELVE

Sweet Young Dreams and Second Time Around

TEENAGE ROMANCE stories really started soon after the Second World War in magazines and weekly papers. It is not surprising that girls aged from ten to fourteen had to wait until then for this branch of the genre to be established, because teenagers, as a distinct group within society having specific needs, were not acknowledged until the 1940s. Until then they were, in the general view, simply neither children nor adults. Judy Garland had summed up their situation in a song ('I'm Just an In-Between') which she made popular during the early part of the decade:

> I'm not a child, and children bore me
> I'm not grown-up, grown-ups ignore me . . .

There were, however, stories providing role-models for young girl readers from as long ago as mid-Victorian times. Many of these had originated on the other side of the Atlantic, and were popular in Britain too. In the main, those that found their way over here were novels about heroines who had made their mark as child characters but had been allowed to grow up in sequels. Girls loyally followed the fortunes of Louisa M. Alcott's Jo March through her late teens into marriage and motherhood; also Susan Coolidge's Katy Carr, Kate Douglas Wiggins's Rebecca, Jean Webster's Judy Abbott, L. M. Montgomery's Anne Shirley, and even Eleanor H. Porter's appallingly sentimentalized Pollyanna.

In Britain, home-grown heroines who grew up virtually by

public demand were erstwhile schoolgirl characters who had adorned the addictive, long-running series by Elsie Jeanette Oxenham (Joy Shirley and the other 'Abbey School' girls); by Dorita Fairlie Bruce (Dimsie and the Anti-Soppists from the Jane Willard); and by Elinor Brent-Dyer (Joey Bettany and other inmates of the Chalet School).

However, although almost all these characters married and produced offspring, readers were permitted few insights into the intimacies of their lives with their husbands. (To have spied into Joy's or Dimsie's bedroom, would have seemed sacrilegious.) There were of course other stories in books, and periodicals such as the *Girl's Own Paper*, about young girls facing the challenge of growing up, going to work and then getting on with the serious business of acquiring partners and settling into domesticity, but on the whole, neither the characters nor the stories that featured them were vivid or memorable.

In 1950 a new mood entered juvenile publishing in Britain. TV had become an integral part of many people's lives and, in newly launched weeklies for girls such as *Schoolfriend* and *Girl*, pictures were firmly *in* while the long text stories favoured in the pre-war papers were definitely *out*. As so often happens with girls' magazines, the readers' ages were sometimes hard to estimate. In 1951 *Girl* had career strips but left romance and any suggestion of physical passion severely alone. By the 1960s, with the establishment of *Jackie* and others, picture-strip stories which rubbed shoulders with pop-star and real-life-problem features began to give prominence to boyfriends and romance.

Over the last three decades, *Jackie*, *Romeo*, *My Guy*, *Fab*, *Blue Jeans*, etc. have catered in varying degrees for the romantic inclinations of readers from ten years old to mid-teens. Drawn strips were largely replaced during the 1980s by photo-strips, which gave a sense of realism to the stories but also cut them off from wilder flights of the imagination. One of *Jackie*'s most memorable black-and-white line picture-strips, for example, appeared in the issue dated 25 June 1977. Called 'A Midsummer Night's Dream', it is visually magical and atmospheric in a way that photo-strips of real-life teenagers could never be. The story owes quite a lot to Shakespeare's play. Fairy Hyacinth's spells go wrong; a stunning young mortal named Mike falls in love with her and temporarily abandons his regular girlfriend, Kate. Hyacinth is eventually able to put things right between the mortal lovers by blowing magic dust into the appropriate eyes at the right moment. She is then free to concentrate her attention on Hal the Hob Goblin, whom she fancies. Despite her gossamer appearance, she uses down to earth idioms: 'Just a little touch of Fairy Rouge on my cheeks ... and I'll knock Hal for six'. There is a neat combination of fairy and human jargon in her response to Mike's admiration of her 'gear': 'Oh, it's nothing special. Just an old thing I tossed together from some rainbow thread and rose petal silk.'

To suit its gently romantic tone, the first issue of *Jackie* in 1964 contained the 'give-way' of a Twin Heart Love Ring. Its original editor, Gordon Small, has commented (*Sunday Times*, 13 June 1993) that the typical 'teen reader' of the 1960s was 'a young girl in love with love', and the aim was to make *Jackie* seem like a reassuring friend. It certainly succeeded in doing so, over a long period.

By the end of the 1980s readers were finding the photo-strip stories slow-moving stuff compared with the pacey soaps on TV, so the teen romance papers began to ditch them and turn to even more pop-star pictures and articles, together with features about girls' 'real-life' needs and aspirations in fashions and jobs, personal hygiene and sex or social problems. *Jackie*, alas, folded in 1993. *My Guy* (now *MG*), *Just Seventeen* and others are still going strong, and providing some measure of the amatory fantasies that appeal to teenagers.

However, it seems that since the early 1980s, simplistic romance and all that goes with it – dreams, dating, dancing, sexual rivalry and experimentation – is as vividly catered for in books as in the weeklies. Teen novels have become big business, with series such as Silhouette's *First Love*, Bantam's *Sweet Dreams* and *Sweet Valley High*, and Pan Macmillan's *Lovelines*. Many of the stories originate in America or Australia but they nevertheless appear to strike the right romantic note with British readers too. Their male-and-female relationships are often social rather than sensual, and they flower – or flounder – in realistic, contemporary settings (at swimming-baths, school, summer camps, gigs, discos and in snack-bars). The interior mood that is quintessential to more mature love-stories has been replaced by fairly slick extroversion. Heroines are resolutely bright, articulate and enquiring, yet 'ordinary' enough for reader identification. As well as coping with a broad variety of romantic vicissitudes, they have to get to grips with the complexities of their own emotional development and possibly also with over-protective or assertive parents.

Titles taken more or less at random from each series indicate the mood and scene: *New Boy In Town* and *Girl in the Rough* (from *First Love*); *Three's a Crowd* and *Clashing Hearts* (from *Sweet Dreams*); *The Great Boyfriend Switch* and *In Love with a Prince* (from *Sweet Valley High*); *All the Right Moves* and *Opposites Attract* (from *Lovelines*). Easy-to-participate-in emotional fantasies were also provided during the mid-1980s by Puffin in a series of Romance Gamebooks, which allowed readers to choose at various points in the narrative the way in which plots should develop and be resolved.

Non-series romances designed for teenagers have also proliferated over the past ten years. These range from purely escapist exploits to serious probing of sexual identity and relationships. They are intended pretty well exclusively for girls: boys feature charismatically in the stories but are not, one gathers, expected to want to read them.

John Rowe Townsend prefaced his *A Foreign Affair* (1982) with an Author's Note that 'This story has no message and no hidden meanings that I am aware of. Don't take it seriously. It is for fun.' He's right: it is an extremely entertaining account of the involvement of Kate, a spirited and no-nonsense teenager, in a 'Ruritanian' adventure (see Chapter 8). Her companion is an up-and-coming journalist, George Ormerod, and on an assignment instigated by her newspaper-editor father they travel together to Essenheim, a somewhere-just-beyond-Switzerland independent state. Here they become caught up in political intrigues, revolution, and a complicated relationship with Rudi, the young, engaging but ambitious and devious Crown Prince. At first Kate fancies him, though she hangs on to her common sense even when his charm is particularly persuasive:

> Rudi flashed the smile.
> 'The English,' he said, 'have a strange taste in women. They like them tall and skinny. Latins like them fat. But in my country we like them . . .' (he looked her up and down appreciatively) '. . . just right.'
> Kate said coldly, 'Do you have to treat us as sex objects? How would you like it if I said that, according to my taste in men, you were "just right"?'
> 'I should like it very much,' said Rudi . . .

By the end of the Essenheim interlude, Kate is beginning to get her priorities right. She sees Rudi's limitations – despite the fact that being with him brings about 'the melting of her insides' – and begins to warm to the homespun but intelligent George: 'Kate felt again the surge of affection she'd had several times for George, and with it another sensation . . . a slight electric sense of physical nearness . . .' *A Foreign Affair* is the stirring stuff of highly imaginative, and just about believable, romantic adventure.

In Gina Wilson's *Just Us* (1988) the sexual responses of the heroine, Lyn Mellor, to the leading man are more explicit. Matthew Beech comes to her school (Gledhill Comprehensive) to teach English, and not only is he mesmerizingly adept at awakening his students to the glories of English Literature, but he is also a natural charmer of women and girls outside the classroom. Lyn's best friend, Beth, develops a crush on him but, aware of this and that he is the focus of several girls' dreams, he shows little sympathy towards her. Then, while he and Lyn are in the process of becoming lovers, he disconcertingly develops an intimacy with Lyn's divorced mum.

The theme of a male teacher seducing one of his girl pupils is, to say the least, a tricky one for the writer of teenage love-stories, but Gina Wilson compels our belief and points out the pitfalls as well as the exuberant peaks that such a relationship might bring about. There is no conventional happy ending, and although Lyn has acquired new strengths from her relationship with Matthew, she is left in a state of irresolution: 'could she have made him stay? Had he wanted her to?. . . she had just stood there . . . letting him go . . . knowing he would never be back. She had made that choice. She *had.*'

The Tower Room by Adèle Geras (1990) also describes an affair between a schoolgirl and an adult. Megan, Bella and Alice inhabit the isolated and enclosed world of Egerton Hall, a girls' boarding school in the heart of the English countryside. They share the Tower Room and from its high windows survey the world outside and dream about the future dangers and delights that may await them. As well as atmospherically evoking the trappings and minu-tiae of school life – desks and lockers, prep and chapel, muddy lacrosse boots, grass-stained tennis shoes, matron's room packed with bandages, iodine and Virol – *The Tower Room* is loosely derived from the fairy-tale, *Rapunzel.* (Its sequels, *Watching the Roses* (1991), focusing on Alice, and *Pictures of the Night* (1992), featuring Bella, are linked respectively with *The Sleeping Beauty* and *Snow White and the Seven Dwarfs*.)

Megan is seventeen and soon to take her A levels. The smooth tenor of her life is disrupted when she meets Simon, the young lab assistant who – athletically and romantically – climbs the tower to be with her whenever they can snatch time together. Megan is convinced that she has the best of both worlds – the everyday security of school routines, and the magical, passionate, transform-ing meetings with Simon.

> I began to feel as though every single one of my nerve ends was singing with pleasure. I was aware of nothing but Simon. It was as though I were drowning: drowning and falling at the same time . . .
> All sense of where I was, or what time it was, or other people, disappeared. The whole universe was now entirely contained in my body, and every beautiful feeling in the world was blossoming and uncurling under my own burning skin, over my flesh and in my mouth made moist and tender by his kisses . . .

278

Their idyll has, of course, to end. They are found out (by Dorothy, Egerton Hall's science mistress who is also Megan's guardian). Simon is sacked, and Megan goes away with him.

The story continues through her letters to her friends, and, after she and Simon have had to live in shabby furnished rooms with blistering paintwork and rusty baths, she begins to wonder whether love *is* the most important thing in the world:

> I used to think that, but now I'm not so sure. Perhaps love needs a whole arrangement of other things to support it, to keep it standing: a kind of scaffolding without which it simply falls to the ground in little shards and splinters . . .

She returns to Egerton Hall, to A levels and the possibility of going to university, but there is a promise that she and Simon are not making a final parting. *The Tower Room* gives truly revealing insights into the plight of a convention-defying schoolgirl, and its power is enhanced by its being set in the early 1960s rather than in today's more permissive climate.

Linking a school story to fairy-tale might seem on the surface to be an awkward contrivance, but in these Adèle Geras novels it works well, providing imaginative glimpses into the interior qualities of the teenage heroines, showing correspondences between apparently very different types of experience, or simply bringing about a broader imaginative horizon for both characters and readers. Virginia Andrews, whose stories became astoundingly addictive to adolescents (as well as adults) during the 1980s, uses fairy-tale resonances with a simmering, brooding violence which gives *Flowers in the Attic* (1979), its sequels and several other of her books the intensity and menace of the early gothic tale. Here are fairy-tales stripped of their magic but emanating the sexuality, distortions and cruelty that underpinned the earliest versions of the folk stories (which did not acquire the liberating and softening elements of magic or faery until much later in their development). There is a profusion or archetypes and archetypal relationships in an uneasy but undeniably 'new age' format. Cinderella, Snow

White, Red Riding Hood, Beauty and the Beast, Bluebeard, witches and warlocks and, in particular, Hansel and Gretel (with some incestuous sibling symbology) lurk just beneath the surface of these modern-day American sagas of forbidden love and lusts. In particular we find sexually predatory but fundamentally weak father-figures, and heroines in dreadful jeopardy. There is also a great deal of emphasis on wealth, power and reversals of fortune, on passion, taboos and astonishing leaps across social divides.

The popularity with teenagers of Andrews's sagas of abuse and betrayal, particularly of young girls by older men and the mothers who would be expected to protect them, suggests that in the context of family relationships and sexual identity she is striking an empathetic note. At their most melodramatic her books can be seen merely as raunchy, lurid and glitzy family sagas, soaps or souped-up versions of *Lolita* expressed in language that is simplistic to the point of banality; but there is no denying their metaphorical imagery and under-the-skin appeal. Teenagers' strong response to them indicates that for many girls they provide clues and landmarks in personal explorations of sexuality, identity and roots as well as in the questioning of parental authority and conformities.

These challenges are the keynote to *More to Life than Mr Right* (1985), a compilation by Rosemary Stones of 'Stories for Young Feminists', which she followed up in 1988 with a further selection, *Someday My Prince Will Not Come*. As the 'blurb' points out, these are not just 'clichéd stories about man-hating lesbians' (although Susannah Bowyer's 'On the Verge' adroitly tackles one heroine's growing realization of her in-built leanings towards single-sex love – see Chapter 10). They give a fresh focus on many important questions for girls-becoming-women, with authors of vitality such as Geraldine Kaye, Michele Roberts, Adèle Geras and Fay Weldon probing with immediacy and zest many aspects of relationships between young women and men. The overall mood is sometimes angry but most often wry, witty and compassionate. It is summed up in a story by Fay Weldon called 'The Year of the Green Pudding', which appeared in the first of these two compilations. This suggests that the absence of guidelines adds considerably to the social challenges which confront girls today but also points out the strength of individuals having to make their own romantic and other decisions always, so to speak, at first hand. In most of these stories the girls do not, at eighteen or twenty or whatever, achieve the conventional happy ending with husbands, homes and babies tucked safely under their metaphorical belts, but, just as love in our society is often short-lived, so too are the effects of a girl's mistakes, stupidities or wrong judgements: doors on opportunity are rarely finally shut. For example, although a guilt-ridden young husband-stealer in 'The Year of the Green Pudding' adds to her sense of inadequacy by publishing a Christmas pudding recipe which turns out to be direly incorrect and loses her a good job, she knows that many career, social and romantic options are still open to her.

The Teens Book of Love Stories (1987), edited by Miriam Hodgson, also looks perceptively at what K. M. Peyton in her introduction calls 'the quivering uncertainties of early love'. As in the Rosemary Stones anthologies, there is an impressive range of authors including Anthony Masters, Alison Prince, Mollie Hunter and Vivien Alcock. The stories move more slowly and reflectively than those designed for the 'young feminists', but in common with them describe 'ordinary' and unusual romantic liaisons without sentimentality but with a touch of passion. A story by Anthony Masters, set in the Cold War period, of a potentially fulfilling but sadly thwarted relationship between an English girl and a Russian boy is particularly moving, and so too is Mollie Hunter's *The Triumph of Love*, which focuses on a love affair in our own society between a Hindu boy and the daughter of an extremely bigoted Christian minister.

Tessa Dahl's *Working for Love* (1988) and Bella Doherty's *Dear Nobody* (1991) are both concerned with young love that quickly burns itself out, or simply dries up under the glare of social pressures and responsibilities. In each case the heroine is left literally and figuratively holding the baby, sometimes distraught and resentful, often fearful of the future, but always determined to build a new and fulfilling life for herself and her child. Both narratives unfold partly through a series of letters: Molly in *Working for Love* pours out her feelings and frustrations in letters to her ex-husband, Jack, while Helen in *Dear Nobody* writes to her child who is still waiting to be born.

Molly's therapeutic, mind-clearing letters to Jack are not intended to be sent to him. They begin only a week after their break-up: he has walked out on her after seven years of marriage. She is thirty and tired of apologizing for her existence: 'I'd tried self-destruction ... I'd tried to be everyone but me and to please the whole male population headed by you and Daddy.' She is deeply bruised and her anger flares up against Jack at intervals: 'Incidentally ... just for the record, I don't need your patronizing, shit-eating company ...' When she married she thought all her problems would be over, and that 'this glorious man, who was so strong and loving' would change her life. She was soon forced to learn, however, that 'no one changes your life but yourself', although Jack did his best to change hers in extremely negative and unpleasant ways: 'We moved to Prestbury. To the mansion with eight bathrooms. A different pot to crap on each day, we laughed. The laughter halted. You crapped on me.'

Apparently he has been a moody, sulky and – possibly worst of all – mean-about-money tyrant. Molly's frustration and anguish under his domination are unravelled layer by layer in these letters, but there are also moments of joy which she recapitulates – the birth of their daughter, for example – and by the end of the book, having probed deeply into herself and dug out new strengths, she is able to bring a note of generosity into her communications with Jack: 'We must never forget the extraordinary moments, the cherishing, the immense power our love had ... We all danced with each other, some of us have changed partners, some of us are alone. But we all grew and we all loved.'

Working for Love provides plenty of food for thought about young marriages, and Bella Doherty in *Dear Nobody* reflects on the physical and psychological restrictions imposed upon her teenage heroine by pregnancy. Her baby is due to be born just at the time when she had originally planned to go away to music college. Her lover, Chris, *does* go to university as planned: he still loves Helen but, somewhere along the months of waiting for the baby to be born, they have both realized that he is just not ready to cope with the demanding commitments of fatherhood. Helen has to rely only on her own gutsy determination to get through: her mother helps reluctantly, but considers that extra-marital pregnancy is 'dirty' and is furious with Helen for not having an abortion.

The change of moods in the letters Helen writes to her unborn baby, ranging from fear to a sense of integration, comes across simply and compellingly, from the early 'Dear Nobody . . . I'm so frightened. I feel as if I'm walking through a wilderness. There's nothing to hold on to. Go away. Please go away . . .' to 'A few weeks away! It's really, really going to happen. I can't wait to meet you.' Helen's story has a happier ending than Molly's: she maintains contact with Chris and, although the wilder edge of their mutual passion has been blunted, love and tenderness remain, and there is the beginning of a new-born capacity in him to meet his emotional responsibilities.

By no means a teenage book, but one which featured a young girl, *The Constant Nymph* by Margaret Kennedy, published in 1924, was to become a literary sensation, as well as being frequently adapted for the stage and filmed three times (in 1927 with Ivor Novello and Mabel Poulton; in 1933 with Brian Aherne and Victoria Hopper, and in 1944 with Charles Boyer and Joan Fontaine). These movie stars played the parts of Lewis Dodd and Tessa Sanger, the appealing and extravagantly romantic hero and heroine whose ardent love affair, had it taken place in an English suburb rather than in the glamorized Austrian Tyrol and other parts of the Continent, would doubtless have shocked many of the readers who were to thrill to it.

Lewis is a young composer and pianist of angry and petulant genius. His appearance lacks the elegance of a Darcy or the ruggedness of a Rochester; he has slightly straggling locks which are rather mundanely described as 'ginger'. This is a surprising choice of colour for, although in the genre all shades of red hair for heroines are considered attractive, it is not usually associated with the hero-image for which black or dramatic blond are the norm. We are told that Lewis has 'observant eyes, so intent that they rarely betrayed him' but a 'thin, rather cruel mouth'. It is the 'wonderful beauty' of his hands 'which gave a look of extreme intelligence to everything that he did' that impresses everyone: 'their strength and delicacy contradicted the harsh lines of his face'.

Tessa is fourteen when we first met her, small, slight, mercurial, audacious, barefoot and garbed in a yellow peasant dress. There is an unusual quality about her; in spite of her heavily laid on girlishness (dissolving into giggles with her sister about practically nothing, and so on) and still childlike body, she has a woman's mind and – though this is never quite spelt out – a woman's desires. These focus on Lewis, although for the early part of the book she makes no special demands upon him. It is enough for her to be near him, to savour their moments of extraordinary rapport, to love him whatever happens. She is one of the seven children (by two or three different wives) of Albert Sanger, another musical genius. He has become a legend in his lifetime both for his creativity and for the unbridled, 'bohemian' behaviour of his family ('Sanger's Circus') in various parts of Europe, but particularly in the rolling mountains and lush meadows of the alpine Tyrol where they are generally based. They are unpredictable, amoral, and irresponsible about pretty well everything except music, which has a semi-sacred significance to all of them – except Tessa:

> Living in a family of artists she had come to regard this implacable thing which took them as a great misfortune . . . alone of the tribe, she was safe from it . . . she rated the writing of music as an atrocious and painful disease . . . To her the thing was a hidden curse, a family werewolf, always ready to spring out and devour them all . . .

But it is made clear that she is no philistine. She has an artist's eye and is rapturously responsive to the natural scene; when, for example, she contemplates the stony crags and snowfields of the nearby Königsjoch she is 'entranced . . . As she looked she had an idea, a passionate hope, which took her breath away. If she could ever see but one thing properly she might quite easily see God.'

Lewis becomes fasincated by the 'wild imginative solitude of her spirit', and by the innocence which she has managed to maintain in the ambitious, individualistic, decadent hurly-burly of the Sanger *ménage*. He starts to wonder what will happen to her, and in sudden fierce protectiveness decides that if he were her guardian he would put her in a convent (though he has no idea of what life there would be like). He senses that one day she will no longer be skipping and dancing on the mountain (there seems an uncannily prophetic note here of the Julie Andrews–Maria character in *The Sound of Music*) and that some man will betray her. Ironically, of course, it is eventually her love for him that brings about her destruction.

By the time that Tessa reaches the age of fourteen, it is obvious that Lewis is in love with her. However, he weakly drifts into an obviously ill-fated marriage when Sanger suddenly dies and Florence, an English cousin, comes out to the Tyrol to look after 'the children'. She is overwhelmed (as are so many British in fact, fiction and film) by the combination of mountain crags, tinkling cow-bells, blue lustrous lakes and meadows strewn with flowers, and even more so by the apparently romantic, but actually self-indulgent and immature, personality of Lewis. They marry, rather astoundingly, because only an imbecile could consider that Lewis would make good husband material. The point here is that inexperienced little Tessa has a stronger grip on reality than the apparently competent Florence: she knows and understands Lewis's weaknesses but nevertheless will love him for ever. She is his constant nymph.

Florence sensibly packs Tessa off to boarding school in England to get her out of her and Lewis's way. Tessa, constant as ever, accepts this for his sake, but he realizes that he needs above all things to be with his now fifteen-year-old inamorata. They spend their first night together in a rather seedy Belgian hotel but, before there is any question of their love being consummated, Tessa develops undefined chest pains and becomes extremely ill. She soon dies – quickly and unmessily; it is implied that her constancy to Lewis has killed her (at first he does not take her illness desperately seriously but thinks she is suffering from sea-sickness as they have just crossed the Channel from England).

Tessa's sudden demise was, of course, a convenient contrivance on Margaret Kennedy's part: in 1924 it was one thing for a mature man and a fifteen-year-old to love each other idyllically but only in mind and spirit; for them to have got into bed together would have been a different matter altogether. Many readers' sense of moral right and wrong would have been flouted, and presumably legalities too.

The Constant Nymph was not only a glorification of youth, innocence and romance, but an endorsement of the fact that love between men and women can flourish even when there is a big age-gap between them. To conform to popular opinion, however, the man should be older than the woman and it should never be the other way round. Bound up with images of the older – and wiser – male are stories of second chances in relationships which have been frustrated some years before.

One of the most celebrated is the account in Jane Austen's *Persuasion* (which was published posthumously in 1818) of the resuscitated romance between Anne Elliot and Captain Wentworth, RN. The story begins eight and a half years after their original period of attraction had ended. Anne is twenty-seven, unmarried and aware that her bloom is fading. Frederick Wentworth, after her rejection of his proposal, had gone away to sea again, with little money and, according to Anne's friend and adviser, Lady Russell, little prospect of making any. (Anne's father had opposed the match for selfish reasons and Lady Russell, in effect standing in for Anne's dead mother, had 'deprecated the connexion in every light', fearing that Wentworth's confidence and wit were misplaced, and that he was headstrong and unreliable.) Anne learns to regret having listened to them rather than following the dictates of her heart, but, even when Wentworth returns to the neighbourhood, she feels that she is now sufficiently past her prime in age and desirability for him to disregard her as a potential partner. (The marriage stakes at the beginning of the nineteenth-century were a tough business.) However, the gallant naval captain has returned with lingering hopes of reactivating their relationship. As well as his manly, appealing person he has a very large fortune ('five and twenty thousand pounds of prize money from the Napoleonic Wars') to offer. After several mishaps and misunderstandings he feels emboldened enough to declare his feelings in a letter which suggests that the intensity of autumnal love glows as brightly as youthful passion:

> You pierce my soul. I am half agony, half hope. Tell me not that I am too late, that such precious feelings are gone for ever. I offer myself to you again with a heart even more your own, than when you almost broke it eight years and a half ago. Dare not say that man forgets sooner than woman, that his love has an earlier death. I have loved none but you . . .

This time all is well; Anne accepts his proposal and there is no doubt that they will experience the 'overpowering happiness' that the text promises, and that Anne's bloom will be fully restored.

Thomas Hardy took up the second-time-around theme in *The Well-Beloved* (1897) which probably provides the most romantic – and the most silly – expression of it in serious literature. The hero, Jocelyn Pierston, starts off as a twenty-year-old sculptor who is obsessed with his concept of ideal beauty, his 'well-beloved'. He clings throughout his long life to the desire to find fulfilment with this 'migratory, elusive idealization' which, although conforming to a constant image, can be found in more than one woman. Accordingly, in his efforts to relate to what Hardy describes as 'a spirit, a dream, a frenzy, a conception, an aroma, an epitomized sex, a light of the eye, a parting of the lips', Jocelyn falls in love with Avice Caro, leaves her for a more opulent beauty, then returns twenty years later for her funeral and meets her daughter, who is physically indistinguishable from Avice. Of course he falls in love with her, but she is already married, so off he goes again. Twenty further years on he returns and meets Avice the third, who is almost identical to her mother and her dead grandmother. Once again Jocelyn falls for his well-beloved . . .

Despite the power of Hardy's prose, surely few hearts could be wrung by all this. More recent authors have done a better job on the returning-to-first-love-theme. Elizabeth O. Peter tackles it in *Compromise with Yesterday* (1946), a novel which covers the period of the two world wars and the years between. Dishy David Allen, who was a pilot in the First World War and has become an RAF air commodore in the second, is a Rupert Brooke-ish figure who never loses his 'sort of lost, searching look'. In the saga, he symbolizes not only the vulnerability of youthful romance but the potency of long-remembered love affairs which are sometimes 'more powerful, more relentless than the living presence, which might disappoint or cease to enchant'. In 1914 he and Lorella, the sister of a fellow-officer, are fervently in love, but their affair is broken up by the selfish connivances of her possessive father. Years later, when the man whom she eventually marries is killed, David hopes to revivify their thwarted romance but Lorella has too much sense to encourage him, knowing that they both have changed considerably. During the Second World War he meets Lorella's niece, Jacky, who strongly resembles her beautiful aunt; he falls for her ('Was he, like Faust, seeking a return of his youth?') and she reciprocates. She is a link with his past, but untrammelled by it – a very practical young woman serving with the WAAF and anxious to get on with the job of winning the war. The author skilfully uses the clichés of wartime fiction when describing snatched meetings between lovers on leave, and the fears of sudden death which then formed the background of so many people's lives. She evokes the genuine atmosphere of the early 1940s when she concentrates on Jacky and David's off-duty moments together: dinner at the Hungaria restaurant; Jacky's sensuousness in a black silk dress instead of her accustomed uniform; the sudden change from lighted café interiors to London's blacked-out shabbiness, and the surprising glamour of the scarred city, expressed through this and other contrasts. The emotive mood of *Compromise with Yesterday* is frequently enhanced by the use of popular music at trigger-points in the text: 'an ordinary little dance tune, with cheap, silly words. All the lost loveliness of youth returning on a wave of bitter-sweet longing and regret.' David sings 'You Made Me Love You' to

Lorella in 1914, and dances to 'the old Missouri Waltz' with Jacky in the 1940s. These songs and their settings convey the insecurity of people caught in an uncertain present, who have to look to the future for fulfilment and to the past with longing.

The fact that David was some twenty years older than Jacky was, of course, no bar to romance. As we so often see, in both fiction and fact an age gap weighted in such a way is acceptable. It can, however, be very much questioned when a young man falls for (and apparently into the toils of) an older woman. Even in romantic fiction this is frequently frowned upon (although both Florence Barclay in *Broken Halo* and Elinor Glyn in *Three Weeks* sanctified it – see Chapters 2 and 3). Elizabeth von Arnim's *Love* (1925) attacks the hypocrisy of society for double sexual standards, and for the taboos it enforces, to the disadvantage of woman, in the name of 'love'. Catherine Cumfrit meets Christopher Monckton at a performance of *The Immortal Hour*: it is her fifth visit to the show and his thirty-second, so, although strangers, they have at least this in common. He is enchanted by her, and undisturbed by – even hardly aware of – their age difference; he is twenty-five while she is forty-seven. Catherine, a widow for some years with a grown-up married daughter, is astounded that at her age she can become the object of Christopher's affections but he woos her, charmingly and relentlessly, and although she never expects a permanent liaison, they eventually marry. From her point of view,

> Vanity had been the beginning of it, the irresistibleness of the delicious flattery of being mistaken for the young, and before she knew what she was doing she had fallen in love – fallen flop in love, like any idiot schoolgirl . . .

However, once love sets in, so does unease and even anguish.

More and more acutely, Catherine becomes aware of the age difference. When she and Christopher go out together they meet people who take it for granted that she is his mother or his aunt; friends and acquaintances whisper behind their hands when the couple attend dinner-parties, and, worst of all, Catherine's daughter, Virginia, and her husband, Stephen, are upset by what they consider to be a thoroughly undesirable relationship. This is particularly hurtful and ironic because Catherine has made great financial sacrifices to help them stabilize their own marriage, and in any case Stephen is thirty years older than Virginia, which neither of them, nor society, ever questions.

Stephen is an astoundingly complacent, domineering and dogma-ridden rector, who preaches regularly on the subject of love, thinks that he adores his wife, but shows little evidence of real tenderness and compassion either in or outside his marriage. When he first realizes that Catherine and Christopher have become serious about each other, he rails at her for three or four pages, but urges her to marry her young lover to keep her good name, for when she was out with him on one occasion and his motor-bike broke down, they spent a night away from home (quite innocently, but of course Stephen thinks the worst). He arrogantly and insultingly insists that they marry, for the sake of respectability, and threatens that if they do not, Catherine will never be able to see his wife (her own daughter!) again. At the same time, he rubs in that 'such a marriage' between an older woman and a young man is 'a disgrace':

> She looked at him, very pale. 'It's at least a mercy, then,' she said, her eyes full of bright tears of indignation at the injustice, the cruelty of the man ... 'That I love Christopher.'
>
> 'You love him!' repeated Stephen, appalled by the shamelessness of such a confession ... 'You dare to use that word in connection with this boy and yourself ...'
>
> 'It is shameful,' said Stephen, beside himself at what seemed to him her ghastly effrontery, 'that some one so much older should even think of love in connection with some one so much younger.'
>
> 'But what, then,' said Catherine, 'about you and Virginia?'

To Stephen this remark is simply an outrage; too contemptuous to reply, he just walks away. For the reader, however, there is an ironic satisfaction which poor Catherine is not able to observe. Virginia begins to realize that it is unreasonable to resent her mother's relationship with Christopher, and when her husband urges her one night – just after they have had sex – 'to pray for her poor mother' she asks him why it is so dreadful that Catherine is marrying Christopher. He sternly replies, 'Do you not see it is terrible to marry some one young enough to be your son?' and she, with a felicitous show of spirit, wounds him to the core by saying, 'But is it any more terrible than marrying someone young enough to be your daughter?'

Sadly, social strictures and gossip have their effect on Catherine. Christopher remains unaffected by them: he loves her and loves being married to her; nothing else seems important. But she embarks on a terrible and humiliating campaign to restore her youthful looks. Inevitably one sympathizes with her wish to look her best for Christopher, but she carries this beyond the boundaries of reasonable behaviour. She sends him away on holiday so that she can progress from regular weekly beauty therapy to taking a crash course (from someone who turns out to be a charlatan). The treatment is electrical and painful, and although guaranteed to make her look young again, fails lamentably, leaving her skin looking duller and more sallow than before. Her chagrin is graphically conveyed, but everything fades into insignificance when she is called to the bedside of Virginia, who is having her first child. The baby is born, but Virginia dies. Christopher returns from Scotland, goes to Virginia and Stephen's house and there meets a 'grizzled little old lady' whom he doesn't recognize – but who of course turns out to be Catherine.

The book ends on a note of irresolution which is entirely appropriate; it is impossible to predict which way their marriage will go. Catherine is all for ending it cleanly and quickly, to save Christopher from disappointment, pain and possible social humiliation. He is more resilient, and his love and optimism bounce back into place at the centre of their relationship once he gets over the shock of realizing that Catherine's dark locks are really grey and that she not only *is* old enough to be his mother but *looks* it. Apparently the story originally sprang from an actual love affair in Elizabeth von Arnim's life after which her young lover married a younger woman, and she was never happy with the ending which she gave the book. However, *Love* works well at several levels:

despite the disparity in age and understanding of Catherine and Christopher, their mutual passion is believable, and suggests the extraordinary enhancement of experience and awareness that can flower from some kinds of unconventional love. It is also a pungent social commentary in which intensity and acerbity alternate with great effect to convey the 'respectable' brutalities of so-called decent society.

In 1935, ten yers after *Love*, Ann Bridge dealt with the same basic theme in *Illyrian Spring*, and it is interesting to compare her treatment of a romance between a very young man and a middle-aged woman with von Arnim's. On the surface there seems little to suggest that received attitudes in 1935 differed significantly from those of 1925. However, the heroine of *Illyrian Spring* is more involved than Catherine in conventional family relationships and responsibilities when she meets the young man who is eventually to call these into question.

Lady Grace Kilmichael is married to Walter, a distinguished economist who has, over the years, remained affectionate towards her in a remote and rather patronizing way. She regrets but ruefully accepts the distance that has developed between them. She feels too that she has no rapport with her self-confident, headstrong, grown-up daughter, Linnet, whom she constantly exasperates. She takes herself off on a painting trip to the Dalmatian coast of Yugoslavia, then unfrequented by tourists, and meets Nicholas Humphries, an aspiring artist whose family are determined that he should leave painting alone and pursue a more stable and remunerative profession. Grace soon discovers that he has a rare talent. At first their mutual interest in art is their only bond, and although Nicholas's social credentials pass muster she is hardly drawn to him in a dynamic way:

> he was rather an off-hand young man, she thought, though his clothes and speech appeared to belong to the class to which she was accustomed . . . He was very young, probably not more than twenty-two, she decided, with blue eyes and a mop of curly strawberry coloured hair; his face was burned a bright raspberry pink by the sun, a most unbecoming combination; in addition, this youthful

face, which should have been cheerful, wore a markedly dissatisfied expression. He was not a very taking person, she felt.

Her coolness about him soon changes to interest, then affection, admiration and attraction. She is forty-two, and resolutely tries to see him as a kind of surrogate son who will give her insights into the working of youthful aspirations and attitudes, thus helping her better to understand Linnet. What actually happens is that his honesty and forthrightness jerk Grace out of her meek acceptance of her rather inferior role in the Kilmichael family. She begins to become much more a person in her own right instead of being 'Linnet's mother' or 'the brilliant Sir Walter Kilmichael's nice wife'. A sign of her increasing independence is that she prolongs her trip in order to spend more time with Nicholas, and they go further and further off the beaten track in pursuit of subjects for paintings, and to relish the prolific beauty of the natural scene. Grace is able to advise Nicholas on several aspects of painting and she determines to try to persuade his family to let him have the art training which will release his vast talents. (Ultimately she succeeds in this.) Still neither she nor Nicholas ackowledges that they are falling in love:

> Yes, it was idyllic, this life she and Nicholas were leading, of hard work and pleasant idleness, of meals in the open air, and – of late – of most serene and unclouded companionship. And for the first time the rarity, the unusual quality of the whole thing struck her. It was very odd that she should find herself wandering through Illyria with this delightful boy.

It is only after Nicholas becomes severely ill with food-poisoning that Grace begins to realize that he is much more to her than just 'a dear, delightful child'. Each is deeply stirred by the other's physical proximity, but too bound by the taboos of the polite society to which they belong to admit it. However, the local doctor who attends Nicholas, and is portrayed as someone of great insight, rapidly assesses the truth of the situation. He has no qualms about suggesting the remedy to Grace:

'He needs ... the experience of love; and this you – older, married
– can give him with grace, with beauty, as a younger woman could
not. Obviously you give him this.'

'Do you mean have a love affair with him?'

'*Natürlich*. You may have to help him considerably; he is nervous,
reserved, and he does not express himself easily. But this is his need,
and you can fulfil it. You will be his mistress.'

Although Grace has considerable respect for Dr Halther, she is
astonished by this conversation, and firmly rejects such dangerous
'continental' attitudes. He is reduced to muttering stereotypically
that 'you English are a most extraordinary people', and she sticks
to the view that between her and Nicholas it is a case of least said
soonest mended:

if once he started to speak of it, she would find it hard, in the face
of his sincerity, not to show an equal truth about herself – and that
could not help. Married, and twice his age, what could come of it?
That was always the point to which she came back. It had never
occurred to Lady Kilmichael to take any but the practical view of
love. Love ought to lead to marriage – if it didn't do that, it could
only lead to disaster or waste.

There is no doubt, of course, that this was the overall attitude of
society, at least overtly. There was room in film and fiction for
older *femme fatales* sexually to titillate and teach young men (in the
manner of 'the Lady' and Paul in *Three Weeks*, see Chapter 3) but
it was not a role which men wanted their wives to play, and most
middle-aged women were reluctant to do so anyway, not only
because of the conventional restrictions but because they doubted
their own erotic capacities and expertise.

At the end of *Illyrian Spring* Grace comes off rather better than
Catherine in *Love*. Nicholas only declares his love after Walter and
Linnet have come out to Yugoslavia to discover what is keeping
the recalcitrant Lady Kilmichael away from home so long. Because
of their presence she is able to deal with his halting, diffident
expression of love with warmth and reassurance, but in the context
of its futility 'there was no outcome possible to love between them;

for them, as them, there was no solution'. However, each is consoled by the wonderfully positive spin-offs of their relationship: he has a new-found tolerance, a broader understanding and, of course, his art course to look forward to, while she, basking in the flame of his ardour, has rediscovered her own strengths and convictions and power to attract a man. There is the implication that the arrogant Walter will no longer be able to take her love and loyalty for granted but will have to put some energy and enthusiasm into their marriage.

Five years later 'Second Marriage', a story by Helen Deutsch in the May 1940 *Woman's Journal*, tackles the subject of love between a young man and an older woman. This time the gap is not so wide: Michael Gravis is nineteen and Antonia Priest is thirty-one when they decide to marry. His passion for her begins as a 'schoolboy crush' but matures into love. In spite of her deeply felt reservations, and the suggestions of her friends that a short-lived affair would be preferable, they go ahead and marry. By this time she is not only relishing 'his unbelievable, extraordinary beauty' but the fact that he is the only person she 'ever knew who seemed wholly strong and wise', and 'the only man who ever made her want to give her life to him'. Alas, marital bliss soon fades in the bitchy, gossiping, connivings of girls of the younger set of their acquaintance, who have their eye on Michael as a second-time-around spouse because he's not only handsome but mega-rich. Antonia, feeling totally inadequate, and that she has no right to hold him, leaves him to precipitate a divorce. He throws his energies into his career and becomes an astoundingly successful playwright. She wrily accepts that 'the world says that these marriages are unwise. I set myself against that idea. I was wrong', and wonders what she is going to do with the rest of her life. There is no question of her taking up a career, but she travels, and then buys a country cottage and raises hollyhocks and delphiniums. She is tempted out of her semi-reclusive situation when, five years after their divorce, she goes to see one of Michael's plays which is to have its West End first night. It is a glittering success but Michael avoids the party which is being held afterwards and creeps away. In so doing he runs into Antonia, who is tremendously touched by his fervent expression of love for her:

> If I were to die and be born again, and die and be born a thousand times, in each new life I'd love only you . . . Here in this one life, by accident of time I was born a little too late. Well, what of it? Why do we punish ourselves for that? We never for a minute loved each other less.

Antonia succumbs to the delectation of remarrying Michael. Readers are assured by the narrative comment (supposedly made many years after their reconciliation) that 'he's fifty now and doesn't look it. But the uncanny thing is that she looks not a day older than he does. If they keep on at this rate, she'll be younger than Michael quite soon.'

What a boost for middle-aged women in the throes or on the verge of late-flowering love! At last, it seems, older women were being allowed to jump off the unsexual, unromantic shelf to which they had for so long been relegated.

In *Second Fiddle* (1988) Mary Wesley unapologetically and triumphantly chronicles the exploits of a middle-aged woman who attracts a young admirer. Laura is forty-five while Claud is only twenty-three. They meet when he has been to university, failed his finals and is living on unemployment benefit. He is an aspiring writer, and Laura suggests that it would be better for him to work on a market stall, as she does, than to live on the benefit poverty line. He does so and continues to write intensively. She becomes impatient with his secrecy about his manuscript: 'You can't be pregnant for ever; somebody has to look at your baby.' Without inhibition she enters more fully into his life:

> I could protect Claud, she thought, then almost laughed outright as she was swept by an irresistible exultant desire to interfere, manipulate, experiment with Claud – by way of protection.

One of the great differences between Laura and the earlier fictional heroines loving younger men is that she does everything with a sense of humour, in which they were somewhat lacking. Almost matter-of-factly (though she is tickled by the fact that he much admires her legs) they become lovers. By the time that he offers to show her his manuscript, she is not quite sure whether she wants to see it: she's happily taken on his body but not necessarily his mind. She succumbs, however, is surprised that it is so good, and is able to offer advice here and there which is helpful. Unlike Elizabeth von Arnim's and Ann Bridge's mature heroines, she is always – or nearly always – in control and cheerfully unruffled by the age gap between Claud and herself. He stuns her a bit by suggesting marriage, but after a quick psychological hiccup she gets things in proportion.

> I underestimated Claud, Laura thought. I used him for pleasure. I even suspected him of being a little camp. Then last night, serve me right, I went overboard, was even ridiculously in danger of believing his suggestion of marriage could be serious, not just froth. I could not have been much stupider than that.

The point is, of course, that Laura has been leading a lively and independent life long before she meet Claud. She knows her own reserves of strength and vitality, is not desperate for any permanent romantic relationship, and in fact has a longer-term love, Martin, of her own age, waiting in the wings of her relationship with Claud.

Laura whisks herself off to London, partly to buy things for her stall and partly to reinforce the fact that she and Claud can be independent of each other but still fulfilled. His book is published to mainly good reviews, but when he collapses and attempts suicide under the impact of a savagely destructive one, she goes back to rally him: 'Listen to this, Claud. You have written a bloody good book, stop whingeing about one idiotic review and get on with the next.'

Martin returns from his secret service work in the USA. He is ferociously jealous of Claud and possessive of Laura but ends up, under orders from her, making tea for his rival who is suffering from alcoholic dehydration, while she takes herself back to London. We do not know when – or if – she will return. Hardly a sentimental ending, but a very satisfying one.

CHAPTER THIRTEEN

Sex, Shopping and Social Responsibility

♡

AT SOME TIME during the 1970s a new urgency came into romantic fiction. There were still of course stories in which the hero's and heroine's feelings for each other took time to flower, and holding-something-back-until-the-final-fervent-clinch remained the pattern, but 'bodice-rippers' were becoming a sub-genre of the love-story, working particularly well in historical romances when frilled, lacy and low-cut bodice tops seemed irresistibly inflammatory to heroes with seduction in mind. And it wasn't only bodices that were being pulled off; over a wide range of emotional tales sexual skirmishes were being described explicitly, and heroes and heroines were increasingly impatient 'to be naked together'.

Kathleen Winsor, as long ago as 1944, had created a leading lady who was to become archetypally associated with bodice-ripping: she was, of course, Amber St Clare, the eponymous central protagonist of *Forever Amber*. She set the pattern for many future heroines, demanding not just to be loved but to achieve success, money and power in her own right. Amber was not exactly endearing; in order to reach the top of the social tree (in fact King Charles II's bedroom) she was prepared to whore, lie, steal and even murder.

Although her place is essentially in historical fiction rather than the general run of love-stories, her impact was felt in these too. Sensual, ambitious and exploitative girls began to crop up more and more frequently as the 1950s and 1960s progressed, and they reached their raunchy zenith in novels by Jackie Collins such as *The Stud* (1970) and *The Bitch* (1979). With these and the author's other books (*Hollywood Wives, The World is Full of Married Men, etc.*) everyone who matters is in the fast lane, jet-setting between and across continents, 'bonking' with gusto, gambling at Vegas, going to glitzy parties, wearing designer clothes and driving stretch limos. Fontaine Khaled at the beginning of *The Bitch* is reduced to wearing last year's sable coat because her 'multi-billionaire' Arab husband has just divorced her and the settlement is not finalized. She wants a pause before she starts looking for another billionaire, but is confident that she will have little difficulty in acquiring one: 'She had never really pursued money, because of her devastating beauty it had always managed to pursue her.' Apparently Benjamin Al Khaled had spotted Fontaine when she was modelling in St Moritz and had 'dumped his first wife quicker than a hooker gives head'. Another reason why Fontaine doesn't want to find a new billionaire immediately is because they tend to be old, and she wants youth: 'she revelled in the male body beautiful and an eight- or nine-inch solid cock'. When she is getting ready to fly back to London from New York her apartment is robbed, so she 'zipped through the ... stores at an alarming pace' to refurbish her wardrobe. 'When it came to shopping for clothes there was nobody better at spending money than she was – except perhaps Jackie Onassis'. She takes her pick from Armani, Cerrutti, Chloe – 'name-designer clothes had always looked well on her' – buys two pairs of boots 'at a hundred and eighty five dollars apiece' and 'a simple black crocodile shoulder bag – four hundred dollars. An art deco necklace and earrings – one hundred and fifty dollars. And three hundred dollars' worth of make-up and perfume'. (The last item is extremely important because it is acknowledged elsewhere in the text that her sexual successes owe a lot to her perfumed thighs.) Although Fontaine must be out of the league of most of her readers, it is gratifying to know that even she, despite her magnificent good looks, has to work at keeping herself in the sort of shape that is likely to attract the next billionaire who happens along. We are given helpful details of her regular vitamin intake and told she has steam baths, facials and massage, and that she exercises.

In fact, instead of a man of fabulous wealth, she finds Nico Constantine, who is rich in magnetism and sex appeal (over ten years he has made love to some '120 fresh-faced beauties') but short on cash. However, we know that once he and Fontaine become a pair, they'll soon use their wits to be back with the high-flyers.

Since the mid-1970s Pat Booth has also been producing novels of 'international high-life' which feature intriguing sexual liaisons and go-getting characters. Her *Big Apple* (1984) is unashamedly described as 'a searing novel of ambition, greed and lust'. Among the most notable and atmospheric of her books are the *The Lady and the Champ* (her first) and *Sparklers*.

Jilly Cooper's accounts of heroines who are romantically inclined but also wry, earthy and at times anarchic are at the far end of the spectrum from those of Barbara Cartland, for example, which are in the more traditional mould. Jilly Cooper has given the modern romance an invigorating and often comic slant. Her six love-stories, published between 1977 and 1978, carry girls' names as their titles, *Emily, Bella, Harriet, Octavia, Imogen* and *Prudence*, and are amalgams of misunderstandings and changing partners, of glamour and good nature in a variety of settings from canal barges to haunted Highland castles. Of her longer novels, *Riders* (1985), *Rivals* (1989) and *Polo* (1993) are social satires in which romance remains a strong ingredient. Jilly Cooper brings an innovative voice both to horsey affairs and bed-to-boardroom exploits.

Romantic and popular fiction of the 1970s and 1980s was reflecting not only freer attitudes towards sex, but change in thinking about women's place in society. In real life, of course, the Pill had brought new freedoms and given couples the possibility of having children only when and if they wanted them. Not surprisingly, many women chose to space their families in such a way that they could either keep their jobs or return to work after a fairly short period at home with babies and pre-school children. It was no longer a case of snatching small pockets of time away from their homes and children in order to do a part-time job to help out the family budget. More and more, society was beginning to accept and indeed become geared to the fact that women were working in full-time, long-term careers. With higher achievement came higher salaries, of course, which made possible the hiring of domestic help, and especially of full- or part-time nannies. Although plenty of women stuck to the old pattern of working for a few years, then having babies and staying at home, equally many others opted for working motherhood as their permanent way of life. Many of these became career high-flyers, competing with each other and with men for senior jobs in many fields.

Fiction mirrored, and frequently glamorized, fact in magazine stories and family sagas about girls starting out in back-street haberdashers or corner grocery shops and eventually building up or taking over enormous international commercial enterprises, or getting top jobs in politics or the media. In real life on the whole women and girls had more money to spend than before – on themselves as well as on homes and families – and popular fiction played up to their new affluence by injecting the gloss of 'designer shopping' into many stories, as we have seen, for example, in the novels of Jackie Collins. Working-girl heroines began to look further than medium-quality off-the-peg clothes and fairly mundane handbags, costume jewellery, and so on. Gucci handbags, Saint Laurent suits, even Cartier glitz, became the norm for the woman who had made it to or near to the top. There is no doubt that this had an enlivening effect on stories across the romantic board. Of course few working women could actually afford to buy the garb and gear which was so mouth-wateringly described, but, together with housewives who didn't go out to work, they enjoyed reading about them.

More than any other fictional saga, Barbara Taylor Bradford's Emma Harte trilogy symbolized the new trend. In *A Woman of Substance* (1979) Emma starts out, in 1905, as a single pregnant kitchen-maid who seems set for a bleak future. However, by the end of the novel, in 1968, she has through her own efforts become one of the richest women in the world, the creator and boss of a business empire 'stretching from Yorkshire to the glittering cities of America and the rugged vastness of Australia'. On the way she has married twice, maintained for sixteen years a great ardour for one particular lover, and had children by each man. However, her success in business has not been achieved without sacrifice; it has cost her the joy of loving relationships with most of her children, who eventually try to betray her and take over the business. She is of course clever enough to counteract their intrigues, and bequeaths the main body of her money and commercial empire to her grandchildren, with whom she *has* been able to build up love and trust. The story is carried on through *Hold the Dream* (1985) and *To Be the Best* (1988). It has been the subject of mini-TV-dramas which were popular on both sides of the Atlantic and it potently focuses on many aspects of the so-called affluent society, and the accepted materialism of the 1980s. It has become synonymous with the 'shopping novel', a phenomenon of the 1980s which has survived, though tenuously, into the 1990s. The text of *A Woman of Substance* is liberally spattered with sleek symbols of success from Cadillacs and clothes to art treasures, Chippendale chairs, Aubusson carpets, fine crystal glasses, exquisite Georgian tea services, and so on.

Two immensely popular American authors, Judith Krantz and Danielle Steel, have created similarly glamorous novels featuring women who move in society's upper echelons, and who tend to be astoundingly beautiful as well as awesomely enterprising and efficient.

Judith Krantz burst on to the publishing scene in 1978 with *Scruples*, the story of 'the best high-fashion boutique in the world'. The scope and influence of this venture have been extended in *Scruples Two* (1993) which allows loyal readers to follow further the fortunes of the central and charismatic characters as well as new ones. The story sweeps (an inevitable word in connection with the Bradford/Krantz/Steel blockbusters) from Beverly Hills to New York and Paris: as before, it is full of the glossy and gorgeous trappings of high fashion and high incomes – but there is a lot of heart as well. Krantz's heroines, in both volumes of *Scruples* and in her other novels, are psychologically larger than life: Billy Ikehorn, the owner of the Scruples chain, is described as 'a tearing beauty' imperious, stubborn, 'too rich,' 'too vulnerable' and 'a creature of rampant sexuality'; Valentine O'Neill, half-Irish but with a Latin soul, is predictably engaging, lively and hot-tempered, as well as being a brilliant designer. So many of Krantz's heroines are memorable. For example, there is the loyal and loving Marguerite Alexandrovna Valensky, the eponymous star of *Princess Daisy* (1980), who starts out as a Russian princess and ends as a Hollywood one in a fairy-tale progression from riches to rags and back again; there is Marie-Frédérique de Lancel ('Freddy'), the Second World War Air Transport Auxiliary pilot in *Till We Meet Again* (1988) whose vivid personality matches her flaming hair, and the much-married, hedonistic, raven-haired Maxi Amberville in *I'll Take Manhattan* (1986), and so on.

In a postscriptorial note to *Princess Daisy*, Krantz says: 'I could never write about a woman who didn't work. I couldn't feel emotionally involved.' She specializes in providing her heroines with splendid jobs that are nothing if not stimulating, command lavish remuneration and take place in ritzy settings which, despite their somewhat over-the-top quality, have actually been well researched and are accurate in essence if imaginative in detail. After the super-shop world of *Scruples*, we see Princess Daisy working in the cut-throat field of advertising commercials, Maxi taking over the fashion trade weekly *Buttons and Bows* and transforming it into the slickest and most successful fashion mag in America, and Fauve, the artist's daughter, following a career in the milieu of modelling agencies and high fashion in *Mistral's Daughter* (1983). It is a measure of Krantz's descriptive skills that, as in *Scruples Two*, she can even make mail-order seem exciting and alluring!

The most exotic elements in her books, apart from the pairings and partings of colourful characters, are the coast-to-coast and overseas trips made by her leading protagonists. A favourite and slightly fantasized location, generally linked with one or another aspect of romance, is France, with which characters are associated at key moments in *Scruples, Princess Daisy, Till We Meet Again*, and most of all in *Mistral's Daughter* which not only provides vignettes of the 1920s ambience of Chanel, Colette, Matisse and Picasso but also the starkly contrasting dramas of Jewish escape bids during the Second World War German occupation.

The dismissive 'shopping and fucking' (S and F) tag has probably been tied on Judith Krantz's novels more than those of many other romantic block-busting best-sellers. She certainly indulges and elevates to the level of wish-fulfilment the enjoyment of luxury shopping with which most women can empathize. As with Jackie Collins and Barbara Taylor Bradford, the cost and opulence of designer clothes and jewellery, fabulous homes, furnishings and cars are mouth-wateringly evoked. The appeal of this kind of shopping is doubtless enhanced just because it *is* so far removed from the tediousness of many women's real-life traipsing around the supermarket and having to stretch inelastic budgets.

Judith Krantz also robustly harnesses the second part of the S and F label. In common with Danielle Steel, another adept at literary window-shopping, she conveys with intensity both physically steamy and softer aspects of sex. Ruthless, savagely exploitative sex scenes occur, but only as and when essential to the plot; they are never prurient. In the career and social context, Krantz and Steel emphasize feminine viewpoints, ambitions and achievements. Similarly, they have brought a freshness and immediacy to their descriptions of sexual activity. They have discarded traditional literary images of women's responses (dreamed up by men and conveyed in the language of masculine experience) and depicted the procedure from an authentic if sometimes idealized feminine orientation of passionate aspirational tenderness.

Danielle Steel's first book, *Going Home*, was published in 1973. It is possible over the twenty or so years of her output to see developments in her style and approach, although, for hundreds and thousands of fans, her stories have been addictive from the beginning. Her heroines, like Krantz's, are usually at the top of the social heap. They get there by birth, marriage or pulling themselves up by their own boot-straps. Even though they are surrounded by the props of the good life, they still often have a tough time, suffering not so much for their own shortcomings as from mishaps and tragedies that engulf the men in their lives. In *Passion's Promise* (1977), for example, Kezia Saint Martin eventually loses Lucas to prison and death, while in *Now and Forever* (1979) Jessica Clarke has to survive the trauma of her husband's trial for rape and his subsequent wrongful spell in jail. From the beginning her books have worked at the colourfully atmospheric level, but those published during the last four or five years have been satisfyingly underpinned by deeper emotional content as in, say, *Heartbeat* (1991) and sharper exploration of both personal and public issues, as in *Message from Nam* (1990).

In *Heartbeat* we find less emphasis than in the early novels on the alluring trappings of life in the fast lane, with Gucci and Saint Laurent gear hinted at rather than drooled over. At first Adrian Townsend, who seems a typically brainy and beautiful Steel heroine, has everything going for her. She is an assistant producer of a news programme on a major American TV network, and the wife of Steven, a 'movie star-handsome' advertising agency executive. However, their glossily fortunate circumstances are dramatically altered when Adrian suddenly finds herself pregnant and realizes that she is psychologically incapable of honouring the contract she had previously made with Steven that theirs should remain a childless marriage. While he heartlessly urges an abortion, she becomes more maternal by the minute and, despite a great deal of agonizing about having to choose between her husband and child, decides to ditch her fanciable but self-absorbed spouse and to have her baby. Steven spitefully makes her suffer at several levels. However, after Adrian grapples with feelings of inadequacy, loss and even guilt (thus attracting empathy from almost every reader), she emerges from romantic – and subsequent economic – reversals with more strengths, inner freedom and, most importantly, more compassion.

When her courage occasionally wilts under the onslaught of Steven's nastiness, she is supported by Bill Thigpen, the dynamic writer and producer of a TV soap-ish drama which always seems to be number one in the ratings. Over-occupied with career success, he has allowed his own marriage to fall by the wayside although he remains close to his two young sons. He has learned to get his priorities straight in time to become a surrogate father to Adrian's baby from the very beginning of its life, and, of course, to prove himself a far more rewarding romantic partner for Adrian than Steven could ever be. *Heartbeat* marks new departures for Danielle Steel in the creation of a heroine who voluntarily embraces more ordinary circumstances than the elegantly affluent 'norm' to which she has been accustomed, and who does not know how she will cope with her new challenges, but is determined to do so for the sake of her child, and from belief in the rightness of having more time to savour experiences which have previously passed her by at the gallop. *Heartbeat* is also surprising in the Steel canon in allowing a great deal of the action and developing relationships to unfold from the standpoint of the male protagonist (Bill Thigpen). There are resonances here of her 1987 *Fine Things* which also unusually focuses on events through the eyes of the hero. Bernie Fine is the well-set-up vice-president of a large department store who has to cope with the cancer and death of his wife, and to involve himself in a bitterly disturbing struggle for the custody of his young step-daughter.

Message from Nam is a *tour de force* and an affirmation of human love and resilience which could easily have drowned in melodrama and sentimentality. Paxton Andrews loses two men she loves in the fighting in Vietnam and goes there as a journalist to find out and report to war-weary readers in America just what is happening. The truth is not easy to uncover; there is ambivalence about who or what is the real enemy, about political power struggles and the whole significance of the war. But above all there is suffering, on the part of the soldiers and by the civilian population with which Paxton increasingly identifies. Like so many military Vietnam veterans, she reaches the point where life 'stateside' appears remote and, in spite of all the killing and maiming and hunger and fear, only life in the embattled Nam seems real. Paxton's newspaper column messages become legendary. She meets Sergeant Tony Campobello, and their mutual passion eclipses all her earlier loves, but, predictably, he is lost in action and presumed dead. Paxton bears his child, and clings to the hope that he might still be alive. She is drawn back to Vietnam, even when the war is ending, to try to find him, a seemingly hopeless task in the chaos and misery that precedes the Americans' pulling out. Eventually, at almost the last possible moment, when everyone is fighting to get on to the helicopters which are endeavouring to evacuate US nationals, she literally stumbles on Tony in the crowd. He is filthy, 'battered, scarred, almost unrecognizable', having lived on the run for two years 'in tunnels he had found and used . . . and survived by wiles and horrors she couldn't have dared to think of'. The nightmare is over, but for Paxton, Tony and all those who fought and worked in those terrible years in Nam, life will never be as it was before.

Message from Nam is Danielle Steel's most challenging work and, because of the extreme contrast of its background with her customary milieu, it comes across with startling directness and intensity. Its language too, comprised of short, sharp almost Hemingwayesque sentences, differs markedly from her usual narrative style, although it is still – astoundingly – the language of romance. It did not exactly set a vogue but, now that America seems better able to come to terms with the frustrations and horror of the Vietnamese war, more books about it are beginning to appear in the romance genre. The theme of devoted women trying, when US government agencies have failed, to rescue their husbands and boyfriends who are prisoners or in hiding is a potent one. Margaret Pemberton conveys the appalling personal conflicts involved in *White Christmas in Saigon* (1991) when the strangely assorted trio of American Abbra, English Serena and part-French, part Vietnamese Gabrielle, 'with a courage born of desperation', set out for Saigon to find out what has happened to the men they love, and whether they can be brought home.

In stories such as these, heroines have to make starkly dramatic choices. More frequently, as we have seen, recent romantic fiction presents heroines with choices focusing on domestic and career issues. Maeve Haran's *Having It All* (1991) breaks the glistening crust of power, money and success which better-off working mothers of the 1980s enjoyed, to reveal something less appetizing underneath. Thirty-six-year-old Liz Ward has her life very much under control. She has a hunky, high-flying newspaper-editor husband, David, two small children (and the essential nanny), and is an ambitious executive and a 'creative power-house' of Metro Television. When she is promoted to become the 'first woman Programme Controller of any major TV company in the UK – possibly the world', things begin to get out of hand. It is not a question of her being unable to do the job; she has the talent and the will, but the struggle to reconcile the ferociously unremitting pressures of her work with the demands of home and husband prove too much. She copes at first, by beavering at all hours in the office and bringing work home, but soon finds she has no time or energy to meet more than basic domestic demands, and knows that she is failing her children, her husband and herself. Most of her female friends and colleagues are career-minded working mothers who think she's got it made, and resolutely refuse to listen to maverick voices which suggest 'that work isn't the Holy Grail, Paradise Regained and Club Med rolled into one'. Eventually, however, up against extraordinary work challenges, professional jealousies and intrigues, and the realization that her marriage is becoming hollow, Liz takes stock and sees that she is being duped by social attitudes which she has never before questioned:

> women had been sold a pup. Having It All was a myth, a con, a dangerous lie. Of course you could have a career and a family. But there was one little detail the gurus of feminism forgot to mention: the cost to you if you did . . .

Liz walks out of her job, but it is too late to save her marriage. David is already heavily involved in an affair with one of Liz's stylish friends, and they break up. Liz, who never does things by halves, moves herself and the children out of London into the country, and tries to manage full-time motherhood as efficiently as she had run the television company. She can't, of course, and it is not long before she realizes that there are also lots of phoney myths about the joys of motherhood unrelieved by domestic help. She is appalled to find herself snapping at her 'whingeing' small son,

Jamie, and not keeping up with the nappy changes needed by Daisy: 'she was amazed at the sheer slog of being a full-time mother. She didn't even seem to be able to cope with the washing and ironing . . .' And orthodox advice on child care provides little help. She is reassured by Ginny, a far more experienced mum, that 'the only use' she has 'for Doctor Spock is to throw it at Ben [her son] when he's just pulled the heads off all the neighbours' daffs or put salt in the goldfish tank'.

Liz misses David terribly but makes the best of her female friendships. This bonding leads indirectly to another change in her circumstances. She ultimately accepts that she is 'a thirtysomething woman who loved her children but who found she needed something else in her life as well', and, in partnership with friends in the same boat, she founds WomanPower, an employment agency for mothers wanting satisfying and reasonably well-paid work. Its slogan is 'Half a woman is the best man for the job!' and it appears to offer Liz, her colleagues and their clients the best of both worlds. Of course, the solution is not as simplistic as it seems, and there are many hurdles of prejudice and self-delusion to jump before Liz succeeds in 'having it all' on her own, not society's, terms. 'All' includes the happy ending of David's return and of a real flowering of partnership at every level between them.

Having It All provides telling and witty social comment, and its success suggests that it reflects a real-life shift of attitudes about women's perpetual balancing act between the demands of home and careers. Perhaps the 1990s really are marking a move away from materialism and high earnings at high psychological cost? At any rate, they have brought changes in the structure and undertow of many romantic stories. At one extreme the huge 500- to 700-page best-sellers seem to be scaling down the larger-and-far-more-successful-than-life aspects of their heroines, giving them more heart and vulnerability and bringing them into closer line with their readers. At the other end of the love-story market Mills & Boon books, which can probably be seen as typifying trademark romances, have become more realistic and challenging.

In the past, of course, M&B novels have been seen as sterotypical of flagrantly escapist, looking-for-Mr-Right-and-not-much-else themes. In a sense they are adult fairy-stories (as are Krantz's and Steel's sagas of transformations from poverty to riches in which virtue triumphs and baddies are punished) with familiar late-twentieth-century backgrounds but happily-ever-after endings that hark back to some mythical age of innocence.

It is only in very recent years that the romantic genre in general has begun to receive any critical comment; until now it has been trivialized and seen as worthless and exclusively 'women's reading'. Men have always had their equivalent literary fantasies, from cowboy and Indian sagas in the 1930s to today's hard-hitting war and espionage tales of torture, violence and brutalized sex, which do not receive such blanket dismissal. M&B in particular are now also beginning to receive attention – though it comes in fits and starts – from reviewers, social commentators and Church dignitaries. In the autumn of 1993, for example, Dr John Habgood, the Archbishop of York, when discussing the soaring divorce rate, informed a Mothers' Union conference that 'those with too many hopes are going into something with quite unrealistic expectations, supported by media hype, Mills & Boon romantic novels, pop songs and screen images of highly romantic and highly sexual love ...' He went on to say that young people are thus conned into believing that marriage 'is heavenly love flowing around you all the time and that you could be on a constant high', but that disillusionment and marital break-up would be likely to follow when the stresses and strains of real-life replaced rosy illusions.

Luigi Bonomi, senior editor at M&B, was quick to reply, pointing out that without exception their stories 'involve the problems of human relationships ... Things don't always work out for the characters and our readers understand that. It may be romantic fiction but it's always underpinned by reality.' One of their most prolific and popular authors, Charlotte Lamb, goes further. She sees M&B novels as '*The* feminist art form, as they are written by and for, and read by, women.' It is certainly true that with a few stalwart exceptions, men have tried their hands without success at the stories which Charlotte Lamb and other female

writers produce with such aplomb. Male would-be M&B raconteurs are apparently unable to identify sufficiently with women's
viewpoints or fantasies; even at the most mundane levels they fall
short, writing about things like cooking, dressing and hairstyling
very differently. To create under the insignia of the Red Rose of
Romance is not the easy option that so many people think it must
be. Those who succeed stress the necessity of sincerity. Among
authors of repute listed in *Million* January/February 1992 as having
written M&B romances at some point in their careers are Sally
Beauman, Georgette Heyer, Victoria Holt, Molly Keane, Mary
Lutyens and Rosamunde Pilcher.

Despite their supposed blandness and unreality, stories and
themes *have* moved with the times. The action now continues –
even in pre-marital relationships – beyond the bedroom door;
heroines are more sophisticated and active in their own interests
and, though still on the naively innocent side, cope slightly more
spiritedly with the heroes. However, although M&B male leads
have undergone alterations in class, costume, settings and nation-
ality (they are now by no means always British), they have changed
rather less than the heroines. In spite of the blond appeal of movie
stars such as Robert Redford and pop idols like David Bowie or
Sting, heroes remain firmly tall, dark and handsome and, on the
basis that women are supposed to be attracted to the strongest male
of the species, always macho and never remotely wimpish.

A few months after the Archbishop had fired his shots across the
M&B bows, the publisher's seminar on romantic fiction at the
London Bookfair made further headlines in the national press. It
had become evident that 'safe sex' was being practised in some of
the stories, which gave reporters, arts correspondents and the *Times*
leader writer something to nudge and giggle about under headings
such as 'Socially responsible bodice-rippers learn to play it safe'
and 'Condom society catches up with heroes of Mills & Boon'. So
it seems that publishers have their knuckles rapped by the Archbishop for producing fiction that is too escapist, but become targets
for journalistic derision when they show realism and a sense of
responsibility. In *A Date with Destiny* and *Knight to the Rescue*, both

by Miranda Lee, the subject of male contraception is referred to for the first time in M&B novels, obliquely and in just a few lines so that appropriate action at the crucial point is not held up long enough to lessen its dramatic and amorous impact.

In fairness, even while laughing at their expense, newspapers were quick (and astounded) to point out that M&B books are almost the only titles which readers ask for regularly each month as soon as they are published, largely regardless of authors' names and with complete confidence in what the publisher offers; that last year M&B sold 15 million copies in the UK alone – one every two seconds, and that their books are translated into twenty-six languages, including Serbo-Croat, and read in 100 countries. It was also suggested that 'well-known Mills and Boon authors, such as Penny Jordan and Charlotte Lamb, have made millions'. Possibly more than any other regular contributors, these two authors have created the pattern of the 1970s' and 1980s' M&B novels. Penny Jordan has specialized in the domineering hero who misunderstands the heroine's actions and motivation, and consequently gives her a tough time. He is, however, always flexible enough to realize that he has done her an injustice, and accordingly to change his attitude towards her and clear the way for the flowering of mutual passion. There are, of course, strong echoes here of old traditions in the genre, though at least the Jordan male leads are not entirely mentally rigid, as the stereotypes of the 1950s were.

Charlotte Lamb's novels helped to precipitate the M&B canon into the period of the so-called sexual revolution and on. Her first book for them, *Follow a Stranger*, was published in 1973, and to date she has contributed well over 100 titles to the series. Her stories are full of gusto and sensation (as titles such as *Desire*, *Scandalous* and *Obsession* suggest), and dark as well as bright aspects of sexual involvement are integral to her plots. She sometimes writes about women as victims: in *Stranger in the Night* and *Seduction* (both published in 1981) her heroines are seduced against their will, and badly damaged psychologically by the experience before their natural resilience begins to reassert itself. There is certainly little escapism about these two novels, and she carries the theme of woman's vulnerability further in *A Violation* (1983) when Clare Forrester, a lively and enquiring young advertising executive, is raped by an intruder who burgles her flat. Her life changes, at first dramatically, and later in subtle and lasting ways. She has to question her relationship with her not very imaginative boyfriend, with her family and workmates; most of all she has to question herself – the confidence which has been so quickly undermined, her residual and unreasonable sense of guilt, and her fear of future physical relationships with men. Although its theme is stark, *A Violation* is not a depressing book. Clare's gradual rehabilitation is persuasively described, while horror and hysteria are balanced by flashes of wit. And, of course, romance is not forgotten. Strong dollops of it come towards the end – and it is the real thing this time.

Charlotte Lamb's heroines are secretaries, businesswomen, artists or actresses. Most of them are romantically unawakened until the hero erupts into their lives. They have to learn how to come to terms with their sexuality, while their men-of-the-world admirers have to sort out the business of learning to become faithful.

Charlotte Lamb also writes as Sheila Holland, Sheila Coates, Sheila Lancaster and Laura Hardy (basically a different name for each imprint to which she contributes). She wanted to write for Mills & Boon because she had read their books since she was a child, and felt that 'other books hadn't got *it*' – something she can't define except as 'an unashamed intensity of feeling'. Sales of her novels are enormous (estimated at between 75 and 100 million so far) and it doesn't worry her that they are so seldom reviewed: 'The readers for whom I write don't give a fig what others think: they form their own opinions . . .' She adds that 'what they want in their fiction is a mixture of warmly observed life and powerful emotion. All fiction is invented; the best fiction is close to reality yet with that added dimension of an escape into dreams.'

Dreams change, of course, and to remain successful romantic authors have to keep up with readers' new aspirations, beliefs and uncertainties. Since the late 1980s there has been a fresh focus on the intelligent, questioning housewife-heroine. Rosamunde Pilcher,

Mary Wesley and Joanna Trollope are prominent among writers who explore the vicissitudes of romance not only before but during marriage and motherhood. In contrast with the extravagant materialism of many 'sex and shopping' blockbusters, their so-called 'Aga sagas' are concerned with 'ordinary' life in which love involves the undertaking of domestic and family responsibilities.

Rosamund Pilcher, whose first stories were written for Mills and Boon during the late 1940s, has continued to keep her finger on the pulse of her audience. As she says in *Twentieth Century Romance and Historical Writers*, over the years that she has been writing 'social conditions, behaviour and expectations have changed drastically'. She also comments that she has incorporated the 'inevitable permissiveness' into her work 'without necessarily condoning it nor encouraging the sort of loveless amorality which was prevalent in the 1960s . . . If the stories do not have a happy ending, then they always have a hopeful one.'

The leading character in her most notable book *The Shell Seekers* (1987), is Penelope Keeling. She is sixty-four, lives alone in the country, and has suffered but recovered from a heart attack. As she considers her present situation, the story of her full and varied life unfolds, jigsaw fashion, in a series of flash-backs. She recollects her happy, bohemian childhood in Cornwall and her open, honest relationship with her French mother, Sophie, and her English father, Lawrence Stern, who was a distinguished artist of the Pre-Raphaelite school. She possesses a few of his sketches and particularly treasures his Cornish beach painting, *The Shell Seekers*, which is not only beautiful in itself but symbolizes the freedom and expansiveness that have always been so important to Penelope: 'the picture shone out into the half-light, brilliant as a stained-glass window with the sun behind it. It was her own personal mantra, pervasive as a hypnotist's charm . . .'

The painting becomes a focus, not only for her reflections about her life and loves, but for family conflict. Its value has increased over the decades until it has become worth a small fortune. Two of her grown-up offspring, Nancy and Noël, are anxious for her to sell it without delay, hoping that they can reap a share in the

financial benefits. Nancy wants the money to preserve her pretentious lifestyle: she and her solicitor husband try to play the role of
country squire and lady but are struggling to maintain an over-
large property and to pay their two children's cripplingly high
private school fees. Noël, unmarried and exploitative in his sexual
relationships, sees himself as an entrepreneurial businessman and,
although most of his schemes have been unsuccessful, hopes that
the picture will be sold to produce urgently needed capital for his
further enterprises.

Penelope's third child, Olivia, has inherited her mother's honesty and independence, and there is an empathic bond between
them. Confident of her own abilities and enjoying career fulfilment
as the editor of a prestigious fashion magazine, Olivia is determined
that Penelope should not be pressurized into disposing of *The Shell
Seekers* or any of Lawrence Stern's works that are in her possession.

Some of Rosamunde Pilcher's most vivid flash-backs centre on
the years of the Second World War when, like so many young
women, Penelope found herself swept up in an affair, pregnancy
and marriage with someone who as she later acknowledged had no
particular affinity with her. It quickly became apparent that
Ambrose Keeling, the naval officer whom she met when she was
serving in the WRNS, was in fact 'a mummy's boy' who, spoiled
and reckless with money, was unable and unwilling to cope with
the challenges of providing for his young wife and family. When
he eventually left her for a younger woman, Penelope's overriding
feeling was simply one of relief.

The real romance of her life had been provided by another
wartime liaison which began fairly soon after her marriage, when
disillusionment about Ambrose had already set in. Almost as soon
as she meets Richard Lomax, a Royal Marine Commando, she
experiences a 'flash of ecstasy' that is frequently to recur when she
is in his presence. He brings her the 'gift of joy', their relationship
seems magical, predestined and 'timeless', and, whether or not they
can persuade Ambrose to give Penelope a divorce, they plan to
spend their lives together.

Richard learns towards the end of May 1944 that he is to be sent into action when the allies launch the Second Front in Nazi-occupied Europe. Buoyed up by his love for Penelope, he writes to her that he has no fear of death, 'the last enemy', and describes himself as a 'happy man who expects to live for ever'. But he is killed on D-Day at Omaha Beach, and Penelope is left having to take consolation from the words of his last letter:

> in this life, nothing good is truly lost. It stays part of a person, becomes part of their character. So part of you goes everywhere with me. And part of me is yours, for ever.

The abiding effects of this brief love affair sustain Penelope over the years and through the usual variety of domestic problems and responsibilities. Her creativity finds expression in bringing up her three children and, later on, in the making and maintaining of her lovely garden. In fact, she never sells *The Shell Seekers* but donates it to the art gallery of the Cornish village in which her father had painted it. Typically, however, she uses money from the sale of some of her father's sketches to help a young couple she has befriended to start the horticultural business for which they are obviously well fitted. Danus, the young man in question, has about him a fleeting resemblance to her long-ago lover . . . Penelope dies of a second heart attack in the garden which has become 'her sanctuary', and in her last moments she feels that Richard is with her.

In this appealing novel, Rosamunde Pilcher deftly balances the ecstasies of young love with the satisfactions of age, and juggles the expansiveness of romance against the demands of everyday life. There is a similarly haunting and persuasive quality about Mary Wesley's *Not That Sort of Girl* (1987). This also has a mature heroine whose long-lasting love is reviewed in flash-back. Rose Peel, at sixty-seven, has just been widowed. Her almost forty-year marriage to Ned seemed to many of her friends and family to have been satisfying and in the conventional mould. No one but she and Mylo Cooper knows that, pre-dating and in parallel with her marriage, Rose and Mylo have maintained an affair of passionate intensity.

Towards the end of the 1930s, largely under pressure from her father who is supposedly dying of cancer, Rose enters into an engagement with the well-off, land-owning and good-looking Ned Peel. He seems to embody the security which her father wants for her and to which Rose is also attracted, as she later on admits to herself: 'Much of me longed for the security, a house in London, the house in the country; the big wedding was tempting, the clothes I had never been able to afford.' She meets Ned at 'a house party for the grouse shooting' in Scotland and feels 'almost in love' with him. But deep down she knows that she has far stronger feelings for Mylo, who is then an impecunious nineteen-year-old with 'no prospects, no money, no family, no job' and without even a university background. His only marketable skill seems to be his fluency in French – the native language of his mother – but, in the eyes of Rose's family 'the speaking of French was somehow derogatory, louche, dangerous.' She succumbs to what she expects might be her last fling with Mylo but, even after their 'tragi-comic abortive attempt at making love' in a lumpy hotel bed, senses that she will never be entirely free of him.

Rose hopefully anticipates a long engagement which might provide time for getting to know Ned better, for reflection and possible changes of mind. However, when the Second World War is declared in September 1939, and Ned is faced with being sent abroad on military service, their marriage quickly takes place. On her wedding she is 'assailed by a sense of desolation' when she recalls the actualities and the potential of her relationship with Mylo, while Ned, less confident of his capacities than he appears to be, makes her swear most solemnly never to leave him.

As she points out, she has already made this promise in church but, surprisingly in view of their lack of affinity and Ned's later infidelities, she remains bound to it. Earlier on, when Mylo had realized that Rose was determined to marry Ned, he too had exacted an undertaking from her:

'Promise me one thing, Rose, you owe me that.'
'All right.'

'When I send for you urgently to come to meet me, you needn't do anything you don't want to, but just come.'

A commitment of this nature in the context of the 1930s would generally have been considered outrageous, but Rose's strength of character is evidenced in her determination to maintain her marriage and to have Mylo too. She bears Ned's son, Christopher, and appears to all intents and purposes a devoted wife and mother. Ned continues to love her in a phlegmatic way, which does not, however, prevent him from pursuing other women. Rose at first resents the snatched nature of her occasional meetings with Mylo, hates it when he eventually marries a colleague from the Intelligence unit in which he served during the war, but never fails to respond to his charms and the idyllic nature of their physical and emotional responses to each other. Eventually Mylo's wife and Ned both die, and after a short period of fairly stringent solitary reflection Rose seeks out her lover, and together they at last seem set for a complete and satisfying relationship in which passion has only slightly dimmed with age:

'. . . I love kissing you.'
'Not forgotten how?'
'If you must know, I'm as hungry as I ever was. I just space the meals out a bit.'

Like *The Shell Seekers*, *Not That Sort of Girl* romantically spans so many years that its appeal is to a wide age-range. Both love-stories are also interlaced with witty and perceptive comments on sexual and marital involvements:

she came out of the wood, stepping on to the footpath along the creek. She remembered with a pang how fast her heart had beat as she looked at Mylo that day, how she had felt sick with desire.

I feel sick with desire just now thinking of him. At my age! I've had no breakfast, perhaps I am confusing my hungers . . .

Joanna Trollope also adroitly balances realism and romance. Anna, the heroine of *The Rector's Wife* (1991) is forty-two years old before she considers having a lover. As the wife of an Anglican rector, Peter Bouverie, she has lived in a variety of parishes from city slum to the country one in which she is now settled. Throughout her marriage she has been almost completely preoccupied with her family and parish commitments. Like so many parson's wives, she constantly finds herself assuming the duties of 'unpaid curate', often doing the boring things, such as delivering parish magazines, that she doesn't like to ask volunteer helpers to do.

The Bouveries live with their teenage son, Luke, and ten-year-old daughter, Flora, in a redbrick rectory 'that looks like a bus shelter', on £9000 a year. Their eldest daughter Charlotte is away at university. Money is so short that Anna has frequently to resort to jumble sale clothes for herself and the children but, although she is a trained language teacher, parish and domestic demands allow her insufficient overflow of energy to pursue her profession, even on a part-time basis. She takes on occasional translation work but is unable to keep this up.

When the novel opens, the family is in a state of crisis. For some time Peter has felt at a dead end in his work, and has been chafing at his inability to provide more adequately for his wife and children. His relationship with Anna has become kindly, passionless and distant. He is driven even more deeply into himself and a sense of failure after his application for promotion to the position of Archdeacon has been rejected. Flora, a sensitive and vulnerable girl, does not fit in at the local comprehensive school; she is being bullied on a regular basis, and Anna despairs at her own powerlessness to intervene. Flora yearns to transfer to St Saviour's, a privately run Roman Catholic school, and, against all financial odds, Anna determines to make this possible. To improve Flora's dire circumstances she is prepared to neglect the demands of the parish (she suspects anyway that certain rector-admiring female helpers will gladly spring into the church-flower-arranging, Brownie-group and Deanery-supper breach). Casting around for some sort of paid job which she feels sure she can cope with, she lands one at the local supermarket, Pricewells, where, starting as a shelf-stacker, she soon becomes 'a star employee'. She is much valued by her bosses and colleagues who, unlike Peter's parishioners, relate easily and directly to her and do not see her simply as 'the rector's wife' but as someone in her own right.

Anna's natural vitality begins to surface once more. Flora transfers to St Saviour's, which is wonderfully suited to her eductional and social needs. Peter, however, hates what he and some of his flock see as Anna's low-level job, which nevertheless makes her less dependent on him, and emphasizes his limitations as the family's provider. A disconcerting discovery causes him to sink further into depression and mistrust of Anna. He learns from the chance comment of a parishioner whose daughter is also at St Saviour's, that Flora has been awarded a full scholarship there. Anna has concealed this from him because she wants to hang on to the independence and interest of the supermarket job and knows that without the necessity of raising Flora's school fees Peter will want her go give this up. Without consulting her, in shockingly high-handed fashion, he stalks into Pricewells and announces that Anna will be quitting.

This solves nothing. Peter still feels inadequate, and Anna cannot resettle herself into the parson's helpmeet role:

'... I can't be an individual, only someone relative to Peter, to the parish, to the Church. I'm forty-two and I don't expect I will ever be myself now. The parish has become the other woman in my life – our lives ... I expect that for other clergy wives whose husbands are less disappointed than Peter, God is the other woman ...'

She becomes more and more restless and dissatisfied, and finds herself strongly attracted first to Daniel Byrne, the extremely understanding man who has secured the Archdeanconship which Peter had coveted, and then to Jonathan, his donnish brother, with whom she has a full-blown affair.

Ironically Peter believes that she has responded to their affluent and forceful neighbour, Patrick O'Sullivan, who can scarcely hide his admiration for Anna but who has actually been firmly brushed off by her. Temporarily blinded by anger and jealousy, Peter crashes his car and is killed. Deeply saddened, Anna realizes that he must have been clinically depressed. She remains refreshingly free from any sense of guilt and knows too that with her 'growing appetite for life' and Peter's 'increasing distaste for it', they could have had no future together.

She is, of course, acutely tempted to make a new life with Jonathan but, rather like the heroine of *A Village Affair* (see Chapter 10) she acknowledges that she is not yet sufficiently strong or inwardly free to commit herself fully to another permanent relationship: 'To be perfectly honest ... I'm desperate for a rest from marriage. And there are Flora's and Luke's needs to be considered ...' *The Rector's Wife* ends on a warmly positive note, despite Anna's indecisiveness about Jonathan which, like her flaws and weaknesses, is empathically conveyed.

One of today's phenomena is that in a materialistic and disillusioned age the demand for love-stories from a wide range of readers increases rather than abates.

As we have seen, throughout the twentieth century, writers in the genre have built on moods and themes established by earlier authors to create a literature which meets the needs of our own time. There have been progressions and deteriorations over the decades, but romantic fiction has generally managed to hold on to some measure of vitality and appeal. The last fifteen years have brought new freedoms and explorations, which reflect the more liberated status of women and girls in real life, and the romance story at its best has inched forward into something far more satisfying artistically and emotionally than the sentimental tales which used to be known as the sub-literature of love.

One question, though: where have all the Darcys gone? And the Rochesters and Rhetts? This is without doubt the age of the heroine rather than the hero: he survives as a sometimes macho, sometimes understanding, hunkily handsome and protective figure, but he is a shadow of his former glory. Pallid Darcy manqués abound, but when will we have the joy of seeing a truly individual new-age hero lift off from the printed page? Or is this a contradiction in terms? Have all the Lovelaces, Darcys, Heathcliffs, Rochesters, Rhett Butlers and Maxim de Winters taken fright in the presence of so many liberated heroines (and so much political correctness) and ridden off into the sunset . . .?